RISK MANAGEMENT AND CORPORATE
SUSTAINABILITY IN AVIATION

This book is dedicated to our families

Risk Management and Corporate Sustainability in Aviation

TRIANT G. FLOURIS

and

AYSE KUCUK YILMAZ

Routledge
Taylor & Francis Group

LONDON AND NEW YORK

First published 2011 by Ashgate Publishing

2 Park Square, Milton Park, Abingdon, Oxon OX14 4RN
711 Third Avenue, New York, NY 10017, USA

Routledge is an imprint of the Taylor & Francis Group, an informa business

First issued in paperback 2016

British Library Cataloguing in Publication Data
Flouris, Triant G.
  Risk management and corporate sustainability in aviation.
  1. Aeronautics, Commercial--Management. 2. Aeronautics--
  Safety measures. 3. Aeronautics, Commercial--Employees--
  Training of. 4. Aeronautics, Commercial--Environmental
  aspects. 5. Risk management. 6. Social responsibility of
  business. 7. Organizational change--Management.
  I. Title II. Kucuk Yilmaz, Ayse.
  387.7'068-dc22

Library of Congress Cataloging-in-Publication Data
Flouris, Triant G.
  Risk management and corporate sustainability in aviation / by Triant Flouris and Ayse Kucuk Yilmaz.
      p. cm.
  Includes bibliographical references and index.
  ISBN 978-1-4094-1199-4 (hardback)
  1. Aeronautics--Management. 2. Risk management. I. Kucuk Yilmaz, Ayse. II. Title.
  HE9774.F56 2011
  387.7068'1--dc22

                                                                      2011011352

ISBN 978-1-4094-1199-4 (hbk)
ISBN 978-1-138-24615-7 (pbk)

Contents

List of Figures and Tables

Figures

Tables

Foreword

TAV Airports is a holding company that operates ten airports throughout the world. Four of these airports are located in Turkey while the remaining six are located elsewhere in the world. TAV Airports undertakes services in most areas of airport operations, namely ground handling, duty free stores, food and beverage, IT, and security.

At the time of writing, TAV Airports Holding provided services to approximately 42 million passengers, 500,000 aircraft, and 8 million cars every year. From these statistics it is easy to see that the company has a diversified and volume-based business model; diversification and mass create complexity and we are aware that complexity provides both opportunities and threats if one is not successful in their management.

In order to be successful, while exploring opportunities, we have to be aware of the threats that we face. Today's best practices may not be the best practices of the future. We at TAV are keenly aware that investors make investment decisions based not only on consideration of the financial performance of a company, but also by monitoring its management style in regard to social and environmental issues. In today's world, where advanced communication technologies exist, every kind of negative occurrence in relation to social and environmental issues is announced rapidly to the whole world. Hence companies are driven to take responsibility in social and environmental matters within the geographical regions that they operate in.

The dynamic, as a result of the "aerodynamic" nature of the aviation industry, is compelling us to adopt more effective and efficient risk management models integrated with strong sustainability practices. On the other hand, sustainability itself requires a dynamic improvement, growth and change of existing systems to dynamically maintain the outstanding performance of a corporation.

Our primary task is to determine the positive or negative effects of economic, social, and environmental aspects of the activities of our corporation. That is why at TAV Airports we do not view risk management as just a means of determining financial uncertainties. Rather, we focus on all dimensions of the risk elements in our businesses, concentrating also on their economic, social, and environmental impacts. We know that, with more than 15,000 employees in our organization, the human factor is one of our key assessment areas. We give much thought to the recruitment and training processes of new employees as we help them to adapt themselves to our organizations and guarantee their continued learning. This is because we are aware that we can add value to our risk management and sustainability systems in this manner.

We believe that TAV Airports Holding possesses one of the best models in the aviation industry in regards to risk management and corporate sustainability; we are committed to responding to the concerns and meeting the expectations of all our stakeholders. The book *Risk Management and Corporate Sustainability in Aviation*, written by Prof. Dr Triant Flouris and Asst. Prof. Dr Ayse Kucuk Yilmaz, is a key reference book for every professional serving in aviation industry with regard to risk management and sustainability. Each line of this book should be read with much attention. The diligent work of the authors will add great value to the practical implementation of risk management and sustainability models in the aviation industry.

Dr M. Sani Şener
TAV Airports Group CEO

Acknowledgments

Sani Sener
Guy Loft, Margaret Younger, Charlotte Parkins and Emily Pace at Ashgate
Nursel Ilgen and Management Team (XE) at TAV Airports Holding
Lorraine Arlan
Sotiria Akritidi

We would also like to acknowledge the very significant contribution to this book of the following individuals and organizations for kindly and generously giving us permission to quote their work:

Aileen Ionescu-Somers
Asuka Hoshikoshi
Brooke Jim
Burr Stewart
EUROCONTROL Information Center
Colin Meckiff
Dave Pollard
Dave Wilkins
Emily Hall
Emma Hollindrake
Geoff Thompson
Graeme Paterson
Iveta Cherneva
John R. McIntyre
Joseph C. Atkinson
Katharine Partridge
Penny Walker
PricewaterhouseCoopers LLP
R. Bruce Hutton

Ruth Tellis
Sinead Porter
Stéphane Oertel
The Economist Group
Tim Johnson
Tim Padfield
Ulrich Steger

Chapter 1
Introduction to Corporate Sustainability: Enterprise-Wide Risk Management Approach to Contemporary Business Management and Organization

Continuous developments and changes in the business world require business planners to rethink the way they organize and manage their businesses for sustainability. Corporate Sustainability (also known as CS) has become a critical issue for today's business organizations. Sustainability requires the corporate system to be improved on a regular basis. Successful businesses offer the most comprehensive crisis risk management programs on the market. Economic, social, and environmental issues are creating both risks and opportunities for businesses. The integrated practice of Enterprise Risk Management (also known as ERM) with Corporate Sustainability is becoming a fundamental principle of business management and organization.

Enterprise Sustainability Risk Management (also known as ESRM) is a necessity for a business which operates in a globally warmed business environment. The implementation of Enterprise Sustainability Risk Management provides a way to address all corporate risks in a timely manner. It introduces an opportunity to turn risk issues into advantages. This book is a guide for business managers on how to apply this advanced managerial approach to their own businesses. Also, Enterprise Sustainability

Risk Management enables businesses to manage the risks and maximize the opportunities through identifying both key financial and non-financial stakeholders and establishing a relationship with them regarding sustainability issues.

Enterprise Sustainability Risk Management is an increasingly accepted concept and growing field in the global business world. Integration of the business world with society is one of the key points for Corporate Sustainability. Enterprise Sustainability Risk Management is core to the business strategy and practice in terms of both opportunities and risks.

Sustainability factors should be considered by managers like any other business risk issues. These factors are expected to have a substantial impact on corporate management. We believe that corporations need a strong sustainability management framework to effectively manage economic, social, and environmental risks; to achieve their Corporate Sustainability objectives; and to meet their stakeholders' demands. Our book offers a new Enterprise Sustainability Risk Management model to fulfill these requirements. In this model, the triple bottom line (also known as TBL) agenda is incorporated into the sustainability management of the business (to control the economic, social, and environmental impact of processes and products).

Enterprise Sustainability Risk Management deals with environmental, social, and ecological risks as well as strategic, economic, operational, and threat risks facing businesses. The best Corporate Sustainability strategies and management approaches require consideration of all corporate risks in both a holistic and systematic way. Our book aims to provide an effective way for managing sustainability risks via a new, well-designed, integrated, dynamic, and flexible framework.

The Enterprise Sustainability Risk Management framework model provides many basic benefits which allow a business to ensure its sustainability. These include:

- managerial approaches and processes such as strategic planning, corporate governance, Human Resource Management (also known as HRM), the decision-making process, reputation management, crisis management, corporate resource planning and management, and financial risk management;

- shareholder acquisition;
- a systematic process for strategic and operational decisions at all levels in business;
- a holistic snapshot of economic, social, and environmental impact factors on Corporate Sustainability for both managers and personnel;
- the integration of economic, social, and environmental factors with strategic objectives according to the triple bottom line concept;
- an understanding of the interdependence between business, society, and the environment.

We envision that Enterprise Sustainability Risk Management will be a core competency for global business management and organization. The new Enterprise Sustainability Risk Management framework offers a flexible strategic approach to anticipating potential problems and resolving sustainability challenges through risk analysis, positive external engagement, and robust management systems.

Twenty-First Century: The Age of Global Awareness

We assume that regulatory changes, financial liabilities, and physical occurrences provide for the highest risks in regard to climate change as perceived by business managers. In the current business environment, reputation risks and litigation risks are considered less pressing by business managers. In addition, business managers have to respond to an increased level of stakeholder benefits, concerns, and close examination. This can be called Stakeholder Risk Management which is embedded in our Enterprise Sustainability Risk Management framework. Basically, the Enterprise Sustainability Risk Management framework is designed with consideration given to the following:

- Enterprise Risk Management
- Stakeholder Risk Management
- Corporate Reputation Risk Management
- Corporate Sustainability Management (also known as CSM)
- Environmental (internal and external) Management
- Value-Based Management

Enterprise Sustainability Risk Management aims to bridge the gap between the Risk and Corporate Sustainability concept in the Contemporary Business and Management field. Enterprise Sustainability Risk Management implementation will increase business managers' trust in themselves regarding optimum management of the sustainability-based corporate risks. Corporate risks include those which are strategic, economic, social, operational, compliance-related, and tactical. Also, the Enterprise Sustainability Risk Management process enables consideration of environmental risks in addition to the other corporate risks as a strategic necessity in a complex fast-changing world and global business environment.

Enterprise Sustainability Risk Management is not just an operational issue, nor is it a financial, strategic, social, environmental, or a compliance-related one. It is a combination of all of them. Experiences in risk management practices show a common cause behind past failures of managing risks. Traditional risk management implementations were dominated by either the financial or operational side of business. The integrated triple bottom line was ignored. However, the implementation of Enterprise Sustainability Risk Management is essential to become and stay sustainable. Consideration of climate change-based issues is critical to survival of the world and corporations. Enterprise Sustainability Risk Management must be part of the corporate strategy and management system. Because of this, Enterprise Sustainability Risk Management tries to bridge the gap between Entity Risk Management and Corporate Sustainability Management. For this reason, Enterprise Sustainability Risk Management is a critical integral part of Contemporary Business and Management.

Since human resources are one of the important risks to business, we focus on Strategic Human Resource Management (also known as SHRM) in this book. For this, we have developed a new Human Factor Risk Management (also known as HFRM) model. We are aware that management of the human factor (also known as HF) is a very risky business, but it is also a very challenging one to both business and risk managers. We offer a well-designed, innovative, and flexible model to manage human resources efficiently in the globally warmed business world.

THINK AND DESIGN HOLISTIC, ACT PROACTIVE AND SYSTEMATIC:
Managerial Methodology to Corporate Sustainability
by Risk Management in Contemporary Issues in Business

This book deals with the main question, "How do we contribute to save both our world and businesses while ensuring Corporate Sustainability?" We assume that triple bottom line-based sustainability risks should be considered in the Corporate Risk Management process since these risks significantly affect the reputation, continuity, and resilience of a business. Businesses should adopt the global approach to be successful in their local business environment.

This book aims to raise awareness of climate change and invites the reader to act as a "global risk manager" to save both our businesses and our world. We are aware that life is a kind of risky business for all of us. This book also invites business managers to act as "sustainability risk managers," achieving sustainability objectives by the effective implementation of Corporate Sustainability Management in their business organizations.

In our opinion, climate change is one of the important reasons for improving the context of Corporate Sustainability Management. Enterprise Sustainability Risk Management provides an efficient way to deal with climate change impacts on the business world. No business operates in an isolated environment, and Corporate Sustainability is embraced as an integrated and proactive management concept. Business organizations can become more sustainable by the implementation of corporate management systems. Enterprise Sustainability Risk Management is a necessity for business organizations to stay sustainable in the globally warmed business world. Enterprise Sustainability Risk Management tries to establish a balance between economic, social, and environmental objectives by minimizing threats and maximizing opportunities. For this reason, business managers should develop their sustainability strategy and process. Also, these efforts will strengthen our ability to save the world via climate change-based strategies.

Climate change is becoming one of the most important sustainability risks faced by humanity as a whole. Everybody has a responsibility in addressing this concept. We should all assume a related responsibility ourselves. We should act as "global risk managers." We prepared this book as an indicator for our efforts in supporting sustainability awareness of climate change issues. Researching the risks and solution practices of global warming issues through industry–academy partnerships is also important to achieving desired results in global and local efforts to save the world.

To clearly understand the costs of climate change/global warming, we searched for answers to the following questions:

1. Is global warming a serious risk for corporations?
2. Do global warming-based factors create sustainability risks for corporations in view of economic, social, and strategic factors?
3. Can a sustainability management-based model applied to global warming issues provide an effective way for managers to achieve corporate objectives?

After our research in preparation for this book, we concluded that global warming presents both risks and opportunities which can create serious sustainability concerns for businesses. A sustainability management model will provide an effective framework for managers to use in addressing these concerns. Business managers must consider not only the financial, strategic, and operational risks of doing business but also the global warming-based risks of social, regulatory, and environmental factors.

Our book presents a holistic and fresh proactive way to manage the enterprise-wide sustainability risks. To go beyond compliance and legal liabilities, businesses have to integrate risk management-based philosophy and culture into core business functions of the company. Sustainability management will succeed only if managers and personnel recognize that the reforms create value for them. Cultural change within the context of an overall sustainability management system must be accomplished within the business in order to provide sustainability management-based benefits, seizing opportunities. The policies and objectives regarding climate change issues should be integrated into an overall sustainability management framework which is an integral part of the firm's business strategy. Integration and a holistic approach are the key concepts for both a successful business and sustainability. The triple bottom line of economic, social, and environmental objectives in the sustainability concept requires more coordination between internal and external stakeholders of the business.

This book of readings in Enterprise Sustainability Risk Management is divided into eight main chapters. Chapters 2 through 7 include opposing views on Enterprise Sustainability Risk Management. First, the new Enterprise Sustainability Risk Management framework model, which we have developed, is presented. This book includes both a model and a risk score formula. These are related to both human factors and airline management. Also, three chapters in the book are derived from articles which are represented in collaborative works of authors from international conferences.

Chapter 2 includes the leading topics in both the "Corporate Sustainability and Enterprise Risk Management" fields such as risk and sustainability, Corporate Sustainability Management, Enterprise Risk Management, crisis management, and global warming. The definition and context of Enterprise Risk Management are given in this chapter. Sustainable business strategies are reviewed in this chapter. We focus on the triple bottom line concept as it relates to Corporate Sustainability. The relationship between Sustainable Development and risk management is reviewed in this chapter. Crisis management is related to risk management and is emphasized in this chapter. The Enterprise Risk Management process is revealed. We emphasize that the crucial point in the globally warmed business environment is Sustainable Business Performance.

Chapter 3 defines and lays out the framework for the new concept: "Enterprise Sustainability Risk Management." We briefly discuss Enterprise Risk Management since companies recognize it as a critical management issue in the current globally warmed business world. Enterprise Sustainability Risk Management is designed as a managerial system and related approach which is used by organizations to manage risks and seize opportunities related to the achievement of their sustainability objectives, in terms of the triple bottom line concept. Enterprise Sustainability Risk Management provides a framework for optimum risk management.

In this chapter, the new Enterprise Sustainability Risk Management conceptual model is offered as the specific management and organizational system to both manage and integrate the corporate goals in order to create economic and financial value and awareness of environmental and social responsibility. Enterprise Sustainability Risk Management has been developed as an important mechanism to improve Corporate Sustainability performance. Enterprise Sustainability Risk Management has a holistic and proactive perspective. Enterprise Sustainability Risk Management provides potential advantages for corporations. It can protect, create, and enhance business value through measurement and management of sustainability threats and opportunities. In addition, this can help businesses to effectively respond to the growing expectations of corporate stakeholders. In the globally warmed business environment, Enterprise Sustainability Risk Management is a necessity for corporations to become and stay sustainable. Enterprise Sustainability Risk Management takes into consideration Corporate Sustainability. For this reason, the new Enterprise Sustainability Risk Management conceptual model is based on the triple bottom line. The drivers of Enterprise Sustainability Risk Management are given in this chapter.

The Enterprise Sustainability Risk Management framework is designed to provide guidance to managers on how to establish a holistic and systematic sustainability risk management process that generates the risk indicators, risk sources, objectives, and reporting systems needed to ensure effective handling of sustainability risks and improved overall organizational performance and value.

The Enterprise Sustainability Risk Management conceptual model offers a strategic road map, which provides a contextual framework for businesses serious about taking on the challenges and opportunities of Sustainable Development.

The process of the Enterprise Sustainability Risk Management conceptual model is given in the remainder of Chapter 3. This process is composed of five main phases and their sub-steps. The main phases are:

- Phase 1: Strategic zanagement: Strategic Plan and Orientation
- Phase 2: Management and Organization: Organizational and Infrastructural Orientation
- Phase 3: Framework Set up: Establishment and Framework Orientation
- Phase 4: Report and Monitor: Internal Control Orientation
- Phase 5: Enterprise Sustainability Performance Optimization: Corporate Orientation

Chapter 4 is about "The Economics of Global Warming" and includes discussion on ways to help "save the world!" The core global risks which are identified by the World Economic Forum in 2007 are listed in this brief chapter. Via this chapter, we aim to make a little contribution to the debate over global warming in order to advance related awareness levels. Economic problems and advantages of global warming are briefly discussed.

Chapter 5 focuses on "Global Warming and Sustainable Aviation". Sustainable Aviation (also known as SA) and the challenges of achieving sustainability are reviewed in this section. Environmental problems create threats for the players in the aviation industry. Improved risk management, business strategy which is integrated with Enterprise Sustainability Risk Management, and a holistic model such as the Enterprise Sustainability Risk Management framework model will assist businesses in achieving Corporate Sustainability and enable them to deal with these challenges faced by aviation business organizations (airlines and airports).

"The Impact of Global Warming on Aviation Business and Management" portion of this chapter discusses our research on the impacts of global warming on business organizations, focusing on the aviation sector in regard to the sustainability's triple bottom line concept (economic, social, and environmental) from the perspective of the Enterprise Risk Management and cost–benefit-based risk analysis. A further aim of this study was the promotion of Environmental Intelligence. The main research question was: "What are the costs and benefits of the global warming debate on airline businesses from an organizational and managerial perspective?" Airline climate change strategies, CO_2 emission and noise-reducing liabilities, corporate social responsibilities, and risk management practices were considered in the research process. The study was designed as an initial step to the management of risk vis-à-vis global warming from an aviation industry perspective.

Climate change, global warming, and risk management for aviation organizations is the other research topic in this chapter. Also, the impacts of global warming on aviation business management and organization are explained. The cost of risk management practice for airline business organizations is reviewed briefly. We review the global warming-based sustainability costs and benefits in this chapter. For this aim, we prepared a list of both the costs and benefits which arise from climate change/global warming.

This chapter also deals with the search for the relationship between Corporate Sustainability, risk management, and the airline business. The aim of this section is, first, to explain the complexity of airline management and then to offer a new Corporate Sustainability Management model for effective and competitive airline business management. We assume Corporate Sustainability Management to be a part of the overall concept of business management and corporate strategy. Corporate Sustainability is placed within a holistic management model. The aim of the new model is to support effective Corporate Sustainability efforts of airlines since sustainability is a major risk for companies in the highly volatile and uncertain business environment. Also, we assume that sustainability risks will be a catalyst for innovation and opportunities. This model should be tailored accordingly to meet the airline business' needs, objectives, and managerial tone, before its implementation. The last topic of Chapter 5 is the importance of managing the climate change-based business risks.

Chapter 6 is about "Modeling human factor-based risks in aviation." Here we offer a new Human Factor Risk Management framework model. Strategic Human Resource Management has an important place in business management and business organizations. Managing the human element is a very risky business and a very challenging one, for both the business manager and the risk manager. We believe the Enterprise Risk Management-based perspective on managing human factors provides a fresh and systematic way of looking at businesses. As both risk sources and managers of risk, human resources have dual roles in corporate management systems and risk management. Human resources are one of the keys to success in corporate management systems. For this reason, the aforementioned dual roles (risk source and risk manager) require a different approach to both the Human Resource Management and corporate management systems. This is due to the fact that the human element has different, highly dynamic, and hardly controllable characteristics from other corporate resources. This Human Factor Risk Management framework model allows managers to effectively apply the combination of human resource and risk management principles.

This chapter addresses the question: "Are human factor-based risks unmanageable in the airline business?" We suggest a Human Factor Risk Management model for airlines, containing a new, full-set of risk shaping/influencing factors (RSF/RIF) taxonomy and a score formula. This model is expected to support corporate risk management and Human Resource Management efforts aimed at identifying and managing human factors and providing a systematic process-based approach to airline management. Managers can provide holistic snapshots of their company's human resources by using this human factor-based risk management concept. We apply our theoretical model to the airline industry and more specifically:

- discuss the importance of human factors in airline management and operations;
- develop a human factor-based risk list for airlines;
- assess the cost of human-based risks on an airline's financial and operational levels; and
- develop a human factor-based risk analysis model for the airline business.

In **Chapter 7,** we present the implementation of "Risk Management, Change Management, and Effectiveness in Aviation Operations". This chapter focuses on providing a theoretical answer to the question: "How can an air carrier effectively implement a Safety Management System (also known as SMS) in its operations?" The core assumptions of this study are:

- the value of a well-structured Safety Management System in enhancing air carrier operational safety is axiomatic; and
- risk management is an integral part of Safety Management Systems in aviation in order to provide for effective aviation operations.

We present a road map for change management, risk management, and their utility and application in transforming a non-Safety Management System compliant system to a Safety Management System one, using change management principles.

In **Chapter 8,** we present "The Integration of Sustainability Risk into Airport Business and Management". To Contemporary Business and Management, sustainability-based initiatives have an effect on corporate reputation and they also affect stakeholder interest. For this reason there is a big potential to increase corporate value. We offer the best practices examples of sustainability management initiatives from two airports in Istanbul, Turkey. İstanbul Atatürk Airport is operated by TAV Airports Holding and İstanbul Sabiha Gökçen Airport is operated by Istanbul Sabiha Gökçen International Airport Investment Development and Operation Inc. (ISG).

The book ends with our concluding remarks where we offer an overview of the Enterprise Sustainability Risk Management and Contemporary Issues in Business fields and provide suggestions for future work.

The reader may be familiar with the concepts discussed throughout the book, while new conceptual frameworks to contemporary business management and organization have been developed by us which include the Human Factor Risk Management model, the Enterprise Sustainability Risk Management model, and the Corporate Sustainability model.

Chapter 2
Corporate Sustainability and Enterprise Risk Management

Sociology ... is a science concerning itself with the interpretive understanding of social action and thereby with a causal explanation of its course and consequences. We shall speak of "action" insofar as the acting individual attaches a subjective meaning to his behavior—be it overt or covert, omission or acquiescence. Action is "social" insofar as its subjective meaning takes account of the behavior of others and is thereby oriented in its course.

Max Weber, *Economy and Society*, 1968, p.4

Corporate Sustainability Management

Water is necessary for soup but soup is more than water!

Edward de Bono, *Sur/Petition* (Turkish Edition), 1996, p.20

Corporate Sustainability (also known as CS) and global competition are vital values to companies. Corporate Sustainability forces companies to move forward, both developing and changing current business strategies, policies, and operations. In regard to this point, integrating sustainability components into business strategy are of critical importance. Business managers aim to provide both high-level efficiency and improved corporate performance by using this kind of integrated and holistic approach. Economic indicators are just one of the assessment criteria in the contemporary business environment. Business managers are aware that there is a need to consider social and environmental indicators in addition to financial ones. These indicators include performance-shaping risk factors in order to move in a sustainable way. There is interaction between economic, social, and environmental performance. Corporate performance is comprised of the economic, social, and environmental components.

The challenge of Sustainable Development for any business is to ensure that it contributes to a better quality of life today without compromising the quality of life of future generations. If industry is to respond to this challenge, it needs to demonstrate a continuous improvement of its triple bottom line (also known as TBL), that is, economic, social, and environmental performance, within new and evolving governance systems (Azapagic, 2003:303). The evidence of the assumed positive relation between corporate sustainable and economic performance is, however, mixed. Moreover, methodologically correlation studies bear no evidence on the causality of how economic performance can be improved by good environmental and social performance (Hahn and Scheermesser, 2006:3).

Edward de Bono said in his book *Sur/Petition* (1996), "Water is necessary for soup but soup is more than water." According to Bono (1996), traditional management approaches such as cost management, quality management, product management, and financial management are important but not enough to contemporary business management and organization. All that is like the water for the soup, but business has to deliver a "value" to the customer just like soup has to deliver a value (Space For Ideas, 2010). The business world achieves the competitive-based assets from the product-based assets. The next point is that holistic values are both an important asset to the future and a baseline to competition. Corporate Sustainability in a competitive and risky business environment includes developing a corporate risk strategy, tone at the top, a creative and proactive approach, *continuing* development, decision making in a timely manner, and a holistic approach: Enterprise Risk Management (also known as ERM).

"Risk" is a fact of life and it is something that is always around us. Moreover, all risks must be handled in some fashion. Any kind of firm or, for that matter, every human being has to act to take protective measures, in various forms (Symreng, 2002:5). Opportunity and risk represent two sides of the same coin: The opportunities embodied in the organization's strategic plan are intended to create stakeholder value, but their pursuit also exposes the organization to risk which may destroy stakeholder value (Sheehan, 2009).

The risks and opportunities that business leaders face are becoming ever more complex and unpredictable. In today's boardrooms, they have the potential to become survival issues. Understanding and responding appropriately to the imperative for Sustainable Development is a very real challenge. Achieving success requires re-evaluation of business strategy and the introduction of new ways of thinking about, measuring, and generating value. Increasingly, they are aware of the interconnections and complexity of economic, social, and environmental issues and recognize they cannot act alone to generate solutions. Stakeholder engagement is rapidly emerging as a vital tool to develop an understanding of what sustainability means for companies and how it can contribute to value creation and the viability of their operations (Stakeholder Research Associates Canada, United Nations Environment Programme and AccountAbility, 2005:10).

New technologies, geographical diversification, and changes in regulatory frameworks may create or increase certain risks. New technologies and globalization provides important possibilities for reduction of risks; the increasing opportunities of geographical diversification and of a more diversified product mix are good and clear examples (Symreng, 2002:4). Generally, sustainability as an outcome is a key goal of the process of Sustainable Development. Sustainable Development merges three important areas (economic, social, and environmental) into an integrated single perspective. The integration of groups of two of the three pillars of Sustainable Development leads to the concepts of eco-efficiency, eco-justice and socio-efficiency (Schaltegger, Burritt and Petersen, 2003:21) (see Figure 2.1).

Sustainability goals posit that private sector companies should not only create economic value and provide goods and services that enhance the standard of living, but that they should also engage actively in mitigating the different environmental and social problems they cause through their activities (Hahn and Scheermesser, 2006:2). The biggest gain in making risk pay off in an organization is improved performance. This results from adopting a strategy which successfully balances the need to pursue profitable opportunities while managing the risk. Boards and management that successfully incorporate both into the

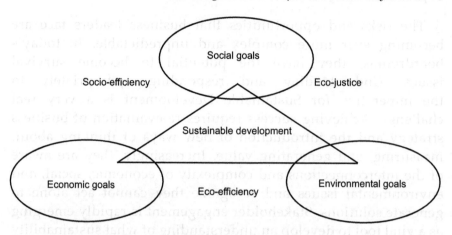

Figure 2.1   The three main goals of Sustainable Development
Source: Schaltegger, Burritt and Petersen, 2003:21.

strategy process will enhance their organization's resilience to risky events, and reduce the variability of its performance, which in turn will enhance its reputation with stakeholders (Sheehan, 2009). The key aim of a sustainability-based Enterprise Risk Management is improving an organization's risk management by integrating strategic planning, operations management, and internal control. Through regular and ongoing communication with an organization's key stakeholders, an Enterprise Risk Management approach will facilitate coordination to provide a unified picture of risk for stakeholders (International Federation of Accountants, 2010).

According to Schaltegger, Burritt and Petersen (2003:28), in simple terms, to be sustainable is to remain in existence and this is the most appealing notion to business managers. Sustainability is and will be a challenge for companies. As a result of this point, business managers need a holistic management and organization system to manage changing risks and to respond to them proactively in a timely manner. The Enterprise or Entity Risk Management approach is highly relative and takes Contemporary Business and Management issues into consideration such as corporate governance, stakeholder management, reputation management, innovation management, performance management, supply chain management, and enterprise resource management and planning. Corporate performance in the economic, social, and environmental dimensions is highly interrelated. Most business managers are aware that success of their organization's economic performance highly depends on social and environmental performance in today's holistic business environment. Businesses also need to integrate sustainability and risk management fully into their strategy—not only to minimize potential losses but also to exploit new business opportunities arising from the sustainability agenda (MicroAgility, 2009:4). In his book, *Management: Tasks, Responsibilities, Practices,* Drucker (1999) said that, "Managers must convert society's needs into opportunities for profitable business. That, too, is a definition of innovation."

Hence, business as a societal actor generating wealth as well as influencing both the ecological and the social sphere can be seen as an important potential promoter of Sustainable Development. Even if this overview is quite general and if there are considerable industry- and even company-specific features, it makes clear that almost every company from a micro-scale business up to a transnational corporation has some influence on the goal of Sustainable Development (Schneider, 2009:6). According to Perrini and Tencati (2006), Corporate Sustainability depends on the sustainability of its stakeholder relationships. The level of this relationship will change according to the group of stakeholders. Stakeholders are sometimes divided into primary stakeholders, or those who have a direct stake in the organization and its success, and secondary stakeholders, or those who may be very influential, especially in questions of reputation but whose stake is more representational than direct. Secondary stakeholders can also be surrogate representatives for interests that cannot represent themselves, for example the natural environment or future generations as per the following list (Stakeholder Research Associates Canada, United Nations Environment Programme and AccountAbility, 2005:11–12):

- investors (primary stakeholders);
- employees and managers (primary stakeholders);
- customers (primary stakeholders);
- suppliers and business partners (primary stakeholders);
- local communities (primary stakeholders);
- government/regulators (secondary stakeholders);

- competitors (secondary stakeholders);
- trade associations (secondary stakeholders);
- media and academic commentators (secondary stakeholders);
- labor unions (secondary stakeholders);
- civil society organizations/non-government organizations (also known as NGOs) (secondary stakeholders).

Figure 2.2 provides details of typical members of primary and secondary stakeholder groups:

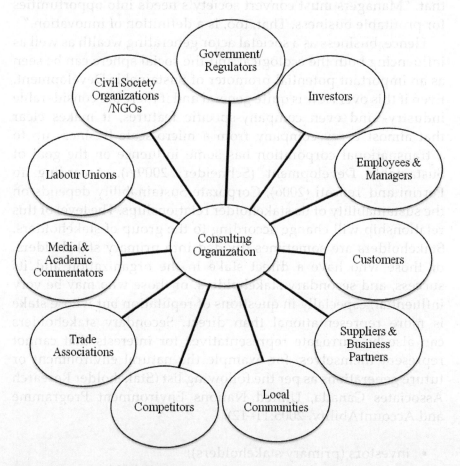

Figure 2.2   Stakeholders

Source: Stakeholder Research Associates Canada, United Nations Environment Programme and Accountability, 2005:12.

Corporate Sustainability is a business approach that creates long-term shareholder value by embracing opportunities and managing risks deriving from economic, social, and environmental developments. Corporate Sustainability leaders achieve long-term shareholder value by gearing their strategies and management to harness the market's potential for sustainability products and services while at the same time successfully reducing and avoiding sustainability costs and risks (Dow Jones Sustainability Indexes, 2010). In general, Corporate Sustainability and Corporate Sustainability Risk (also known as CSR) refer to company activities—voluntary by definition—demonstrating the inclusion of social and environmental concerns in business operations and in interactions with stakeholders. This is the broad—some would say "vague"—definition of Corporate Sustainability and Corporate Sustainability Risk (van Marrewijk, 2003:102). Sustainability addresses not only social and environmental issues but also economic issues that lie at the core of any company when everything is interconnected in today's global economy. Perhaps it's the only viable strategic and tactical option to succeed while addressing the complexity, volatility, and ever-broadening spectrum of risk when operating within global markets, relying on global energy supplies, and depending on global supply chains (MicroAgility, 2009:4).

The quality of a company's strategy and management and its performance in dealing with opportunities and risks deriving from economic, social, and environmental developments can be quantified and used to identify and select leading companies for investment purposes. Leading sustainability companies display high levels of competence in addressing global and industry challenges in a variety of areas (Dow Jones Sustainability Indexes, 2010):

- *Strategy*: Integrating long-term economic, social, and environmental aspects in their business strategies while maintaining global competitiveness and brand reputation.
- *Financial*: Meeting shareholders' demands for sound financial returns, long-term economic growth, open communication, and transparent financial accounting.

- *Customer and product*: Fostering loyalty by investing in customer relationship management and product and service innovation that focuses on technologies and systems, which use financial, natural, and social resources in an efficient, effective, and economic manner over the long term.
- *Governance and stakeholder*: Setting the highest standards of corporate governance and stakeholder engagement, including corporate codes of conduct and public reporting.
- *Human*: Managing human resources to maintain workforce capabilities and employee satisfaction through best-in-class organizational learning and knowledge management practices, and remuneration and benefit programs.

Corporate Sustainability performance is an investable concept. This is crucial in driving interest and investments in sustainability to the mutual benefit of companies and investors. As this benefit circle strengthens, it will have a positive effect on the societies and economies of both the developed and developing world (Dow Jones Sustainability Indexes, 2010). Operating sustainably does not only entail containing risks. For leading businesses, assessing the risks that all stakeholders face can yield rich opportunities (PricewaterhouseCoopers, 2009a:4). The three most frequently cited benefits that firms expect from sustainability policies relate to improved business outcomes: the ability to attract and retain customers (named by 37 percent of respondents) and improved shareholder value (34 percent). The third was straightforward increased profit (31 percent) (Figure 2.3) (Economist Intelligence Unit Survey, 2008:9). It seems like the term sustainability can be found everywhere these days—in corporate annual reports, in government policies, in community organizations' mission statements, in speeches of national and world leaders, in the business press (Banerjee, 2004). Current financial crises and ecological issues indicate that short-term planning and unsustainable practices do not seem to work in the Contemporary Business and Management concept. There are many examples, especially in west European countries and the United States, which show that leading companies are not adversely affected by global crises since these companies have internalized sustainability practices.

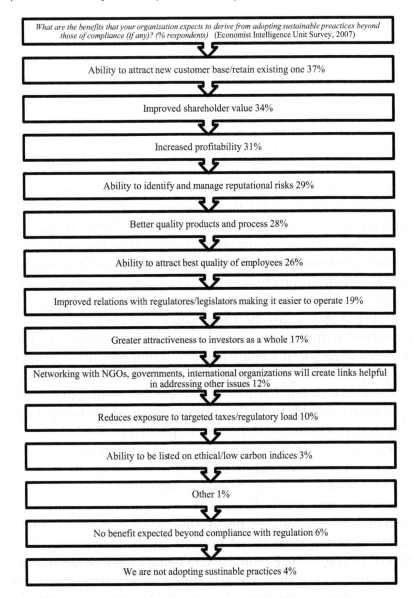

Figure 2.3   Biggest benefits from sustainability adopted practices

Source: Economist Intelligence Unit Survey, Doing Good: Business and the Sustainability Challenge, 2008:9.

The roles of companies are increasing day by day. Companies have a responsibility that is directed toward Sustainable Development. Also, sustainability-related responsibilities need to be institutionalized by companies. The concept of Corporate

Sustainability exists on agendas for boards of directors. It is assumed that society will not achieve Sustainable Development if it gets support from companies since companies represent productive sources of the economy.

Corporate Sustainability is a new and developing managerial approach to Contemporary Business and Management. In viewing Corporate Sustainability, there is agreement that company growth and profitability are important, but a company should follow societal objectives related to Sustainable Development such as environmental protection, economic development, social rights, and justice. (Wilson, 2003:1). According to Banerjee (2004), an examination of the Corporate Sustainability literature indicates that the rationale and assumptions behind this discourse are: (1) corporations *should* think beyond making money and pay attention to social and environmental issues; (2) corporations *should* behave in an ethical manner and demonstrate the highest level of integrity and transparency in all their operations; (3) corporations *should* be involved with the community where they operate in terms of enhancing their social welfare and providing community support through philanthropy or other means. The normative core of this discourse is not hard to ascertain: the assumption is that corporations should do all these things because: (1) being a good social and environmental citizen is positively related to good financial performance (despite very weak empirical evidence, if any; and (2) if a corporation is a bad citizen then its license to operate will be revoked by "society." Both of these are simplistic assumptions with little theoretical or empirical support. Large transnational corporations responsible for major environmental disasters and negative social impacts in the developing world (Union Carbide, Nike, Exxon, Shell to name a few), rather than lose their license to operate, have actually become stronger and more powerful whether through mergers, restructures, or relentless public relations campaigns (Banerjee, 2004).

Sustainability will not work as an add-on. It needs to be integrated into corporate structures and processes. Such change can be hard to manage, but is a key element of getting this right. Sustainability does not involve a simple checklist of activities but an alignment of social, environmental, and financial goals. A good assessment of what sustainability issues a company should be addressing requires an accurate idea of how company activities are affecting those around it. These need not be negative. Moreover, such analysis should include all aspects of the triple bottom line—environmental, social, and financial (Economist Intelligence Unit Survey, 2008:7).

Companies profit from the ecological and the social sphere by using natural resources and workforce to generate profit in the economic sphere. Logically sustained economic success can only be achieved if the company can resort to an intact ecological and social sphere. Reducing negative impacts on these two domains is therefore a necessary condition for sustained economic success. Moreover, companies concentrate considerable financial resources as well as technological knowledge and institutional power, and this combination makes them indispensable for Sustainable Development (Schneider, 2009:5). In his work, van Marrewijk (2003) differentiated the Corporate Sustainability definition into five interpretations. Each definition relates to a specific context, as defined in *Spiral Dynamics*. Also, the motives for choosing a particular ambition are provided for (Marrewijk, 2003:102–103):

- *Compliance-driven Corporate Sustainability*: Corporate Sustainability at this level consists of providing welfare to society, within the limits of regulations from the rightful authorities. In addition, organizations might respond to charity and stewardship considerations. The motivation for Corporate Sustainability is that Corporate Sustainability is perceived as a duty and obligation, or correct behavior.
- *Profit-driven Corporate Sustainability*: Corporate Sustainability at this level consists of the integration of social, ethical, and ecological aspects into business operations and decision making, provided that it contributes to the financial bottom line. The motivation for Corporate Sustainability is a business case: Corporate Sustainability is promoted if profitable, for example because of an improved reputation in various markets (customers/employees/shareholders).
- *Caring Corporate Sustainability*: Corporate Sustainability consists of balancing economic, social, and ecological concerns, which are all three important in themselves.

Corporate Sustainability initiatives go beyond legal compliance and beyond profit considerations. The motivation for Corporate Sustainability is that human potential, social responsibility, and care for the planet are as such important.

- *Synergistic Corporate Sustainability*: Corporate Sustainability consists of a search for well-balanced, functional solutions creating value in the economic, social, and ecological realms of corporate performance, in a synergistic, win-together approach with relevant stakeholders. The motivation for Corporate Sustainability is that sustainability is important in itself, especially because it is recognized as being the inevitable direction progress takes.
- *Holistic Corporate Sustainability*: Corporate Sustainability is fully integrated and embedded in every aspect of the organization, aimed at contributing to the quality and continuation of life of every being and entity, now and in the future. The motivation for Corporate Sustainability is that sustainability is the only alternative since all beings and phenomena are mutually interdependent. Each person or organization therefore has a universal responsibility toward all other beings.

By implementing a sustainability program, an organization can have first-mover advantages and can create obstacles in the path of other firms that may want to enter into a given market (MicroAgility, 2009:4). Too few companies are integrating their supply chains into their sustainability policies. Just as with the financial side of operations, poor performance by suppliers here can harm a company's sustainability record—and very quickly its public reputation—while a sustainable supply chain can greatly enhance an organization's ability to deliver its own high social and environmental performance (Economist Intelligence Unit Survey, 2008:7).

Sustainability is about the relationship of business to other elements of society. This means that a successful company will frequently cooperate with a range of stakeholders (Economist Intelligence Unit Survey, 2008:7). Discussions have also coalesced around the three principles that ground Sustainable Development: environmental integrity, economic prosperity, and social equity. Each of these principles represents a necessary, but not sufficient, condition; if any one of the principles is not supported, economic development will not be sustainable. These principles are described below (Bansal, 2005:198–199):

1. *Environmental integrity*: The environmental integrity principle ensures that human activities do not erode the earth's land, air, and water resources.
2. *Social equity:* The social equity principle ensures that all members of society have equal access to resources and opportunities.
3. *Economic prosperity:* Economic prosperity involves the creation and distribution of goods and services that will help to raise the standard of living around the world.

Organizations must apply these principles to their products, policies, and practices in order to express Sustainable Development. Below, the three principles underpinning Sustainable Development are extended to the level of the firm. As with the societal notion of Sustainable Development, it is assumed that corporate Sustainable Development is achieved only at the intersection of the three principles. As a result, all three of the principles listed and then defined below are necessary conditions for corporate Sustainable Development (Bansal, 2005:199–200):

1. Environmental integrity through Corporate Environmental Management

Corporate Environmental Management is an effort by firms to reduce the size of their "ecological footprint." Every firm has an environmental impact, whether it is merely by lighting office buildings or, more significantly, through the waste and emissions generated by production processes. Sound corporate Environmental Management practices are likely to be related to strong corporate environmental performance (Bansal, 2005:199).

2. Social equity through Corporate Social Responsibility

Corporate Social Responsibility requires that firms embrace the economic, legal, ethical, and discretionary expectations of all stakeholders, not only financial shareholders. Corporate Social Responsibility involves three processes: environmental assessment, stakeholder management, and social issues management (Bansal, 2005:199).

The right balance of strategy, brand management, and Corporate Social Responsibility leads to a sustainable competitive advantage for the firm. For this result to occur, however, Corporate Social Responsibility must be effectively integrated throughout a business' operations (Werther and Chandler, 2005:322). Corporate Social Responsibility is about incorporating common sense policies into corporate strategy, culture, and day-to-day decision making to meet stakeholders' needs, broadly defined. It is about creating strategies that will make firms and their brands more successful in their turbulent environments (Werther and Chandler, 2005:324). Environmental assessment or scanning enables firms to identify economic, social, and environmental issues and respond to them accordingly. Through stakeholder management, firms respond to individuals, outside organizations, and even the natural environment, that have a legitimate stake in the organization. An important aspect of stakeholder management, then, is building strong stakeholder relationships through transparent operations, representing stakeholder interests in decision making, and distributing the value created by firms equitably among all relevant stakeholders (Bansal, 2005:199). Stakeholder and corporate reputation-based concerns can be useful to developing the Corporate Sustainability strategy.

A sustainability-oriented company is one that develops over time by taking into consideration the economic, social, and environmental dimensions of its processes and performance. Therefore, financial and competitive success, social legitimacy, and efficient use of natural resources are intertwined according to a synergetic and circular view of the company's aims. In this perspective, value creation processes are broad and shared and meet, in different ways, the stakeholder expectations (Perrini and Tencati, 2006:298). Social issues management is the process of addressing social issues, such as the decision not to employ child labor, not to produce socially undesirable products, and not to engage in relationships with unethical partners. While these practices may uphold social causes, they may not be consistent with the views of all stakeholders (Hillman and Keim, 2001), but by acting in societal interests, the firm is acting responsibly. A high standard in Corporate Social Responsibility is often related to high corporate social performance (Frederick, 1994).

3. Economic prosperity through value creation

Organizations increase the value created by improving the effectiveness of those goods and services efficiently. Value is created, then, by producing new and different products that are desired by consumers, by lowering the costs of inputs, or by realizing production efficiencies. The high-value creation is not always related to high financial performance. For example, Napster was not able to capture the value it had created through its web site portal that allowed users to share music. Cooperatives create value for their members, but do not capture that value directly through revenues. When a firm does create and capture value, it distributes this value to consumers through its goods and services, to shareholders through dividends and equity, and to employees through salaries.

Integrating Enterprise Risk Management with Corporate Sustainability

In the words of Metcalf (2010), "enterprise risk management is business critical." Many companies and sectoral organizations are actively involved in the sustainability debate, trying to identify ways in which they could improve their triple bottom line and contribute to Sustainable Development. One of the main driving forces for this interest in Corporate Sustainability has been legislation, which is increasingly being tailored toward promoting Sustainable Development. However, increasingly, a second major reason for incorporating sustainability into business practice is starting to emerge; it makes business sense to be more sustainable (Azapagic, 2003:303). Sustainability opportunities and risks spanning economic, social, or environmental performance should be considered as part of an Enterprise Risk Management framework, rather than as specific risks that are managed outside the existing risk management strategy and framework and related policies (International Federation of Accountants, 2010). The Enterprise Risk Management-based approach provides a proactive, systematic, and holistic way to develop a Corporate Sustainability framework. It is directly related to business strategy. According to International Federation of Accountants (2010), a key challenge in Contemporary Business and Management is integrating Sustainable Development issues into a rigorous and adaptive risk management approach.

Risk management is the act or practice of dealing with risk. It includes risk planning, assessing (identifying and analyzing), handling, and monitoring. The risk management problem is primarily a problem in decision making: deciding what a firm should do about the pure risks it faces. Unfortunately, it seems to be more difficult to recognize risk events than to solve them once they are recognized. If the advantages outweigh the disadvantages and viable financial returns are likely, the risk becomes more attractive. Risk may seem to be a negative force, however, monitored it could be a competitive tool providing the edge over competitors if managed carefully (Kuo, 2005:9). Today's challenge for the business and management world to be competitive is in integrating sustainability, reputation, and stakeholder-related issues into a proactive and holistic Enterprise Risk Management system since Enterprise Risk Management is critical to business.

You face uncertainty, and the challenge for management is to determine how much uncertainty to accept as it strives to grow stakeholder value. Uncertainty presents both risk and opportunity, with the potential to erode or enhance value. Value is maximized when your management sets strategy and objectives to strike an optimal balance between growth and return goals and related risks, and efficiently and effectively deploys resources in pursuit of corporate objectives. Enterprise Risk Management could enable your management to effectively deal with uncertainty and associated risk and opportunity, enhancing the capacity to build value (Treadstone 71, 2010).

According to PricewaterhouseCoopers (2009b), Enterprise Risk Management may cover one or more of four objectives allowing an organization to focus on relevant aspects (see Figure 2.4).

When analyzing the relationship between corporate reputation risk, stakeholder risk, and Corporate Sustainability, we see that the Enterprise Risk Management perspective gives the best solution for optimization of this relationship. Integrating sustainability, reputation, and stakeholder-related issues into a proactive and holistic Enterprise Risk Management approach is a fundamental challenge to the Contemporary Business and Management concept.

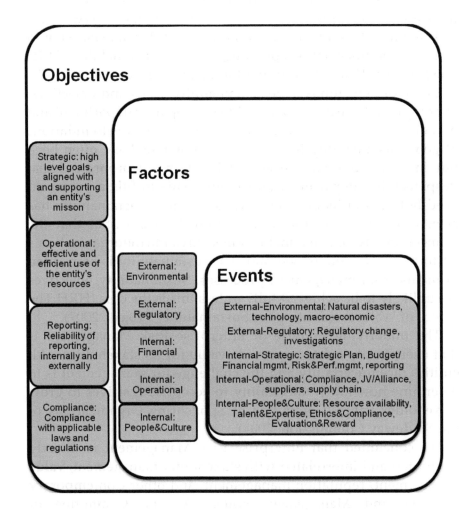

Figure 2.4   Objectives and factors in the Enterprise Risk Management

Source: Adapted from PricewaterhouseCoopers LLP. Not for further use without the prior permission of PricewaterhouseCoopers LLP.

Today's global companies are taking a more holistic approach to the notion of "green" than solely meeting the bottom line. Business leaders are faced with the challenge of how to achieve a competitive advantage while promoting the prosperity and wellness of their stakeholders (Parekh, 2008).

No organizations have unlimited resources to dedicate to addressing sustainability risk issues. It is, therefore, important for each organization to determine which sustainability areas are the most important for it and to understand how sustainability in these areas affects profitability, brand, and relationships with key stakeholders. It is, of course, important that this analysis should focus on the financial or operating case for sustainability (HRH The Prince of Wales Accounting for Sustainability Project, 2007).

Many organizations have sustainability plans and objectives, but they tend to be the responsibility of a separate department and part of a separate mindset. To put it another way, the foundations of good sustainability information and actions have often been put in place, but have been sidelined in a Corporate Social Responsibility department and report. This fulfills a perceived need but fails in its broader purpose because sustainability has been isolated within the organization. It is essential that the connection between sustainability measures and the organization's performance is understood and that sustainability is embedded in mainstream management processes. Sustainability objectives are unlikely to be achieved fully unless this is the case (HRH The Prince of Wales Accounting for Sustainability Project, 2007).

The underlying premise of Enterprise Risk Management is that every entity exists to provide value for its stakeholders. All entities face uncertainty and the challenge for management is to determine how much uncertainty to accept as it strives to grow stakeholder value (Committee of Sponsoring Organizations of the Tradeway Commission, 2004).

We concluded that Enterprise Risk Management is directly supported and interrelated with stakeholder management, value management, reputation management, and other Contemporary Business and Management issues. As the Committee of Sponsoring Organizations of the Tradeway Commission (2004) said, Enterprise Risk Management provides reasonable assurance to get business objectives and goals.

Organizations that proactively identify and manage risks tend to be in a better position to seize opportunities. This applies to managing Sustainable Development opportunities and risks, which include economic, social, and environmental issues. These opportunities and risks are best considered as part of an existing risk strategy and approach, rather than as a newly created layer of risk management focusing specifically on sustainability issues. Integrating Sustainable Development opportunities and risks into an existing framework and strategy should allow for a better understanding of their relationship to an organization's business goals and other activities. A good measure of whether Sustainable Development is embedded into organizational operations and general good management is the extent to which organizations: (a) astutely manage risks, attuned to social and environmental sensitivities; and (b) recognize the opportunities for improving both its financial and sustainability performance (International Federation of Accountants, 2009).

In their research, Benson and Davidson (2009) have examined the relation between firm value, stakeholder management, and compensation. Benson and Davidson find that stakeholder management is positively related to firm value. They also find an endogenous relation between compensation and firm value. Their results are consistent with Jensen's enlightened value maximization theory. Managers are compensated for achieving the firm's ultimate goal, value maximization. However, managers optimize relations with stakeholders to accomplish this objective (Benson and Davidson, 2009).

A strategic perspective promotes the integration of sustainability issues at a strategic level, so that they are embedded in organizational development covering strategy, planning, Enterprise Risk Management, and organizational learning processes. Part of the challenge for society and many organizations is dealing with the nebulousness of the issue of sustainability and Sustainable Development. Although most people recognize a need for action in this area, action itself is often lacking, or is poorly executed. This often manifests itself in well-presented promotional material, but with little indication of whether Sustainable Development is embedded in the organization's business model or whether senior management takes sustainability issues seriously. Thinking about sustainability issues strategically is an opportunity for organizations to establish or re-establish the "why" of sustainability, and to recognize what Sustainable Development stands for, that is, what we enjoy today will impact the livelihood and enjoyment of future generations. Organizations can find it easier to integrate sustainability where there is a clear understanding of its meaning and how it relates to the organization. Definitions are covered in some detail because different terminology is frequently used to refer to the same or similar issues, and can cause confusion. Strategy development covers the critical driving factors and activities that help organizations to embed sustainability. These include (International Federation of Accountants, 2009):

- defining and clarifying the terminology that an organization has decided to use (sustainability, Corporate Responsibility, or Corporate Social Responsibility) and what it means in relation to the organization;
- establishing leadership, vision, values, and behaviors;
- effective stakeholder engagement;
- setting goals and targets;
- establishing the business case;
- integrating risk management and assessment; and
- engaging suppliers.

Organizations that have successfully embedded sustainability from a strategic perspective tend to be those that also convert increased sustainability performance into commercial advantage. This is particularly the case when dealing with specific issues such as climate change that can present strategic risks and opportunities. Taking a strategic perspective helps an organization to develop an awareness of its sustainability risks and opportunities, foster a commitment to deal with these, and to manage difficult choices and trade-offs that might have to be made between financial, environmental, or social performance. A strategic perspective also helps to provide a systematic approach to ensuring checks and balances, and identifying and developing the skills required to address sustainability issues (International Federation of Accountants, 2009).

The King Report on Governance for South Africa 2009 (King III) emphasizes the fact that risk management should be seen as an integral part of the company's strategic and business processes. The board remains responsible for risk management and should pay particular attention to a number of specific risks, including reputational risk, sustainability risk, IT risk, and the risk of the unknown. King III proposes that companies institute measures to ensure that they are able to proactively manage the relationships with all their stakeholders (including shareholders), and the company should encourage constructive stakeholder engagement. The Board should strive to achieve the correct balance between the interests of all its various stakeholder groupings and promote mutual respect between the company and its stakeholders (Deloitte, 2009). Stakeholder identification is an unfolding process over time. Every company has (or should have) its own stakeholder map (Bouma, 2007). The sustainability of a firm depends on the sustainability of its stakeholder relationships: a company must consider and engage not only shareholders, employees, and clients, but also suppliers, public authorities, local (or national, according to a firm's size) community and civil society in general, and financial partners. Now and more and more in the future, the quality, that is the sustainability, of stakeholder relationships must be the guiding principle for the managerial decision-making process and the pillar of a more comprehensive corporate strategy (Perrini and Tencati, 2006). The following five steps are taken from the Australian and New Zealand Risk Management Standard (ASNZ 4360:2004), and you may wish to apply these when analyzing possible risks. Throughout these five steps you should be consulting and communicating with stakeholders and monitoring and reviewing the process (National Communications Branch of the Department of Immigration and Citizenship, 2008):

1. Establishing the context: you need to understand the situation clearly and without blinders. Ask yourself what type of stakeholder engagement this is, for example, is it a high-level strategic project or a localized initiative?
2. Identifying the risks: take the time with your team to brainstorm the risks, thinking strategically and outside the square.

3. Analyzing the risks: what is the likelihood that this risk will occur and what broader implications will ensue?
4. Evaluating the risks: draw all the information together in a written document and prioritize them.
5. Treating the risks: action is required now, not after the issue has arisen. Look for methods to mitigate or dissipate the risk.

Entity Risk Management and Corporate Sustainability

Most businesses today are under severe pressure to proceed with needed organizational transformation in order to cope with increasing rates of environmental change and turbulence. The law of requisite variety in cybernetics stipulates that for any system to preserve its integrity and survive, its rate of learning must at least match the rate of change in its environment. Organizations are living systems that are subject to this law. Their management faces the challenge of managing change toward a more or less accepted form. The new organization must be responsive, flexible, adaptable, and value-adding for all stakeholders (Dervitsiotis, 1998).

Organizations are not merely structures of units and departments but living fields of creative intelligence of the people who constitute the organization. In other words, business organizations are similar to living organisms like humans. They need to adapt to the changes within their environment (Dunphy, Griffiths and Benn 2002:197). In recent years, businesses have stressed the importance of Corporate Sustainability. Because of this, adaptation to the changing business environment in a timely manner is critical for corporations. This is possible via Enterprise Risk Management since its framework has both a human centric systematic approach and it supports the organizational transformation process by risk culture. Business managers can achieve a sound organizational transformation in their companies by sustainability-based Enterprise Risk Management. The human factor (also known as HF) is the most important corporate risk en route to both the best practice of Enterprise Risk Management and Corporate Sustainability.

At this point, Max Weber's ideas can provide the best guidance for us. Max Weber earned recognition for applying a conceptual framework to sociology. In other words, Max Weber is the founder of modern sociology as a distinct social science. He offered a philosophical basis for the social sciences, a general conceptual framework for sociology, and a range of learned studies covering all of the great world religions, ancient societies, economic history, the sociology of law and of music, and many other areas (Marshall, 1998). According to Weber (1968), social action depends on the human subject who can select proper tools to achieve objectives. The individual (human) is able to create history since he is capable of creating his own realities. Social action is directly intended for the human subject who is the individual in the cultural process. We can adapt this idea to Corporate Sustainability. The organizational transformation is one of the key elements of Corporate Sustainability. Enterprise Sustainability Risk Management (also known as ESRM) requires organizational transformation in order to adapt to the globally warmed business environment in a timely manner. Enterprise Sustainability Risk Management has the penetrating ability to shape human behavior into the desired organizational transformation. Enterprise Sustainability Risk Management is made successful by the person who has a holistic and systematic view point regarding corporate risks. This is in agreement with Weber's ideas since the individual specifies the society. Enterprise Sustainability Risk Management considers the importance of leadership to management in a sustainable way.

Weber emphasized the *"approche compréhensive"*. According to Weber (1968), the ability to be comprehensive is important. The manager who has a comprehensive ability has power to have an impact on the economic dynamics of the business world. This shows the necessity to incorporate Weber's ideas into those of risk management. For this reason, Enterprise Risk Management needs to find its own place. This book is a response to this necessity.

Max Weber embraced the *"approche compréhensive."* In this approach, the important thing is to be able to both understand and to explain human behavior. According to Weber (1968), the perception of the human as a determined element is not true.

Weber was against the thought that "the society specifies the human." The important thing for Max Weber is human behavior. He generated the Ideal Types of human behavior to help us understand human behavior better.

According to Weber (1968), economic determinants are important to societal change, but thoughts and beliefs are influential to the same degree (Yildirim, 2009). Similarly, economic and operational risks are important to Corporate Sustainability, but social factor-based risks are influential, too. For this reason, our Enterprise Sustainability Risk Management framework is based on the triple bottom line concept. This is well-matched with the sustainable business strategy which is embedded in our Enterprise Sustainability Risk Management conceptual model. We incorporate business and societal interests (or sustainability factors) to achieve corporate objectives within the triple bottom line concept via our Enterprise Sustainability Risk Management model.

Our Enterprise Sustainability Risk Management model is designed as a general conceptual framework to provide Corporate Sustainability in a more systematic way. Like Weber's work, our Enterprise Sustainability Risk Management framework has a philosophical basis to support achievement of the organizational transformation which moves Corporate Sustainability forward. The Enterprise Sustainability Risk Management model is designed to be a kind of value-based approach to management in the globally warmed business environment. According to Weber (1968), an individual specifies the society. Similarly, the individual or human factor is the key element to our Enterprise Sustainability Risk Management model. The human factor is influential on both organizational transformation and Corporate Sustainability. The Enterprise Sustainability Risk Management model offers a systematic and holistic way to both organizational transformation and Corporate Sustainability via a human-centered approach. Max Weber attempted to re-establish society based on relationships between individuals. Correlatively, our Enterprise Sustainability Risk Management model is designed to re-establish the relationship between all of the corporate risks which include strategic, social, economic, environmental, and operational risk categories.

Max Weber provided major contributions to sociology. He has been described as the founder of the general conceptual framework of sociology as a science. He developed a consistent social science philosophy. In the same manner, we have developed a consistent Enterprise Risk Management philosophy based on a new Enterprise Sustainability Risk Management conceptual framework. The modern sociology framework that was founded by Weber requires continuous development in order to adapt to environmental changes. Similarly, the risk management framework needs to adapt to the changes within the globally warmed business environment. For this reason, we have developed a new Enterprise Sustainability Risk Management conceptual framework that has a flexible and systematic composition. This characteristic provides a modern framework to the risk management process. Our inspiration comes from Weber's conceptual framework for modern sociology.

The conceptual framework of sociology, as described by Weber (1968), sheds light on the necessity of a "modern framework" for risk management. Our book intends to fill the gap in the risk management field.

Charles Darwin once concluded in the *Origin of Species* (1859): "It is not the strongest of the species that survive, nor the most intelligent, but the ones most responsive to change" (van Marrewijk and Merre, 2003:109).

Like biological systems, business organizations need to have a system of "sensors" or metrics that will probe the environment and provide the necessary signals to the entity to react in a timely fashion. Metrics are essential not only for measuring how the entity is doing at the present time but also for monitoring its risks associated with conducting business in this ever-changing world of the Internet. A profitable strategy today does not necessarily guarantee profitability tomorrow. The Internet is not only affecting how businesses conduct their routine transactions (placing orders, making payments, receiving cash) but also creating new types of products and services that were never envisioned. Moreover, the ease of information accessibility globally through the Internet has created a global economy. In this new environment, businesses have to compete globally. Another characteristic of this Internet environment is the rapid change in technology, which changes every few months. Thus, to stay profitable, businesses need to monitor and manage risks associated with the changes in the environment (Srivastava, Kogan and Vasarhelyi, 2001). To attain strategic sustainability, managers must develop ecological and human capabilities within the organization. These capabilities enable the organization not only to keep abreast of sustainability issues but to obtain sustainable competitive advantages (Dunphy, Griffiths and Benn, 2002:197).

Although Sustainable Development has been interpreted primarily as a national (or global) goal, there is increasing discussion of the "sustainable city," the "sustainable sector," and the "sustainable business" (Atkinson, Hett and Newcombe, 1999). In today's consumer marketplace being "green and ethical" are no longer options but a necessity. New legislation, voluntary standards, and customer expectations are making businesses more and more accountable for the impact of their products on the environment and society. Consumer demand for eco-friendly and ethically-made products continue to grow. As environmental and social issues enter mainstream thinking, most major brands and retailers are beginning to focus on the "triple bottom line:" economic, social, and environmental responsibility. Yet, many companies are unsure where and how to begin. Enterprise Sustainability is a business approach that creates long-term shareholder value, improves performance by removing waste, and manages risk. It considers the interrelationship of economic, social, and environmental issues (Bureau Verita, 2009).

Achieving Corporate Sustainability is a challenge that will increasingly occupy the attention of chief executive officers (also known as CEO), senior executive teams, change agents, and key stakeholders of twenty-first century organizations. This leading-edge topic will enable managers to understand the challenges and opportunities that exist for business by engaging with and designing a strategic approach to sustainability (The University of Queensland, 2009c). Assessment of the business world is necessary to understanding, with high-level awareness, the sustainability risks for companies. Today's companies are faced with many challenges that can get in the way of their objectives. These can be listed as follows:

- uncertainty of the market;
- difficulty of source management;
- protection of the company's reliability;
- survival in the long term;
- enterprise value, prestige, and reputation;
- Corporate Sustainability;
- competitive advantages;
- the need to increase sales;
- different positioning;
- creation of the corporate identity.

The effective solution to dealing with these vital issues is implementation of Corporate Sustainability Management (also known as CSM). Corporate Sustainability Management is the best way for business managers to achieve the following objectives:

- Financial: efficient and profitable.
- Legal: compliance with regulations and laws.
- Ethical: compliance with social norms and expectation.
- Social and environmental: contribution to the solution of societal and environmental problems.

Corporate Sustainability Management has a potential to provide vital potential benefits for companies as follows:

- increase/growth in value of the company brand and market;
- decrease in turnover of company's qualified personnel;
- increase in corporate learning;
- increase in innovation;
- facility to gain trust of sensitive investors;
- growth in share value;
- decrease in debt cost;
- access and entrance into new markets;
- increase in customer loyalty;
- increase in value gained by approval of social and regulatory authorities;
- growth in efficiency and quality;
- decrease in operational costs;
- increase in use of raw materials;
- reduction in cost of production and service;

- increase in market share and competitive power;
- advanced product design;
- use of clean technologies.

Economic, social, and environmental issues are creating risks and opportunities for companies. The Corporate Sustainability Management approach and its implementation can provide a way to identify this and turn these issues into advantages. This book can help business managers apply this advanced thinking to their own businesses. Corporate Sustainability Management provides sustainability in the economic, social, and environmental aspects of business in order to achieve a "sustainable company" target (see Figure 2.5).

Figure 2.5   Corporate Sustainability components

Source: Adapted from Nemli, 2004.

The crucial point: The sustainable business performance

Sustainability of a company's performance and success indicators is of crucial importance to introducing the company's performance and its future value. Corporate Sustainability is an important indicator which includes both internal and external factors and its assessment. Sustainability indicators cover economic, social, and environmental criteria, and performance of the corporate and financial management. For this reason, Sustainable Business Performance not only includes a company's financial performance but also its profitability and growth rate. These are highly related in the short-term or current position. However, Corporate Sustainability performance metrics present a long-term and more detailed framework. Corporate Sustainability is highly interrelated and connected with the effective managing of risks which are based on economic, social, and environmental sources. Also, organizational and financial-based risks should be considered and managed to effect Sustainable Business Performance. The Corporate Sustainability Risk Management process and framework provide maximized shareholder value by adding value to the company.

Environmental and social issues pose strategic risks and opportunities for businesses. Corporate Sustainability is a business approach that creates long-term shareholder value by embracing opportunities and managing risks deriving from economic, social, and environmental developments (Wikipedia, 2009b). Corporate Sustainability encompasses strategies and practices that aim to meet the needs of stakeholders today while seeking to protect, support, and enhance the human and natural resources that will be needed in the future (Australian Government, The Department of the Environment, Water, Heritage and the Arts, 2009).

Challenges such as increasing fossil fuel and food prices, climate change, and diminishing natural resources are evolving in a complex environment where staying internationally competitive requires great skill and expertise. But there are also immense opportunities, and Corporate Sustainability Management brings exciting solutions such as new markets for environmentally sustainable products, improved business development techniques, and better relationships between business and society. Corporate Sustainability Risk Management aims to produce business managers with an understanding of how businesses can be competitive and profitable while at the same time demonstrating environmental and social responsibility (The University of Queensland, 2009c).

Companies are faced with an imperative to undertake Enterprise Sustainability as a critical strategy. A convergence of factors—increasing regulation, changing customer expectations, competitor advances, brand equity protection, and global risk management—requires that companies move rapidly to address these complex issues (Deloitte, 2007a). A convergence of factors, technologies, and social and environmental issues make it critical for companies to consider making the transformation to "green" as a way of life. The principles embodied in developing the sustainable enterprise are responsive to these factors, and are, at the same time, necessary to address and resolve many of the issues we face. What factors today create risk for those companies that are not addressing sustainability on an enterprise-wide basis? These factors may not have been as obvious even a few years ago, but with the acceleration of activity, news, and public awareness of these issues, it is reasonable to assume that the time for action is now (Deloitte, 2007a):

- increasing regulatory requirements;
- changing consumer expectations;
- advancing technologies;
- risk management: hedging against major disruptions;
- competitive positioning: keeping up;
- value chain leadership (the Wal Mart effect);
- changing employee values: gen X and Y values;
- the moral imperative (it's the right thing to do).

In the global business environment, stakeholder value—based on the economic, ecological, and social impacts a company has on its diverse constituents—is becoming a way to achieve competitive advantage (Laszlo, 2008).

In his research, Kelly (2007) has developed a process that addresses the value of sustainability (Sustainability Value Process). According to Kelly (2007:6) twenty-first century business drivers can be viewed through two different lenses:

Conventional and Sustainability. The Conventional business lens includes "business-as-usual" strategies while the Sustainability lens focuses on "sustainable business" strategies. According to Kelly, the Sustainability approach is superior to the business-as-usual approach as it aids organizations in improving overall shareholder value with decreased costs, decreased risks, increased opportunities, increased market share, and better products (Kelly, 2007:6).

The above mentioned Sustainability Value Process presents a value-based approach to Corporate Sustainability Management. Sustainable business strategy is an important factor in shaping a company-specific risk management process and framework. Desired business outcomes depend on the effective implementation of risk management techniques. Business Enterprises of today are at a critical crossroad of strategic change. The assumptions and material conditions that gave rise to the industrial revolution —plentiful natural resources, infinite sinks for waste, smaller populations with relatively low levels of consumption, people as disposable inputs to the production process, and wealth and capital concentration as the natural order of things—stand in stark opposition to today's growing recognition and awareness of environmental degradation, polarization of economic development, and social inequity. Yet, we believe that this radical shift presents an opportunity of immense proportion to forward-looking businesses—an opportunity to re-imagine the processes and business models by which firms extract and acquire resources, produce products and services that meet the needs of culturally-diverse people at all socio-economic levels, and conceive of and manage "waste." Clearly, the challenge of responding to these conditions with the "next industrial revolution" calls for novel and radical business models that align practices with the diverse interests of society, the environment, and shareholders. This perspective can be conceptualized as a "triple bottom line" of social responsibility, financial accountability, and environmental sustainability (Johnson, 2004).

Crisis Management

The crisis in world markets, even if brought under control, is already changing the way business is conducted. Accounting professionals are becoming far more cautious and as credit becomes tighter, risk management and cash flow will take a much higher prominence (Australian Broadcasting Corporation, 2008).

In today's global economic environment, emphasis is falling on efficient and systematic crisis risk management capabilities. Organizations that wish to remain competitive must ensure sound crisis risk management for business continuity in the event of any serious disruptions. Research indicates that the ability of an organization to respond effectively during a crisis is a great factor in ensuring its survival. Crises are inevitable; however, they are not always entirely unpredictable. There is often a narrow window of predictability that provides opportunities for organizations to prevent and to mitigate the impact of crises as well as the consequences of emergencies. Enterprise Sustainability Risk Management is the top priority of Chief Financial Officers (also known as CFO) and Chief Research Officers (also known as CRO) in reaction to the current financial crisis. It is also designed to minimize the negative impacts of business interruption, disruption, or severe loss and enables better crisis management when required. The Enterprise Sustainability Risk Management model will support crisis and risk awareness and preparedness. Also, it will offer managers a step-by-step framework to execute crisis management from the initial pre-planning stages and will help navigate their efforts through to actual implementation, disaster recovery, and, eventually, post-action stages to minimize the chances of reoccurrence and ultimately to achieve business continuity.

Dealing with risk and crisis is not a new challenge for business managers, however new challenges are emerging. For instance, globalization, a volatile and highly uncertain business environment, global warming, and developments in world economy raise the need for managing risk and crisis in a proactive manner to be able to grasp opportunities for economic development and Corporate Sustainability. This book provides the background and rationale for the new conceptual framework for sustainability risk and crisis management.

Risk and Sustainability

This part introduces risk and sustainability and reviews the relationship between them. This section will compare the concepts "Sustainable Development" and "risk management". While there are many differences between these two frameworks, the comparison is necessary because they operate alongside each other and often represent potential alternative approaches to the same problems. They form different frames, which particular actors (for example, different companies, scientists, and government departments) bring to bear on similar problems (Gray and Wiedemann, 1999).

Sustainable Development refers to the fulfillment of human needs through simultaneous socio-economic and technological progress and conservation of the earth's natural systems. Sustainable world progress is dependent upon continued economic, social, cultural, and technological progress. To achieve this, careful attention must also be paid to preservation of the earth's natural resources. Sustainable Development is a term generally associated with the achievement of increased techno-economic growth coupled with preservation of environmental and natural resources. It requires the development of enlightened institutions and infrastructure; the appropriate management of risks, uncertainties, and information; and a knowledge of imperfections to assure inter-generational equity, intra-generational equity, and conservation of the ability of earth's natural systems to serve humankind (Sage, 1998).

According to Gray and Wiedemann (1999), both risk and sustainability are nominally future-oriented—that is, they assess present actions according to what they may lead to—but risk management is typically concerned with shorter future time spans. As we have seen, both concepts are also concerned with potential loss in some sense. However, a major difference is that sustainability is closely associated with the idea that certain needs ought to be met. By contrast, risk, in the context of environmental risk management, does not directly include a "benefits" component, as previously remarked. Both areas have to take into account the uncertainty associated with future outcomes, but they do this differently. In estimating risks, the uncertainty of given outcomes is a central concern which it attempts to capture in explicit probability estimates. In sustainability studies, although uncertainty can be factored into economic estimates and also appears in some environmental predictions (notably those concerning global warming), it is often treated implicitly or qualitatively, if at all.

Further differences become clear in terms of the types of loss typically considered. Risk tends to be concerned with injury and death of humans, and (more rarely) of other species. Sustainability has a broader concern which emphasizes more global issues such as biodiversity and social effects. More importantly, at least in its narrower forms, sustainability relates mainly to systems rather than individuals. Risks are of most interest in regard to sustainability when they affect the environment, or human society, or societies in aggregate. This is a matter of emphasis, however, and not an absolute difference. Thus, (un)sustainability is both a more comprehensive concept than that of risk, and, correspondingly, less detailed in respect to direct physical risks to humans.

Interestingly, the perception of risks by laypeople seems in some respects to correspond more closely to the concept of sustainability than does the technical concept of risk employed by experts. For instance, factors which laypeople tend to judge as risky seem to include effects on future generations, catastrophic potential, persistence, tampering with nature, and so on. Formal risk assessments tend to be limited to more proximate, immediate consequences. It is also worth noting in this connection that laypeople seem to identify positively with the values behind the sustainability concept (Gray and Wiedemann, 1996), while experience suggests that they tend to be more skeptical about risk management.

Different tendencies can also be detected in relation to decision making. Within Sustainable Development the application of the precautionary principle is emphasized. In risk management, despite the emphasis on losses mentioned earlier, one strong tradition argues for the explicit weighing of risks and benefits in decisions for example, using cost–benefit analysis (also known as CBA). Admittedly there are other examples where this does not occur, for example, in the USA's regulation of carcinogens. There seems to be no logically necessary reason for this difference to exist; it seems to arise from historical and "cultural" grounds.

Finally, the typical format of messages for public communication differs between the two approaches. While risk estimates are normally given in terms of quantities, especially probability-based estimates, or categories (for example, safe/ dangerous), public messages about Sustainable Development tend to have a broader content including qualities, quantities, visions, and strategies (Gray and Wiedemann, 1999).

Businesses today need to fully integrate sustainability and risk management into their strategy—not only to minimize potential losses but also to exploit new business opportunities arising from the sustainability agenda. These may include new products and services to meet developing sustainability needs, new technologies to improve sustainability or risk performance, or new business models to access and develop emerging markets and support the creation of sustainable communities.

Sustainability performance today has become an investable concept that effectively and efficiently balances profits and fundamentals for competitive advantage in complex and dynamic environments. It is a forethought business approach dedicated to creating long-term value through better embracement of opportunities, reduction of sustainability costs, and management of hidden risks by paying heavy emphasis on economical accountabilities toward those who bear financial risks, well-being of societies and societal agents, and proper care toward the eco-system. Today, it has become an important means to ensure long-term security of investments and to manage enterprise risk exposure in the current socio-economic and political environment (Liyanage, 2006).

Corporate Sustainability Management is emerging as a core competency for business leaders. The ability to create value from, and mitigate risks associated with, Sustainable Development increasingly impacts markets, access to capital, company reputation, and shareholder value. Managers who understand the need for a strategic approach to Corporate Sustainability Management will perform across the "triple bottom line" of environmental, social, and financial performance to preserve value and create new business opportunities.

Corporate Sustainability is a business approach to create long-term shareholder value by embracing opportunities and managing risks deriving from economic, social, and environmental developments (Sanchez, 2008).

The increasingly complex business environment that we currently face is creating a paradox. Risk is more significant than it has ever been, and yet it is less understood than ever before. In the past, most organizations tended to see risk as something to avoid with the objective of preserving value. Past conventions and attitudes about "risk as a threat" have resulted in a narrow view of the role of risk management in a business, a view that ignores reality. Unless companies take risks, they die. To be successful, they must be open, positive, and proactive about the risks they face. That is why the traditional risk management model, while perhaps good for companies in the past, is no longer good enough as they face an uncertain future. Companies and investors that see risk management as a differentiating asset are focused on the future and on the possibilities of what could happen if they manage risk effectively, not just what might go wrong if they don't. Thus, companies need to be more systematic in their approach to assessing and managing risk (DeLoach, 2004).

DeLoach has developed a "Risk Management to Sustainability Process" to aid organizations in systematizing their risk assessment and management practices. This process appears in the *Handbook of Business Strategy* (DeLoach 2004:31). According to this process, risk management has six main steps and every step is supported by information for decision making as seen in the list below (Deloach, 2004:31):

    i.   Establish Business Risk Management Process:
         a.   goals and objectives
         b.   common language
         c.   oversight structure;
    ii. Assess Business Risks:
         a.   identify
         b.   source
         c.   measure;
    iii. Develop Business Risk Management Strategies;
    iv. Design/Implement Risk Management Capabilities;
    v.   Monitor Risk Management Performance.

The Enterprise Sustainability Risk Management Concept

Business "Sustainability" is defined by Wirtenberg et al. (2006) as, "A company's ability to achieve its business goals and increase long-term shareholder value by integrating economic, environmental and social opportunities into its business strategies."

Sustainability grounds the development debate in a global framework, within which a continuous satisfaction of human needs constitutes the ultimate goal. When transposing this idea to the business level, Corporate Sustainability can accordingly be defined as meeting the needs of a firm's direct and indirect stakeholders (such as shareholders, employees, clients, pressure groups, and communities) without compromising its ability to meet the needs of future stakeholders as well. Toward this goal, firms have to maintain and grow their economic, social, and environmental capital base while actively contributing to sustainability in the political domain (Dyllick and Hockerts, 2002:8).

Risk is a part of everyday life. There are many types of risk that will be encountered in business. Some will have a minimal impact and can be managed easily; others may threaten the longevity of a business. Understanding the principles and processes for effective risk management will help a business owner make the decisions necessary to ensure the best possible outcome for the business (Global Risk Alliance Pty Ltd and NSW Department of State and Regional Development, 2005).

One of the most pressing areas for companies in today's global business environment is the assessment and management of risk. Managing risk is cited as one of the primary objectives of firms operating internationally. The science of risk management has made remarkable advances in the past 20 years on the financial side, developing new tools for offsetting risk exposures to foreign exchange, interest rates, and liquidity, for example. However, few companies seem prepared to deal with the emerging issues of political risk that today's new geopolitics presents. In today's world of rapid change, growing uncertainties, instant communications, and unstable political environments, traditional portfolio planning models and financial risk assessment methods are likely incomplete and even unrealistic. The risk assessment and management too often focus on a particular set of uncertainties to the exclusion of other interrelated uncertainties. Both financial and strategic corporate risk management must be considered together and treated as interdependent (Hutton et al., 2006).

The main objective of integrated Corporate Sustainability Management is to provide reasonable assurance and significant contributions to the achievement of business objectives regarding economic, social, and environmental factors and thereby providing the key to Sustainable Development. Sustainability advantages can be obtained by best practices in Corporate Sustainability Management.

Sustainability management offers various advantages to enhance the triple bottom line of People–Planet–Profits in the globally warmed business environment. These can be listed as follows (Wirtenberg et al., 2006):

- greater employee engagement;
- better recruitment and retention of talent;
- increased employee productivity;
- reduced operating expenses;
- reduced risk/easier financing;
- increased revenue/market share;
- the "fortune at the bottom of the pyramid";
- increased social/reputational capital.

Leading companies are aware that stakeholders have a large and increasing impact on how organizations perform. Corporate Sustainability is the management of the social, cultural, environmental, and economic factors that are most important to a company and its shareholders (Rowland, 2008). Enterprise Sustainability Risk Management is more than just getting better at identifying and assessing risk. The true value of Enterprise Sustainability Risk Management is that it can help organizations operate more effectively in environments filled with risks. Enterprise Sustainability Risk Management is not about constraints; it's about helping organizations get where they want to go. Most large companies have risk management processes in place. They know taking risks is part of doing business, and managing risk is critical to success. But Enterprise Risk Management practices vary greatly and the term itself has meant different things to different people. As a result, Boards and senior executives who are responsible for overseeing the identification, analysis, and management of risk have not had comprehensive guidance from a single source by which to evaluate their approach to Enterprise Sustainability Risk Management (Martens, 2005). A business owner chooses to take risks every day. Often business owners rely on experience and intuition to manage risk. However, the more complex the business, the more important it is to identify risks that may prevent a business from realizing its potential, and to manage them in order to minimize adverse outcomes and maximize positive outcomes (Global Risk Alliance Pty Ltd and NSW Department of State and Regional Development, 2005:9). Risk may have positive or negative outcomes, resulting in either an opportunity or a loss for a business. Risk management is the way in which adverse effects from risk are managed and potential opportunities are realized. Therefore, risk management involves (Global Risk Alliance Pty Ltd and NSW Department of State and Regional Development, 2005:9):

- minimizing those things that may negatively impact upon a business; and
- identifying and harnessing those things that will help to achieve the goals and objectives of a business.

Figure 2.6 illustrates the components of each step of the basic integrated risk management process and illustrates the cyclical nature of the process. A most current, best Enterprise Risk Management framework and process such as the one from AS/NZS 4360:2004 can be shaped and tailored to focus on Corporate Sustainability-based factors. The new Enterprise Risk Management model for Corporate Sustainability already takes into consideration the managing of sustainability risks.

"The New Enterprise Risk Management Model for Corporate Sustainability" (Kucuk Yilmaz and Yilmaz, 2008) process consists of a series of steps that, when undertaken in sequence, enable continual improvement in decision making. Communication and consultation will be reflected in each step of the process. Monitoring and review is an essential and integral step in the risk management process.

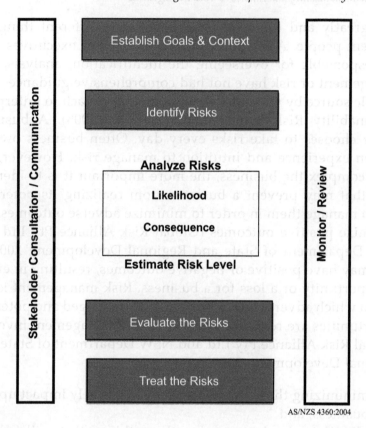

AS/NZS 4360:2004

Figure 2.6   Details of the risk management process: AS/NZS (4360:2004)

Source: Global Risk Alliance Pty Ltd, and NSW Department of State and Regional Development, 2005.

The Sustainable Management System and Sustainable Business Strategies

Sustainable Development is a process of change in which the exploitation of resources, direction of investments, orientation of technological development, and institutional change are in harmony and enhance both current and future potential to meet human needs and aspirations. Sustainable Development seeks to find the balance between economic, social, and environmental performance. Organizations following the Global Reporting Initiative's (GRI) reporting guidelines use specific performance indicators to identify reportable sustainability achievements and challenges. The GRI also requires that the organization describes its sustainability management system. In addition to having a sustainability policy and strategy, such a system should include four phases (Nieuwlands, 2007):

1. planning and risk management;
2. implementation and operations;
3. checking and corrective action; and
4. management review and continual improvement.

Sustainable Development is a systems-based concept with a long time horizon, a tendency to apply precaution in decisions, and a positive normative "mission" (development). Risk management focuses on specific, linear chains of cause and effect over short time periods, is typically associated with cost–benefit decision making, and concentrates on avoiding negative outcomes. However, risk management is also potentially a tool for informing and implementing sustainability. Both risk and sustainability are multidimensional constructs which can be indicated in varied ways. The selection of indicators in both fields depends on technical (for example, robustness, problem-orientation) and communicative criteria (for example, truthfulness, informativeness, relevance, clarity, and resonance) (Gray and Wiedemann, 1999). Business strategies for Sustainable Development mark the final phase in the journey. The aim is to seek win–win situations which can achieve environmental quality, increase wealth, and enhance competitive advantage. Companies integrate Sustainable Development into their business strategies. Sustainable Development is a natural extension of many corporate environmental policies. In the pursuit of economic, environmental, and community benefits, management considers the long-term interests and needs of the stakeholders. Sustainable Development strategies uncover business opportunities in issues which, in earlier stages of the journey, might be regarded as costs to be borne or risks to be mitigated. Results include new business processes with reduced external impacts, improved financial performance, and an enhanced reputation among communities and stakeholders. For the business enterprise, Sustainable Development means adopting strategies and activities that meet the needs of the enterprise and its stakeholders today while protecting, sustaining, and enhancing the human and natural resources that will be needed in the future (BSDglobal, 2009). Growing environmental concerns, coupled with public pressure and stricter regulations, are changing the way people do business across the world. Industry is on a three-stage journey from environmental compliance, through environmental risk management, to long-term Sustainable Development strategies. In the initial phase of the journey, the need to comply with environmental regulations drives improvements in environmental performance. Businesses adopt a more proactive approach in the next phase. Environmental risk management is introduced, to reduce environmental liabilities and to minimize the costs of regulatory compliance. A substantial number of companies recognize that the implementation of sustainable business strategies can lead to new opportunities and improved results—the business and Sustainable Development phase (BSDglobal, 2009) (see Figure 2.7).

Corporate Sustainability strategies create flexibility to accommodate an uncertain future in which social and environmental drivers become increasingly important. Thus, many sustainability strategies can be seen as (Gilding, Hogarth, and Reed, 2002):

- providing flexibility to accommodate stricter environmental and social regulations in the future;
- building product platforms that serve as the basis for a range of new products with sustainability attributes;
- preserving reputation and brand integrity that will give the company added leeway with stakeholders; and/or
- protecting a company's right to operate and renewing the license to grow.

Sustainable Development and Risk Management

The main question is, "How does a sustainability strategy create value for the firm?" While there is a good deal of discussion regarding the triple bottom line, the fact is that the company has a single bottom line—profitability. Strategic environmental and social actions feed this single bottom line, increasing firm

Step 1: regulatory compliance

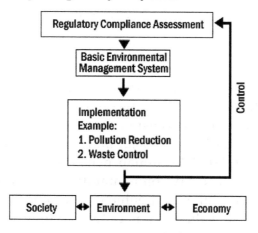

Step 2: environmental risk management

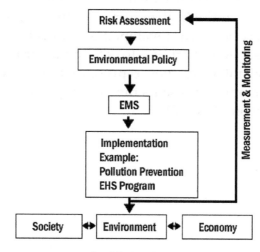

Step 3: sustainable business strategies

Figure 2.7   Three-stage journey

Source: BSDglobal, The Sustainable Development Journey, 2009.

value through environmental stewardship and promoting social equity in ways that serve both shareholders and the larger social good. By doing so, the value of the firm is enhanced through an improved reputation and brand image among key stakeholders (Hutton et al., 2006). The Sustainable Development process model (Hutton et al., 2006) presented in Figure 2.8 attempts to address these and other issues important to the successful implementation of Corporate Responsibility strategies aimed at contributing to Sustainable Development.

According to Hutton et al. (2006), Sustainable Development Strategy is the heart of the model. Sustainable Development has three main components: economic, social, and environmental. Sustainable Development is represented by the circles in the model. The economic dimension recognizes the value of the market as a foundation for social and environmental progress and for signals related to human needs, demand and supply, risk, and scarcity. The environmental dimension recognizes the necessity of maintaining and enhancing ecological systems for both their intrinsic value and as critical to long term economic and social progress. While the social dimension was given little attention in Rio, it represented the growing social problems later articulated in the Millennium Development Goals, world-wide inequities between developed and developing countries, and the subsequent barriers to economic progress and the environmental integrity they represented. The overlap of the circles in the model represents the interdependency of the three pillars (Hutton et al., 2006).

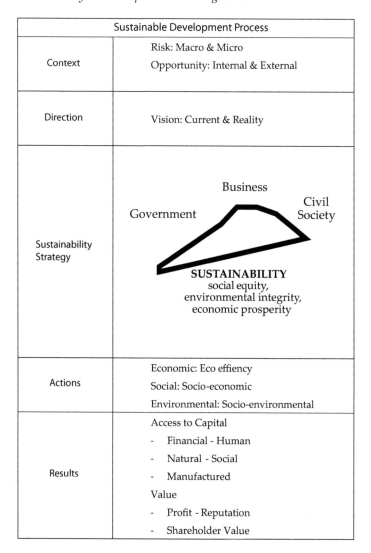

Sustainable Development Process	
Context	Risk: Macro & Micro Opportunity: Internal & External
Direction	Vision: Current & Reality
Sustainability Strategy	Business Government Civil Society **SUSTAINABILITY** social equity, environmental integrity, economic prosperity
Actions	Economic: Eco effiency Social: Socio-economic Environmental: Socio-environmental
Results	Access to Capital - Financial - Human - Natural - Social - Manufactured Value - Profit - Reputation - Shareholder Value

Figure 2.8 Sustainable Development process

Source: Hutton et al., 2006, 17.

Chapter 3

The Enterprise Sustainability Risk Management Conceptual Model: A Holistic and Proactive Perspective

Enterprise Sustainability has been defined in management literature in many ways. A very appropriate working definition for our purposes has been proposed by the Australian Government, Department of the Environment, Water, Heritage and the Arts (2009) as encompassing "strategies and practices that aim to meet the needs of stakeholders today while seeking to protect, support and enhance the human and natural resources that will be needed in the future" (Australian Government, 2009).

Enterprise Sustainability Risk Management (also known as ESRM) includes Corporate Sustainability (also known as CS) based aims. For this reason, our new Enterprise Sustainability Risk Management concept is based on the triple bottom line (also known as TBL) concept, and it also includes strategic, compliance-related, and cultural dimensions of business management:

- financial;
- social;
- environmental.

Businesses must consider these dimensions of Corporate Sustainability in order to be competitive in the global business world. Deloitte (2007a) developed a working definition of sustainability: "The continual improvement of business operations to ensure *long-term resource availability through environmental, socially sensitive, and transparent performance* as it relates to consumers, business partners, and the community."

Corporate Sustainability Management (also known as CSM) is defined by Salzmann, Steger, and Ionescu-Somers (2005) as a "profit-driven corporate response to environmental and social issues that are caused through the organization's primary and secondary activities." From a more focused business perspective, Corporate Sustainability can be defined as "a business approach that creates long-term shareholder value by embracing opportunities and managing risks derived from economic, environmental, and social developments" (Dow Jones Sustainability Indexes, 2009).

Companies are focusing on Corporate Sustainability in very different ways. However, successful sustainability programs methodically address strategic, operational, collaborative, and governance requirements (Deloitte, 2007b). The United Nations Environment Programme (UNEP) Finance Initiative addresses the interaction between financial institutions and four broad groups of stakeholders: suppliers, internal (employees), clients and shareholders, and society and the environment. Also, four primary ways in which implementing Sustainability Management and Reporting (also known as SMR) can provide benefits to financial institutions, especially in emerging and developing economies, are identified by the UNEP Finance Initiative (2006) (see Figure 3.1):

- revenue growth;
- risk management;
- access to capital;
- cost savings and efficiency.

Enterprise Sustainability Risk Management Drivers

The decision to undertake sustainability is a relatively easy one. However, implementing sustainability in a way that balances opportunity and risk is a significant challenge requiring fundamental business model innovation. Breakthrough thinking is necessary to incorporate sustainability into every aspect of the business model. Leading companies factor changing

Matrix of Sustainability Management and Reporting SMR drivers				
Stakeholders Benefits	A. Suppliers	B. Internal	C. Clients & Shareholders	D. Society/ Environment
i. Revenue growth	Opportunities for new business developments	Improve competitiveness and business	New products and services	Boost local economic growth
ii. Risk management	Reduce risk of supply chain reputational damage	Governance— improve compliance and transparency	Manage environmental risk	Manage reputational risks
iii. Access to capital			Improve access to finance	Meet stock exchange listing requirements
iv. Cost savings & efficiency	Build better relationships	Reduce waste Motivate workforce	Build better relationships	

Figure 3.1   The matrix of Corporate Sustainability Management drivers

Source: United Nations Environment Programme Finance Initiative, 2006:4.

technologies, emerging consumer demands, and evolving regulatory requirements into sustainable strategies and operations. Companies are focusing on sustainability in very different ways. However, successful sustainability programs methodically address strategic, operational, collaborative, and governance requirements. Leading companies take a top-down, sequential approach when implementing sustainability into their organizations. Leadership commitment is the most important first step. Then, through non-traditional collaborations, systematic assessments of value–chain impacts, and robust governance structures, leading companies ensure that sustainability is woven into the very fabric of the company (Deloitte, 2007a).

Corporate Sustainability involves both financial and non-financial measurement and it can be built on (Salzmann, Steger and Ionescu-Somers, 2005:3/24):

- cost reduction achieved through improved environmental, health, and safety performance (for example, fewer accidents, fines, and lost workdays);
- revenue increases achieved through gain in market share due to new environmentally sound products;
- positive effects on intangibles or, as referred to in Figure 3.2, value constructs, which do not increase financial performance per se but are yet to be leveraged accordingly.

Companies will not be able to dictate the timeframes or expectations for managing sustainability. Shareholders, federal and state agencies, and consumers are driving the evolution of sustainability. The time is now to undertake initiatives and integrate sustainability into the organization. However, sustainability need not be a reactive response to environmental or regulatory threats. As sustainability develops in the business world, companies can move from short-term risk avoidance and regulation compliance to long-term development of brand, competitive, and operational advantage. Proactive sustainability initiatives are an opportunity for companies to differentiate themselves as leaders in the industry, the environment, and society, ensuring long-term business success (Deloitte, 2007a).

We have developed this new conceptual Enterprise Sustainability Risk Management framework model as a specific management and organization system to manage integration between the corporate goals of creating economic and financial value and the aspects of environmental and social responsibility. The Enterprise Sustainability Risk Management framework has been developed as an important mechanism for improving Corporate Sustainability performance. It can protect, create, and enhance business value through measurement and management of sustainability threats and opportunities. In addition, this can help businesses effectively respond to the growing expectations of the corporate stakeholders.

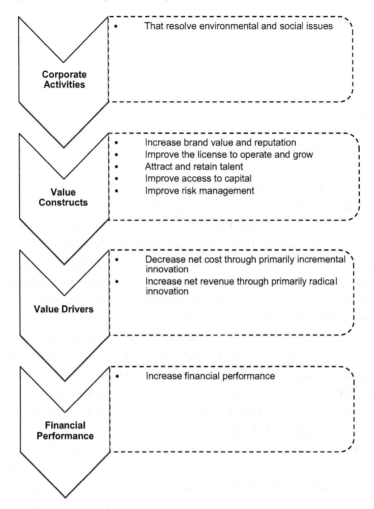

Figure 3.2   Systemization of value drivers and value constructs

Source: Salzmann, Steger, and Ionescu-Somers, 2005:3.

The Enterprise Sustainability Risk Management framework provides guidance to managers on how to establish a holistic and systematic sustainability risk management process that generates the risk indicators, risk sources, objectives, and reporting systems needed to ensure effective handling of sustainability risks and improved overall organizational performance and value.

We believe that integrating sustainability considerations into existing corporate systems and processes is the most effective way to embed sustainability into corporate business rather than creating new systems and processes. The Enterprise Sustainability Risk Management model enables companies to enhance their competitiveness and future orientation while minimizing their business risks.

Managing business processes by using a Corporate Sustainability-based approach is crucial in today's global business environment. Companies should incorporate a sustainability-based approach in their decision-making process and activities in pursuit of corporate objectives.

The Enterprise Sustainability Risk Management framework is a logical model that offers a strategic road map, which provides a contextual framework for businesses serious about taking on the challenges and opportunities of Sustainable Development.

The Enterprise Sustainability Risk Management conceptual framework aims to provide a systematic process for integrating sustainability into all company functions, including strategic and business planning, business development, corporate governance, project management, risk management, resources, human resource processes, stakeholder management, performance management, and corporate social responsibility. The Enterprise Sustainability Risk Management process provides a framework for Corporate Sustainability factors to be built into corporate systems, functions, and operations.

We assume that Enterprise Sustainability Risk Management is a kind of Enterprise Risk Management (also known as ERM) which is not just for building and maintaining the capacity to understand the risk of new socio-environmental businesses. In a world where new regulations and expectations of the social responsibility of financial institutions are growing, Enterprise Sustainability Risk Management assists in appropriately assessing these risks within the institution's overall credit risk analysis and other financial decision making (United Nations Environment Programme Finance Initiative, 2006). "Integrating sustainability" means that environmental, social, and broader economic factors, as well as more traditional financial factors are incorporated into business decision making, actions, and performance. Companies are increasingly integrating sustainability into their key business processes for different reasons, whether to manage new risks, gain business opportunity, or extend their role in society (Stratos, 2007).

Corporations are now redesigning themselves in order to integrate sustainability principles into their business strategies and policies. Global companies increasingly recognize that sustainability is an integral part of good Enterprise Risk Management and affects the bottom line and long-term profitability. Corporate Sustainability requires companies to address the issues of economic prosperity, social equity, and environmental quality simultaneously. No individual company can be fully "sustainable" within an unsustainable economic system. Managing for long-term success requires a full integration of the principles of sustainability into an organization's Enterprise Risk Management processes. Working toward the goal of Corporate Sustainability is a complex journey in which different process concerns may be emphasized at different phases.

The Enterprise Sustainability Risk Management model helps managers to employ tools such as Environmental Management systems, cleaner production, environmental auditing, life-cycle assessment, and environmental accounting. These tools can be applied to reduce risk, reduce costs, identify opportunities, and enhance business reputation and stakeholder interest. The findings of Deloitte (2007b) indicate that leading companies focus on the following critical success factors in order to have a successful, long-term sustainability program. Importantly, the sequence in which these efforts are undertaken is crucial to implementation success.

> Suggestion: Enterprise Sustainability Risk Management should be made an integral part of the corporate strategy.

The new Enterprise Sustainability Risk Management framework model (Figure 3.3) is designed as a process to help mainly with the following:

- improve awareness of the necessity for sustainability risk management;
- identify sustainability risks and opportunities;
- promote innovation and operational efficiency;
- develop a company-specific sustainability risk management model, policy, and guideline;

- integrate sustainability considerations into the decision-making process and practices;
- manage sustainability funds;
- proactively manage risk and achieve competitive advantages;
- increase value and innovative capacities;
- move toward sustainable business practices;
- promote corporate social investment, citizenship, and social responsibility;
- increase financial, social, and environmental contributions;
- improve the corporate reputation.

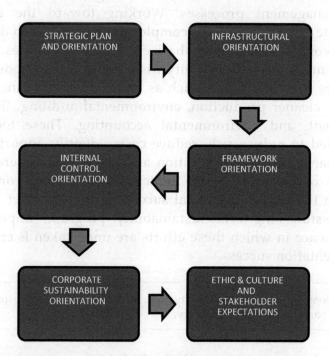

Figure 3.3   The Enterprise Sustainability Risk Management framework model

The main expected benefits of our Enterprise Sustainability Risk Management model are as follows:

- achievement of balanced and integrated economic, social, and environmental performance;

- full integration of sustainability-based topics into business strategy, management, and organization at all levels;
- corporate value optimization;
- reasonable assurance to achieve the corporate objectives in the triple bottom line concept;
- corporate resource optimization;
- corporate risk optimization;
- effective and proactive management of the sustainability-based risks.

The new Enterprise Sustainability Risk Management model is designed as a conceptual process, consisting of six main phases as shown in Figure 3.3. The sub-steps of each phase are presented below.

Phase 1—Strategic plan and orientation

Objective: Establishment of strategic orientation to practice use of the Enterprise Sustainability Risk Management model.
Sub-steps of Phase 1:

- set strategic Sustainability Strategy and determine the related objectives: economic, social, and environmental (triple bottom line concept);
- define business objectives in terms of sustainability;
- demonstrate leadership;
- stakeholder analysis: identify stakeholders and stakeholder expectations;
- define strategy, targets, and plans;
- define company policies: economic, social, and environmental considerations;
- search competitive advantage fields: current and latent;
- look to create innovation-driven Corporate Sustainability strategies;
- examine current strategies from a sustainability perspective;
- examine operations from a sustainability perspective;
- examine current risk culture from a sustainability perspective;
- improve strategic plan in terms of Enterprise Sustainability risks;

- improve business plan in terms of Enterprise Sustainability issues;
- improve operational plan in terms of Enterprise Sustainability issues;
- link up with like-minded companies.

Phase 2 — Management and organization: infrastructural orientation

Objective: Integration of Enterprise Sustainability Risk Management into key corporate activities and functions — sustainability-based approach.

Sub-steps of Phase 2:

- check over infrastructural situation related to corporate resources in view of financial, social, and operational processes;
- mobilize corporate resources;
- develop guideline of Enterprise Sustainability Risk Management model;
- develop measures and standards of business performance;
- assign Enterprise Sustainability Risk Management committee and alignment of roles and responsibilities;
- Enterprise Sustainability Risk Management organization: identify roles and responsibilities;
- training: familiarize personnel with Enterprise Risk Management, Corporate Sustainability, and related practices; train Enterprise Sustainability Risk Management team on emerging approaches and techniques; hold executive seminars on Enterprise Risk Management, Corporate Sustainability, and integration of Enterprise Risk Management and sustainability;
- create and improve a corporate culture supportive of sustainability;
- sustainability in Human Resource Management (also known as HRM) issues: attract and retain talent;
- set up Corporate Sustainability performance criteria;
- set up stakeholder engagement plan and its process.

A stakeholder engagement process: This sub-step has critical importance for Corporate Sustainability. Engagement is a means to help build better relationships with the stakeholders. This is today's necessity to improved business planning and performance for companies. Stakeholders can add value to the business. *Engagement* is but one form of stakeholder relations along a spectrum of possible interactions that also include activities like message delivery, media outreach, deal negotiations, lobbying, coalition development, advocacy, damage control, research surveys, focus groups, issue management, and benchmarking (Altria Corporate Services, 2004). The content of stakeholder engagement is generally described as an obligation to inform stakeholders on company performance. Although not much clarity is provided on the content of what should be communicated, it is clear that information on the financial and non-financial performance of companies should be disclosed. It is, however, widely emphasized that such communication and disclosure should be prompt, open, relevant, and transparent (Rossouw, 2005:100).

The stakeholder engagement process model includes the following activities (Katsoulakos and Katsoulakos, 2006):

- identification of key stakeholders;
- definition of stakeholders relations map and objectives;
- definition of stakeholder-related responsibility and sustainability key performance and risk indicators;
- definition of transparency policies and strategies;
- definition of stakeholder participating roles and tasks;
- integration of stakeholder roles/tasks in existing and new processes;
- provision of role-based information and training;
- supervision of stakeholder interaction and implementation feedback;
- monitoring of transparency and stakeholder company understanding/perception;
- obtaining stakeholder feedback on responsibility and sustainability and monitoring stakeholder satisfaction;
- updating the relations map and indicators.

Phase 3 — Set process step: framework orientation

Objective: Systemization of sustainability issues, corporate value drivers, and relevant corporate activities by setting up the risk management framework.

Sub-steps of Phase 3:

- identify threats and opportunities which affect Enterprise Sustainability: determine sustainability issues affecting both strategic and operational risks which are related to not meeting and meeting business objectives;
- create Scenario Analysis for potential sustainability risk events;
- prioritize sustainability-based threats and opportunities;
- establish strategic plan to achieve business objectives;
- establish thresholds and targets according to enterprise risk appetite;
- analyze impact, cost, and benefits of sustainability-based risks;
- prepare corporate risk map and holistic picture of the company;
- exercise decision making to optimize risk handling options;
- implement risk handling plans for enterprise risk optimization.

Phase 4 — Report and monitor: internal control orientation

Objective and related activities: Collection, analysis, and dissemination of risk data for relevant levels of management; communication and reporting in a timely manner.

Part of the effort to integrate innovation for sustainability throughout the organization is achieved through regular communication. Both within and outside the organization, a systematic process should be in place to spread the word about any achievements being made, in as solid and quantifiable a way as possible, to encourage everyone involved and give those associated with the company something to boast about and identify with.

Phase 5—Corporate Sustainability check: Corporate Sustainability orientation

Objective and related activities: Establishment of internal control of model and related activities toward effective implementation of sustainability practices.
   Sub-steps of Phase 5:

- create gap analysis: performance optimization aimed at assessing and comparing triple bottom line-based performance results and risk factors according to planned and desired Enterprise Sustainability Risk Management model outputs;
- assess progress toward sustainability goals;
- determine overall score;
- adjust strategies to ensure goals are met.

Overall Enterprise Sustainability check

This phase (abovementioned as Phase 6) includes assessment of Enterprise Sustainability Risk Management implementation performance by control and measurement of sustainability variables according to the determined criteria (Esquer-Peralta, 2006) as follows:

- sustainability leadership;
- planning for sustainability improvement;
- employee involvement;
- process management;
- product/service management;
- information and analysis management;
- customers and supplier involvement;
- other stakeholder involvement;
- sustainability results.

In this final step, performance is measured according to the criteria in three main groups—Economic and Strategic, Social, and Environmental, as follows:

1. Economic and Strategic
   - business value;
   - customer loyalty;
   - reputation;
   - total assets;
   - financial performance;
   - innovation;
   - efficiency;
   - revenues;
   - diversification;
   - improved risk management;
   - new markets;
   - cost and liability reduction;
   - increase in competitive advantage;
   - market performance;
   - sales volume and growth;
   - operating income growth;
   - compliance level with laws and regulations;
   - participation;
   - stakeholder dialogue;
   - transparency;
   - value creation;
   - long-term economic sustainability;
   - orientation toward needs;
   - improved business management.
2. Social
   - employee interest;
   - health and safety;
   - global and local responsibility and global citizenship;
   - encouraging company staff to develop, test, or practice environmental protection measures;
   - human resource sustainability;
   - corporate social performance: reputation and corporate social responsibility activities;
   - respect for local/regional culture.
3. Environmental
   - products and processes;
   - environmental impact associated with output;
   - eco-efficiency;

- using more renewable energy sources;
- recycling strategy;
- benefiting economic, social, and environmental stakeholders to the same degree;
- minimizing use of resources;
- reducing environmental load.

Final overall score

Sustainability has become a core part of business for many leading companies. Leaders are integrating sustainability into the full cycle of business processes, from strategic and business planning to business development, risk management, project management, disclosure, and assurance. Strong governance and accountability structures, as well as stakeholder engagement and human resource processes, provide the foundation for this integration of sustainability factors (Stratos, 2007).

Strategic Plan: A three-to-five year plan that is designed to lead, manage, and change an organization in a well-integrated fashion based on core strategies. The strategic plan should drive and inform the business plan.

Business Plan: A one-to-three year plan that serves as the principal operating tool for an organization and outlines strategies for operational and financial sustainability. An effective business plan will include plans/strategies for (The Calgary Centre for Non-Profit Management, 2001):

- governance;
- marketing and communications;
- human resources;
- resource/fund development;
- financial management;
- administrative procedures; and
- technology supports.

The business plan should drive and inform the operational plan.

Operational Plan: A one-year plan that provides details of annual operations linked to the budget.

Corporate Sustainability Committee (CSC): Sustainability should be an integral part of the corporate culture and behavior in business. As such, each employee is responsible on an individual level for upholding the corporate principles, and line management is responsible for ensuring alignment in business activities and processes within their area of responsibility. To ensure a close link to the operational part of the business and a full commitment from management, membership reflects the group management model of a cross-functional team approach using an integrated network within the organization to make use of all relevant resources, experience, and knowledge from all levels (Roche, 2009).

An effective strategy for Sustainable Development requires good management. It must provide coordination, leadership, administration, and financial control, harnessing skills and capacities and ensuring adherence to timetables. The roles, responsibilities, and relationships between the different key participants in strategy processes must be clearly defined and understood (Organisation for Economic Co-operation and Development, 2001).

Chapter 4
The Economics of Global Warming

Climate change economics has produced new methods for evaluating environmental benefits, for determining costs in the presence of various market distortions or imperfections, for making policy choices under uncertainty, and for allowing flexibility in policy responses. Although major uncertainties remain, it has helped generate important guidelines for policy choice that remain valid under a wide range of potential empirical conditions. It also has helped focus empirical work by making clear where better information about key parameters would be most valuable (Goulder and Pizer, 2006).

The economics of global warming refers to the projected size and distribution of the *economic costs and benefits* of *global warming* and to the economic impacts of actions aimed at the *mitigation of global warming*. Estimates come from a variety of sources, including integrated assessment models which seek to combine *socio-economic* and biophysical assessments of *climate change* (Wikipedia, 2009a).

Climate change poses a major risk to the global economy. The increasing frequency of severe climatic events, coupled with social trends, has the potential to stress insurers, reinsurers, and banks to the point of impaired viability or even insolvency. Worldwide economic losses due to natural disasters appear to be doubling every ten years, and, with current trends, annual losses will reach almost US$150 billion in the next decade. The greenhouse gases (also known as GHGs) which create this problem are long lived, so action is urgently needed. A long-term international political framework for climate stability is essential. The Kyoto Protocol, under which many industrialized nations have pledged to curb their emissions of greenhouse gases by 2012, is an important step but does not go nearly far enough. To ensure future economic development is sustainable, it must be based on the principles of precaution and equity. This will be achieved more quickly, and with less economic dislocation, by harnessing market mechanisms with a skillful blend of policies and measures. The financial sector therefore has a key role to play in delivering market solutions to climate change. Examples include greenhouse gas emissions trading markets and finance for clean energy technologies. By some estimates, the former could be aUS$2 trillion/year market by 2012 while the latter could be worth US$1.9 trillion by 2020 (United Nations Environment Programme Finance Initiative (FI), 2002).

Global warming has become one of the most pressing issues of modern society. Once dismissed as the ravings of a fringe movement, people are increasingly realizing that global warming is something that cannot be ignored. In particular, the economic effects of global warming are very significant. Economic problems and advantages of global warming (Economics Help, 2009) can be listed as follows.

Economic Problems of Global Warming

- *Rising food prices*: Global warming is causing desertification of agricultural land. This is compounded by a shortage of water. This will cause problems in supplying food leading to rising prices. This will particularly affect countries which are net importers of food.
- *Rising sea levels*: Global warming is causing sea levels to rise. This will cause structural damage and loss of land. To fight rising sea levels is expensive in terms of flood defenses. But, also, even the best flood defenses may not be able to prevent rising sea levels.
- *Storm damage*: It seems that global warming is leading to an increased propensity for flooding and storms. This has led to huge insurance payouts. In 2007, the floods in the UK could have been due to global warming. This will lead to higher insurance premiums. Some areas may become uninsurable.
- *Loss of wildlife*: Changing temperatures can cause havoc for wildlife. The economic cost may be hard to evaluate, but

if species go extinct, it may prevent future medicines from being invented.

- *Migration*: Global warming will cause migration from some countries to others. Those that suffer the most from global warming will see depopulation. There will be overcrowding in the other countries.

Advantages of Global Warming

- *Improved agricultural output*: It is argued that higher temperatures may lead to increased food production in some countries. This conflicts with the issue of desertification. Some areas will have increased production while some areas will have lower production.
- *Lower heating bills for cold countries*: But there will be higher air conditioning costs for warm countries.
- *The rise in temperatures is only temporary*: Some argue that world temperatures have always fluctuated and these rises in temperatures will only be temporary.

The challenge of coping with global warming is particularly difficult because it spans many disciplines and parts of society. Ecologists may see it as a threat to ecosystems, marine biologists as a problem arising from ocean acidification, utilities as a debit to their balance sheets, and coal miners as an existential threat to their livelihood. Businesses may view global warming as either an opportunity or a hazard, politicians as a great issue as long as they don't need to mention taxes, ski resorts as a mortal danger to their already short seasons, golfers as a boon to year-round recreation, and poor countries as a threat to their farmers as well as a source of financial and technological aid. This many-faceted nature also raises challenges to natural and social scientists who must incorporate a wide variety of geophysical, economic, and political disciplines into their diagnoses and prescriptions (Nordhaus, 2007:5).

The concept of "sustainability" is presented as an ideal state of social development for harmonizing the global environment and human society. The science, technology, and economic systems in the twenty-first century are known together as the "environmental

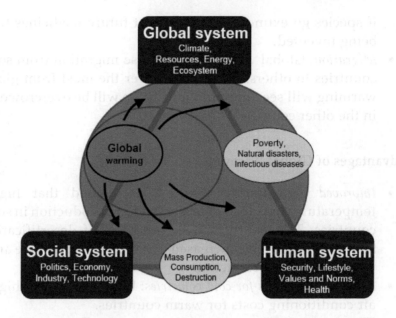

Figure 4.1   Sustainability science topics and change of global warming issue status

Source: Maeda and Hibiki, 2008.

era," and this concept is the keyword for developing discussions during various opportunities in government and business sectors or in cross-border situations. At first, the global warming problem was one of the sustainability science subjects along with the North–South Poles and poverty issues. Now, as the negative effects of the global warming problem are increasing and deepening, it has become, accordingly, the current central issue (Maeda and Hibiki, 2008) (see Figure 4.1).

Risks are idiosyncratic—a risk to one group may present an opportunity to another. The qualification of global risks lies in their systemic nature: their impacts challenge the integrity of the system. Their consequences are harder to predict, frequently disproportionate, difficult to contain, and present challenges to us all. The Global Risk Network identified 23 core global risks which the international community will face over the next ten years (World Economic Forum, 2007) (See Table 4.1.).

These core global risks were assessed in terms of likelihood and severity by the World Economic Forum (2007). In addressing

Table 4.1   Core global risks

Economics	Oil price shock/energy supply interruptions US current account deficit/fall in: US$ Chinese economic hard landing Fiscal crises caused by demographic shift Blow up in asset prices/excessive indebtedness
Environmental	Climate change Loss of freshwater services Natural catastrophe: tropical stroms Natural catastrophe: earthquakes Natural catastrophe: inland flooding
Geopolitical	International terrorism Proliferation of weapons of mass destruction Interstate and civil wars Failed and failing states Transnational crime and corruption Retrenchment from globalization Middle East instability
Societal	Pandemics Infectious diseases in the developing world Chronic disease in the developed world Liability regimes
Technological	Breakdown of critical information infrastructure Emergence of risks associated with nanotechnology

Source: World Economic Forum, 2007.

likelihood, actuarial principles were applied in the few cases where sufficient data existed; in most cases only qualitative assessments, based on expert opinion, were possible. In assessing severity, two indices were considered: destruction of assets/economic damage and — where applicable — human lives lost. Although some risks are inherently long term (such as climate change), and others (such as an oil price shock) could occur in the near term, all risks were evaluated within a ten-year time frame (World Economic Forum, 2007). In addition to risk assessment in terms of likelihood and severity, the Global Risk Network developed a qualitative global risk "barometer," based on expert judgment of the outlook for global risks. This is essentially a forward-looking measure: it does not look at how the risk has played out over the last year; rather, it assesses whether the seriousness of the risk for the next ten years has become more or less acute. For example, while 2006 saw fewer tropical storms than 2005, expert consensus was clear that the risk trend is moving upward, with growing agreement on the impact of climate change on severe meteorological events (World Economic Forum, 2007).

Chapter 5
Global Warming and Sustainable Aviation

The air transport sector is of great importance for worldwide socio-economic development, facilitating access to goods and services, and playing a major role in tourism. The role of the aviation sector in Sustainable Development is increasingly the focus of governments, the civil society, and the aviation industry itself. These stakeholders recognize that the right balance between economic, social, and environmental values must be found if the sector is to play its part in the necessary move to Sustainable Development. Over the past decades, the air transport sector has reduced specific emissions through continuously improving technology and operational procedures. With a growth rate of about 4–6 percent, however, the increased demand for air travel has outpaced these improvements. Therefore, new strategies need to be designed and implemented. Balancing the three pillars of Sustainable Development is a complex task that requires action from all stakeholders involved, almost at the same time. Therefore, partnerships involving all relevant stakeholders are crucial to developing and successfully implementing innovative and meaningful ideas for action (United Nations Environment Programme, 2009).

A strong and growing demand, significant environmental and social costs, and impacts of global warming create growth challenges for aviation, and these impacts threaten to constrain airline/airport growth.

The challenge for government and industry is to ensure adequate environmental protection while, at the same time, delivering social and economic development (Thomas, 2006). Corporate Sustainability (also known as CS) requires a new business strategy and model in order to deal with these challenges to aviation business organizations: airlines and airports.

Aviation's impact on the environment and climate change is one of the most important challenges now facing the industry. Addressing aviation's impact on the environment has become one of the most significant challenges facing the aviation industry. Increased media and stakeholder interest, coupled with increased calls from government to the industry means that we need to do more than ever to reduce aviation's impact on the environment. In June 2005, the aviation industry produced its strategy for a sustainable industry. Sustainable Aviation (also known as SA) marked a step-change in the industry's response to environmental issues and signaled its commitment to long-term Sustainable Development (Society of British Aerospace Companies, 2008). Sustainable Aviation addresses sustainability issues such as climate change, noise, local environmental impacts, and social and economic development.

Flying by jet plane is the least environmentally sustainable and fastest growing way to travel and transport goods (Grayling and Bishop, 2001:7). Air transport has undeniable social benefits. However, growth in air transport also comes at a cost to the environment and with potentially increased accident risk (Grayling and Bishop, 2001:26).

Aviation has a number of impacts on the environment, including local air pollution (nitrous oxide (NO_x), hydrocarbons (HC), and toxins), climate change (carbon dioxide (CO_2), NO_x, contrails, cirrus clouds, and sulfur dioxide (SO_2)) and noise. The impacts of aviation on climate change are mostly exempt from any regulation. In addition, aviation is largely exempt from kerosene taxation, thus contributing to inefficiencies in the transport system as a whole. In order to combat climate change, developed countries and economies in transition reached an agreement, under the Kyoto Protocol, to reduce their greenhouse gas (also known as GHG) emissions to about 5 percent below 1990 levels, between 2008 and 2012. While domestic aviation emissions are accounted for in these countries' emissions totals, emissions from international aviation are not. Currently representing 3.5 percent of total anthropogenic radiative forcing, aviation's total human-induced climate change impact could represent as much as 15 percent by 2050 if no measures are taken to reduce these emissions, even after accounting for expected technological improvements, according to the Intergovernmental Panel on Climate Change (IPCC) Special Report on Aviation and the Global Atmosphere (International Coalition for Sustainable Aviation, 2003).

Civil aviation, like most other economic activities, gives rise to environmental problems of various kinds. In 1999, the International Civil Aviation Organization (ICAO) Secretariat compiled an inventory of environmental problems that may be associated with civil aviation, to assist the ICAO Council in identifying future priorities in the environmental field. It was assumed that "the environment" means all those natural and man-made surroundings which may be adversely affected by the presence of civil aviation but which are not directly involved in the aviation itself. The inventory, therefore, excluded problems concerning the conditions for passengers and crew or problems concerning the working conditions of airline or airport employees. It also excluded aircraft-manufacturing processes because such processes fall outside ICAO's ambit. Environmental problems associated with aviation include (International Civil Aviation Organization, 2001):

- aircraft noise;
- the impact of aircraft engine emissions, at ground level and globally;
- other local problems at airports, including problems arising from construction and expansion of airports and associated infrastructure, water and soil pollution, and management of waste.

The effects of airport activity can be classified under three categories: social, economic, and environmental. Any analysis of the effects of airports should therefore examine these three aspects (Campbell et al., 2005):

- Economic effects of airport operations and activity may be summarized under direct economic impacts, indirect or induced economic impacts, and catalytic economic impacts. Direct economic impacts of airport operations and activity include employment and income generated in the airport areas' supply chains of goods and services, for example, the revenue and employment created within the actual airport, shops, and restaurants. Indirect or "induced" economic impacts include employment and income generated within the airport area and derived from the spending of incomes by the direct and indirect employers, for example revenue channeled into hospitality or car hire. Catalytic economic impacts are derived through the role of the airport in attracting other economic activities, for example tourism and the inward investment from multinational technology firms.

- Social factors include issues like noise pollution, the quality of life for nearby residents, and the possible physical encroachment of the airport on to nearby communities in order to accommodate for airport expansion, increasing and/or decreasing land and house valuations. Additionally, there are the various positive social/cultural links with other nations. As any airport expands and diversifies, there is likely to be a significant increase in jobs available, and this can inevitably lead to large numbers of outsiders moving into nearby communities. This pattern can be found in many other forms of economic development where large-scale job creation has occurred in close proximity to already independently existing communities. In some cases, this has come to be known as "gentrification," and its affects are well documented. Of all the potential negative spin-offs of an expanding airport, community upheaval presents possibly the biggest challenge to local sustainability. If this cannot be achieved in a local sense despite all mitigation measures, methods must be devised to tailor the expansion in order to achieve sustainability in a broader sense of the term.

- Environmental concerns include the airports' physical "footprint" (the area of land covered by the airport and surrounding infrastructure), the emissions generated by the airports' operation, inefficiencies created in the airports' operation, as well as the destruction of surrounding habitats. Airports of this scale are often dependent on more than one runway (which can be up to two miles long), a large terminal building, large hangers and other support and maintenance structures, and thousands of parking spaces, to name a few things. Due to the sheer scale and complexity of an airport and its operations, not all of the solutions will come under the remit of planning, for example, the fuel efficiency of an aircraft's engine, but planning, more so than in many other professions, can negotiate a balance between the often conflicting goals of social, economic, and environmental factors.

The Impact of Global Warming on Aviation Business and Management

Climate change—often referred to as "global warming"—is one of the most significant emerging risks facing the world today, presenting huge challenges to the environment and to the world economy. It is also one of the most difficult risks to mitigate (Marsh, 2009). Climate change presents physical, regulatory, and competitive risks to companies, but it also provides significant competitive and reputational opportunities for businesses that decrease their carbon footprint and take advantage of burgeoning global markets for low-carbon products and technologies. As demonstrated by recent reports from scientists, economists, and companies alike, climate change will have an unprecedented impact on corporations in a variety of sectors around the world, jeopardizing the profitability and shareholder value of companies and entire industries (Lubber, 2008). These risks can be estimated by the implementation of proactive Enterprise Risk Management. The Enterprise Risk Management-based framework and strategy provide a reasonable assurance for managing these risks.

Corporations face increased financial risk from emerging carbon-reducing regulations at the international, federal, and regional levels which will make carbon emissions prohibitively expensive. With the Kyoto Protocol now in force, imposing limits on global warming pollution in many industrialized countries—the European Union (also known as EU) operating under a carbon cap-and-trade system and many US states, including California and the Northeast states—smart US companies are taking notice and taking action. For example, in anticipation of federal climate regulations, some US businesses are already backing away from new projects considered to have high carbon exposure. Construction of dozens of coal-fired power plants has been postponed or cancelled in the past year due to regulatory risks and other factors. With all arrows pointing to regulations and placing a cost on carbon emissions, the rules of the game will soon change in a big way for many firms. Directors need to think seriously about how this new reality will impact outmoded "business as usual" models (Lubber, 2008).

Global warming is both a global business and a risk management issue. The debate over global warming has focused on the three big "Es": environment, energy, and economic impact (Knickerbocker, 2007). Air travel is the world's fastest growing source of greenhouse gases, such as CO_2, which cause global warming. The huge increase in aircraft pollution is largely due to the rapid growth in air traffic which has been expanding at nearly two and a half times the average economic growth rates since 1960. It is expected that the number of people flying will virtually double over the next 15 years. This means there will be increasing airport capacity, more flights, more pollution, and increasingly crowded airspace (Friends of the Earth, 2009). However, the civil aviation sector is also a cornerstone of our global economy. For this reason, global warming requires a holistic approach from civil aviation business. Global warming legislation brings new operational, financial, and legal risks for civil aviation business organizations. These risks have a potential impact on Corporate Sustainability for the above-mentioned organizations via means such as new taxes, regulations, and investment requirements; aircraft noise regulation; and night-flight restrictions of airports. These new requirements mean new costs and decreasing returns. Global warming is a reality that will increase the operating costs of aviation business organizations. For this reason, global warming is truly a corporate financial risk management issue. Risk managers of civil aviation businesses should analyze their business' threats and opportunities regarding global warming-based risks.

This part of the chapter aims to present a core set of ways in which global warming impacts civil aviation management. It is designed as the initial step to supporting environmental and operational sustainability efforts for civil aviation business organizations in view of the costs and benefits of global warming.

Airlines and airport operators must now have expertise in Environmental Management. Like the current global financial crisis, global warming has the potential to create various threats and opportunities for business organizations. Airlines and airport businesses should develop and practice sustainability strategies and risk management and integrate sustainability into their operating models, business strategies, and critical processes. The risk management-based holistic approach—which encompasses strategy, design, and execution—enables managers in the aviation industry to grow revenue, reduce costs, manage risks, and enhance their brand and reputation. This must include global warming-based issues. Global warming-based sustainability costs and benefits should be identified for effective management of sustainability risks in the aviation business organization. This section presents the initial step to a risk management system for the aviation business organization via determination of costs and benefits.

The aim of this part is as follows:

- Research the impact of global warming on both aviation business management and organizations, such as liabilities which are raised by the Kyoto Protocol.
- Review both cost and benefit-based parameters for aviation business organizations regarding global warming influences.
- Offer a new conceptual approach for parameter analysis.
- Raise awareness of the impact of global warming and risk management on aviation business organizations.
- Help to raise environmental awareness and contribute to the community both domestically and internationally.
- Establish a cost–benefit "triple bottom line" (also known as TBL) regarding climate change issues for the sustainability concept of aviation business.

Climate change is an important aspect of the long-term risk management strategy for aviation organizations, like any other global business. Companies should seek long-term solutions that mitigate the adverse impact of global warming-based events before they become more extensive. The various aspects of global warming have an effect on company brand and reputation.

Corporate social responsibility-based practices should demonstrate the company stakeholders' sensitivity regarding global warming issues. The risk management-based approach aims to provide economic sustainability, environmental sustainability, social accountability, and sustainability integration to companies.

The hypotheses of this part are as follows:

Hypothesis 1: Global warming creates the only threat to the sustainability of companies. The costs of global warming are always greater than its benefits for companies in the short, mid, and long term.

Hypothesis 2: Global warming creates opportunities for the sustainability of firms. The benefits of global warming are higher than its costs for companies in both the mid and long term.

Hypothesis 3: Global warming-based costs and benefits can be compared to each other for aviation business organizations.

Hypothesis 4: Global warming is one of the important topics on today's corporate risk management agenda. This issue affects Corporate Sustainability, brand, and marketing management. It was found at the end of this study that although global warming costs appear to be greater than benefits in the short term, benefits will be greater than costs in the long term, regarding the Corporate Sustainability concept. Also, global warming-based costs and benefits could not be compared to each other directly since related parameters have different characteristics and time tables.

For this reason the null portions of Hypotheses 1 and 2 are, "Global warming creates the only threat to the sustainability of companies," "The cost of global warming is always greater than its benefits for companies in the short, mid, and long term," and "Global warming-based costs and benefits can be compared to each other for aviation business organizations."

Aviation Industry, Climate Change and Global Warming

Airports and aviation generate greenhouse gases in three main ways (Aviation Environment Federation, 2009):

- *Flights* are by far the largest source. Aircraft emit large quantities of CO_2 and NO_x during flights, particularly during take-off and landing. NO_x emissions at high altitudes react to either increase ozone concentrations or decrease methane concentrations in the atmosphere. While this leads to global warming and cooling respectively, the two occur in different regions and latitudes and do not cancel each other out. Water vapor from combustion also contributes to the formation of condensation trails (contrails), and persistent contrails are also thought to cause additional cirrus cloud formation (although the scientific certainty of the precise impact is less, compared to other greenhouse gases).
- *Ground traffic* is the second largest source. Vehicles (including construction vehicles) traveling to and from the airport and around the airport generate CO_2.
- *Airport buildings* require electricity and heating. Unless this comes from sources that do not use fossil fuel (for example, hydro or wind power), the energy production will generate greenhouse gases. Airport construction also generates CO_2 through embodied energy.

Aviation is a global industry and requires global solutions. This is especially true with climate change since greenhouse gas emissions are long lasting and ubiquitous. Any environmental measures affecting aviation should be in conformity with the policies being developed cooperatively by the 190 contracting states of the Chicago Convention through the ICAO, including the prohibition against taxing fuel used in international operations. The integrity of the international aviation system is based on the establishment of limits on the ability of any one country to impact the flying rights of another country. The EU's unilateral decision to subject non-EU aviation to its emissions trading scheme (also known as ETS) puts this principle at risk and preempts the international treaty rights of other countries (Experimental Aircraft Association, 2009).

The aviation industry contributes to global warming in a number of ways. It is the burning of fossil fuel in flight that causes the aviation industry's biggest impact on the climate, but ground emissions from airport vehicles and the vehicles used by passengers and staff to get to and from the airport also contribute. Finally, greenhouse gas emissions are generated by the production of the energy used in airport buildings. The effects that aircraft have on the climate are not solely a result of CO_2, but also include effects linked to emissions of NO_x, the creation of contrails, and the potential impact of contrails on cirrus clouds. These effects are complex and there is still scientific uncertainty over them. The IPCC has estimated that aviation's total climate impact resulting from these effects is some 2.7 times the impact of its CO_2 emissions alone. Of course other sectors, from road transport to agriculture, also have a non-CO_2 impact which must be taken into account. The IPCC has estimated that aviation is responsible for around 3.5 percent of the total human contribution to climate change. The IPCC's central case estimate is that aviation's contribution could grow to 5 percent of the total contribution by 2050 if action is not taken to tackle these emissions, although the highest scenario is 15 percent. If other industries achieve significant cuts in their own greenhouse gas emissions, then aviation's share as a proportion of the remaining emissions could also rise (BAA, 2006a).

The negative impact of airports and aviation includes land take, noise, air pollution, climate change, water use, and effects on the social structures of local communities. Positive impact includes direct and indirect employment and social (and economic) benefits for people who fly. These can typically be split into the following groups (Aviation Environment Federation, 2009):

- *Construction* versus *operation* of airports and associated projects, and possibly closure if, for example, a runway is relocated.
- *Airport terminal and ground operations, flights, access to the airport* (cars, buses, trains, parking, and so on) and *associated projects* such as hotels and airport-related office developments.

Figure 5.1 shows the key ways in which each of these activities typically causes an impact. (Not all airport development will have an impact in all of these ways, and any given airport development may also have other forms of impact.)

Key Impacts - Negative impact + Positive impact	Terminal & ground operations		Flights	Airport access		Associated projects	
	construction	operation	operation	construction	operation	construction	operation
Air pollution			-		-		-
biodiversity impacts	-	-	-	-	-	-	
climate change		-	-		-		
employment and economic benefits	+	+	+			+	+
heritage	-		-	-	-	-	
land take	-			-		-	
landscape	-	-		-		-	-
noise		-	-	-	-		
risk and public safety zones			-				
social costs to nearby communities	-	-			-		
traffic	-	-		-	-	-	-
water pollution		-			-		
water use		-					-

Figure 5.1   Key impacts caused by airport and aviation activities

Source: Aviation Environment Federation, 2009:2.

Cost–benefit analysis (also known as CBA) is essential for aviation management and organization. Any proposed measures to address aviation's impact on the environment should include a rigorous analysis of the expected benefits weighed against the cost to the economy, industry, jobs, communities, and the transportation infrastructure and should take into account the costs and benefits of inter-modal substitution. Likewise, they should address possible trade-offs between environmental effects, such as those between emissions and noise (Experimental Aircraft Association, 2009).

Civil aviation requires huge investments which include time, financing, and human resources. Investments of civil aviation business organizations will require the analysis of risks and a strategy for dealing with global warming/climate change-based issues. For certain investments, as in the fossil fuel, utility, and air transportation industries, insurer investment managers will need to carefully monitor global warming/climate change risk exposures. Opportunities will exist from technological developments that act to slow global warming. Managing global warming/climate change risks will present many business opportunities for insurers. With their expertise in risk assessment, mitigation strategies, crisis management, and innovative risk financing schemes, opportunities are present and competitive advantages can be gained. Insurers can contribute to managing global warming/climate change risks, as well as helping societies deal with the impact of these risks (Anderson, 2007).

The objective of Enterprise Risk Management (also known as ERM) is to assess, mitigate, and finance the portfolio of risks facing the firm. A new and evolving set of sustainability risks are critical and very different from those found in most Enterprise Risk Management schemes. More importantly, many businesses, and their insurers, have not incorporated sustainability risks into their Enterprise Risk Management structures. More generally, corporations are increasingly being asked or required to become more transparent in regard to sustainability risks. Environmental and social exposures and adverse activities are becoming more difficult to hide (Anderson, 2007). Generally, risk topics can be listed as follows:

- shareholder risks (corporate social responsibility);
- corporate governance risks (transparency);
- reputation risks;
- investment risks;
- compliance risks;
- liability risks;
- fleet improvement investment risks, for example, fleet planning.

In the strategic framework of risk management, greenhouse gas reductions can reduce financial risks. According to the Coalition for Environmentally Responsible Economies (CERES), US$7.4 trillion in corporate assets today are potentially threatened by climate change. This leads the Coalition to conclude that corporate Board members, senior executives, and institutional investors can no longer ignore such costs, and they would be negligent in their fiscal responsibilities, should they do so. The risks are enormous. They are both physical (the results of droughts, floods, and hurricanes) and financial (the effects of greenhouse gas liabilities on share price and asset valuation) (Hoffman and Toffel, 2007).

Most of the studies on this subject are based on a macroeconomic viewpoint or on a prospective analysis of the possible consequences of global warming for business activities. Thus, after explaining the greenhouse effect and its global impact, Packard and Reinhardt emphasize the social responsibility of managers and the importance of assessing risks and opportunities arising from ongoing climate change (Boiral, 2006).

According to Hoffman (2002), the economic and strategic impact of climate change will depend mostly on capital asset management, the global competitiveness of countries, the anticipation of institutional changes stemming from the Kyoto Protocol, and the ability of the market to take advantage of the emergence of new opportunities related to climate change policies. Hoffman stresses that companies can benefit from voluntary greenhouse gas reductions through seven aspects: operational improvement, anticipating and influencing climate change regulations, accessing new sources of capital, improving risk management, elevating corporate reputation, identifying new market opportunities, and enhancing Human Resource

Management (also known as HRM). These benefits are not systematic, and organizational responses to global warming issues are not perfectly linear and monolithic. These organizational responses depend on contingent factors, particularly the expected economic impact of greenhouse gas reductions, the political and regulatory context surrounding global warming, scientific or technical aspects, and social pressures. Because of the uncertainties and interdependence of these factors, corporate response to global warming remains a complex issue, requiring foresight and vision from managers rather than reactions to existing constraints (Boiral, 2006). The risk management-based approach is the set of elements in the business management system concerned with managing global warming-based risks. It describes the systems, processes, attitudes, and commitment needed to successfully integrate risk management with existing business management processes in order to ensure that the risk management program can assist a business in achieving its corporate objectives and global warming targets.

The Impact of the Aviation Business on Global Warming

Aviation is a user of fossil fuels and contributor to man-made greenhouse gas emissions. Although aviation currently only contributes some 3 percent of global greenhouse gas emissions, there are reasons for concern: the sector faces strong growth rates in demand, and alternative low-emission technologies under development may not be sufficient to compensate the growth effect. Due to this, the share of global emissions from aircraft might double during the next couple of decades (Unione delle Università del Mediterraneo, 2009). Although the impact of aviation on climate change is projected very differently in the press around the globe, all parties agree that aviation's contribution to climate change is growing. Globally, more business communities favor action on climate change. The aviation industry is increasingly in the spotlight and expected regulations on emissions trading will have a financial impact on the industry. The industry is preparing for more defined Corporate Responsibility policies to maintain corporate reputation and to ensure favorable bottom line results. Understanding the risks and opportunities in the carbon market is vital to this preparation (Deloitte, 2007a). The aviation industry in particular is now facing enormous pressure since the IPCC and environmental campaign groups have singled out the responsibility of air travel in accounting for a considerable portion of global greenhouse gas emissions. Globally, the world's 16,000 commercial jet planes generate more than 600 million metric tons of CO_2 per year, almost as much as from all human activities in Africa each year. The huge increase in aircraft pollution is largely due to the rapid growth of tourism and related air traffic. A World Wildlife Fund (WWF) briefing paper entitled "Tourism and Climate Change" (2001) states that the actual metric tonnage of CO_2 emitted will increase by over 75 percent by 2015; concomitantly, from almost 700 million international travelers in 2000, numbers are expected to jump to over 1 billion by 2010 and 1.6 billion by 2020. "As a consequence, the role of air travel within the tourism industry is likely to expand, cause considerable environmental damage, and to have knock-on effects on the tourism industry itself," concludes the WWF. Given the recent negative publicity, tourists in western countries are changing their behavior and tend to fly less. There are now voices in Europe, even, that go so far as to suggest that flying away on holiday is immoral and should be stopped altogether. Growing consumer awareness on these issues and a burgeoning citizens' movement calling for fuel taxes and stricter regulation of the transport industry can severely curb future tourism growth targets and thus cut deep into the profits of plane-makers, airlines, travel agencies, cruise ship operators, and other tourism-related businesses. It is no wonder that companies are now scrambling to talk about hard-earned environmental advances and new initiatives to protect the environment. At the Paris Air Show in June 2007, for example, Airbus' top salesman, John Leah, told a press conference that Airbus is "saving the planet, one A380 at a time." The company's promotional brochures featured a silhouette of the new two-deck super-jumbo—dubbed the "gentle green giant"—set against images of dolphins, rain forests, and fishing boats on a misty pond. Boeing representatives were also keen to display ecological bona fides and claimed the industry has reduced fuel consumption by 70 percent since the jet age began, reported Dow Jones Newswires (Pleumarom, 2007).

A carbon-trading scheme implies a direct and indirect impact on the aviation sector (Llewellyn and Chaix, 2007):

- *Direct impact*: If the sector is included in a carbon-trading scheme, all carbon emissions represent a cost, obliging airlines either to invest in low-carbon-emitting technologies or to buy emissions rights.
- *Indirect impact*: The emissions trading scheme implies an increase in the price of carbon and thereby an increase in the price of fuel. In the aviation sector, fuel costs represent a large part of the total cost structure.

The impact of a carbon-trading scheme is likely to be characteristic of industries with limited ability to pass on additional costs. Hence, the net increase in costs to airlines will likely necessitate capacity reductions relative to what would have been obtained otherwise. For established full-service airlines, this could mean lower utilization of the existing fleet in the near term, and slower capacity growth over the long term. For the low-cost segment, a segment of the industry that prices aggressively to drive volume, higher costs will likely lead to reductions in growth. Higher energy-related costs will also likely drive continued interest in fuel-saving technologies, such as winglets, and in more fuel-efficient operating procedures, such as single-engine taxiing (Llewellyn and Chaix, 2007).

Basically, three actions are recommended to achieve objectives regarding global warming and climate change. The first is to promote coordination and communication among stakeholders. The second is to develop more effective tools and metrics for guiding policy decisions and for planning research investments. The third is to establish a vigorous program to develop specific technological, operational, and policy options that support a balanced approach to long-term environmental improvements (Waitz, 2006).

Economists have been trying to analyze the overall net benefit of the Kyoto Protocol through cost–benefit analysis. There is disagreement due to large uncertainties in economic variables. Some of the estimates indicate either that observing the Kyoto Protocol is more expensive than not observing the Kyoto Protocol or that the Kyoto Protocol has a marginal net benefit which exceeds the cost of simply adjusting to global warming. However, a study by De Leo et al. (2001) found that "accounting only for local external costs, together with production costs, to identify energy strategies, compliance with the Kyoto Protocol would imply lower, not higher, overall costs."

The Kyoto Protocol would slow down the process of global warming, but it would have a superficial overall benefit. Defenders of the Kyoto Protocol argue, however, that while the initial greenhouse gas cuts may have little effect, they set the political precedent for bigger (and more effective) cuts in the future (McKitrick, 2000). They also advocate commitment to the precautionary principle. Critics point out that additional higher curbs on carbon emissions are likely to cause a significantly higher increase in cost, making such defense moot. Moreover, the precautionary principle could apply to any political, social, economic, or environmental consequence which might have an equally devastating effect in terms of poverty and environment, making the precautionary argument irrelevant. The Stern Review (a UK Government-sponsored report on the economic impact of climate change) concluded that 1 percent of global gross domestic product (GDP) is required to be invested in order to mitigate the effects of climate change, and the failure to do so could risk a recession worth up to 20 percent of the global GDP (Stern, 2006).

One problem in attempting to measure the "absolute" costs and benefits of different policies on global warming is choosing a proper discount rate. Over a long time horizon such as that in which benefits accrue under the Kyoto Protocol, small changes in the discount rate create very large discrepancies between net benefits in various studies. However, this difficulty is generally not applicable to the "relative" comparison of alternative policies under a long time horizon. This is because changes in discount rates tend to equally adjust the net cost–benefit of different policies unless there are significant discrepancies of cost and benefit over the time horizon (Farber and Hemmersbaugh, 1993).

The Aviation Portfolio Management Tool (APMT) by Waitz (2006), takes aviation demand and policy scenarios as inputs and simulates the behavior of aviation producers and consumers to evaluate policy costs. Detailed operational modeling of the air transportation system provides estimates of the emissions and noise outputs. Then a benefits valuation module is used to monetize the health and welfare impact of aviation noise, local air quality, and climate effects. These modules jointly enable a cost–benefit analysis of policy alternatives (Waitz, 2006).

Modern jet aircraft are significantly more fuel efficient (and thus emit less CO_2 in particular) than they were 30 years ago. Moreover, manufacturers have forecast and are committed to achieving reductions in both CO_2 and NO_x emissions with each new generation of design of aircraft and engine. The accelerated introduction of more modern aircraft, therefore, represents a major opportunity to reduce emissions per passenger kilometer flown. Other opportunities arise from the optimization of airline timetables, route networks, and flight frequencies to increase load factors (minimize the number of empty seats flown), together with the optimization of airspace (Wikipedia, 2009c).

Airlines continue to invest in safety—the number one priority. While holding safety and security paramount, efficiency and cost reduction are critical. Cost efficiency is basic for any business. Competition imposes it on airlines. Airlines achieved amazing results in the last four years, but losses will decrease despite the rise in fuel prices. Inefficient air traffic management results in 12 percent extra CO_2 emissions. At current fuel prices this 12 percent inefficiency is a US$13.56 billion cost. The International Air Transport Association (IATA) has a fuel efficiency strategy involving more direct routings, improved terminal operations, less radar vectoring, more reliance on avionics, more efficient fuel management by airlines, and more effective operations. They achieved some impressive results last year. Three hundred air route improvements saved 6.1 million metric tons of CO_2 emissions. Working with airlines on best practice for fuel management saved 4.3 million metric tons of CO_2. Their "Save One Minute" campaign improved airspace design and procedures and saved 1.5 million tonnes (metric tons) of CO_2. The bottom line—savings totaled US$2.4 billion. Asia Pacific has delivered some impressive results in recent years with the redesign of South China Sea airspace and the introduction of the reduced vertical separation minima (RVSM) in many regions (Bisignani, 2006).

The Cost of Risk Management Practice for Airlines

Airlines are spending at least US$8.36 billion a year on risk management, with around 70 percent or US$5.86 billion going on insurance premiums, according to new research into airline risk management trends. Terrorism and new business risks are also fueling airline concerns about premiums. The threat of dirty bombs, plus the lack of a stable, competitive capacity for war and terrorism risks, will have an impact on future insurance costs. "Additionally, new perceived risks, directors' and officers' responsibilities, credit risks, overbooking and operating risks, loss of use, credit card acquirers risk, etc. will increase the components of the insurance bill and make it difficult to come back to the glory days of pre-9/11." With terrorism risks at the forefront of everyone's mind, it is not surprising that 24 percent of risk managers in the study cite war and terrorism in general as the major risk facing the aviation industry and a further 30 percent believe it is specifically war and terrorism insurance and restrictions on coverage. The majority 55 percent believe that government insurance/limitation of liability is the most realistic way to go forward. High jet fuel costs result in more airlines having to develop fuel hedging programs or hedging more intensively (Airline Business, 2006).

According to the research, the top five insurance risk priorities are aircraft accidents, aircraft-related war/terrorism, property damage, general liability, and directors' and officers' liabilities. This is not very surprising, considering that insurance covering most of these risks is mandatory for many airlines. However, looking beyond operational essentials, airlines are earmarking extra risks to insure against in the future, with 37 percent planning to insure against computer crime, 30 percent against credit risks, and 22 percent against loss of reputation. Although loss of reputation is at the bottom of current airline insurance policies, branding is an increasingly big issue for airlines, and fears about loss of brand and reputation can be tied into the emergence of highly branded low-cost carriers and frequent flyer branding for the big alliances (Airline Business, 2006). Global warming-based Corporate Responsibility practice can support corporate brand risk management.

All business organizations and aviation businesses need to be aware of and manage their operational and strategic risk when it comes to global warming. Global warming provides threats and challenges, such as to find ways to decarbonize their operations, increasing insurance costs. At the same time, it provides new business opportunities for new markets and entrepreneurial ventures. New opportunities such as climate-friendly behavior or Corporate Responsibility-based practices can have a tangible impact on corporate reputation and company efficiency. For this reason, global warming may become a source of competitive advantage for business organizations. Global warming is an important risk (threat and/or opportunity) factor and global warming-based risk management is important for business organizations.

The cost of risk management practice is redeemable by companies in the mid and long term. Also, business organizations need to use risk management practices for Corporate Sustainability and to handle global warming-based costs and benefits.

The Costs and Benefits Analysis of Global Warming

Cost–benefit analysis has been used as a tool to conduct economic analysis of environmental mitigation measures across many areas of economic activity, but some difficulties have arisen in its application to aviation, primarily because of measurement and information problems. Cost–benefit analysis provides a framework for balancing the economic and environmental impact associated with different policy options (Intergovernmental Panel on Climate Change, 1999).

Companies, especially those exposed to strong environmental pressures, should make provisions for Environmental Intelligence or the appointment of specialists to anticipate the impact of global warming and assess how to capitalize on opportunities that arise as a result. Such services or specialists would contribute to monitoring the economic, political, social, and scientific or technical issues that could affect an organization's activities, as well as keeping a watching brief on related opportunities and threats. These issues are interdependent and require an interdisciplinary approach, integrating a wide variety of information. The complexity of this type of information has led some organizations to cooperate in sharing Environmental Intelligence (Boiral, 2006). To support the formulation of environmental goals and air transportation policies, government and industry should invest in comprehensive interdisciplinary studies that quantify the marginal costs of environmental protection policies, the full economic benefits of providing transportation services while reducing the costs (in terms of noise, emissions, and congestion), and the potential of financial incentives in order to encourage the development and use of equipment that goes beyond regulatory standards (Aeronautics and Space Engineering Board, 2002).

Global warming offers aviation organizations with significant risks an increasing number of market opportunities. As with all global organizations, aviation organizations face the necessity of compliance with international and regional laws and regulations. There are many unknowns about potential regulations and liabilities which produce risks for the strategy and management of aviation organizations. Aviation organizations are looking at these changing preferences, creating effective relationships with their stakeholders, and seizing market opportunities proactively, improving risk management by the implementation of global warming-based risks. An improved Enterprise Risk Management-based approach is critical at this point. Enterprise Risk Management presents an effective way to minimize the costs and maximize the benefits of global warming since it affects global warming-related corporate strategies and organizational integration. Also, if aviation organizations would like to be sustainable, they should be doing a careful cost–benefit analysis of the global warming-based risk issues. For this reason, this is only our initial work. Our future plan is to work on implementing the new Enterprise Risk Management-based framework in aviation organizations.

The costs or benefits associated with climate change depend on many factors, such as the sector of activity, environmental objectives and firm capabilities, corporate management systems, technologies and operational processes, firm size, industry market structure, and return expectations, all of which can vary significantly from one case to another. Understanding these factors is difficult as they are embedded in a political, social, and scientific context that can vary from one sector or one region to another (Boiral, 2006).

Risk and uncertainty take place at the center point of climate change analysis: in practice, considerable uncertainties surround both the incremental costs and the incremental benefits, making it impossible at present to determine with certainty the value of the "social, environmental, and economic" cost of climate change/global warming. Calculation of the cost–benefit to climate change/global warming ratio is limited for the following reasons (Llewellyn and Chaix, 2007):

- scientific uncertainties;
- economic uncertainties about the valuation of the impact, particularly in non-market sectors;
- methodological uncertainties, particularly concerning the extent to which it may be appropriate to discount expected damages.

In our opinion, cost of inaction on global warming-based risks will be higher than managing these risks.

While the basic theory is straightforward, the practice is likely to be more complicated. First, it is difficult to assess adaptation costs, because adaptive capacity depends on a range of economic, sociological, technological, and developmental conditions. Second, there is an inter-relationship between expenditure on adaptation and the appropriate amount to spend on abatement (see Figure 5.2) (Llewellyn and Chaix, 2007). The initial cost of global warming-based liabilities and investments is and will be a high cost for corporations, but benefits gained from global warming-based investments can pay off related costs in the midterm. Also, companies will gain stakeholder interest via global warming-based efforts. These efforts take part in corporate social responsibility practice and are highly effective on stakeholder perceptions of the company.

Business leaders must first understand the importance of global warming in general and that of carbon emissions more specifically in terms of their operations, customer preferences, and the changing regulatory and economic landscape. They must then weigh the long-term commercial and environmental

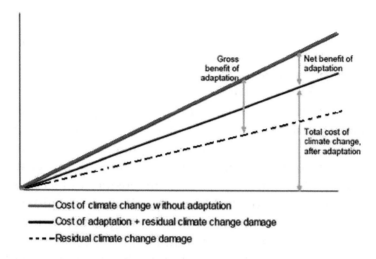

Gross benefit of adaptation

Net benefit of adaptation

Total cost of climate change, after adaptation

——— Cost of climate change without adaptation

——— Cost of adaptation + residual climate change damage

- - - -Residual climate change damage

Figure 5.2   Climate change and adaptation costs

Source: Llewellyn and Chaix, 2007:34.

benefits of reducing their carbon footprint against the costs to their companies and, ultimately, their shareholders (Gremouti, 2007). Managers should be considering the complex cause and effect chain in order to effectively manage global warming-based risks since climate change and global warming are directly linked with Corporate Sustainability, and they have a serious impact on businesses and their stakeholders (see Figure 5.3).

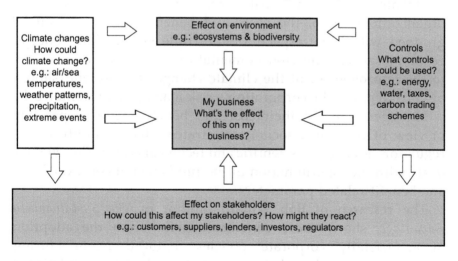

Climate changes How could climate change? e.g.: air/sea temperatures, weather patterns, precipitation, extreme events

Effect on environment e.g.: ecosystems & biodiversity

Controls What controls could be used? e.g.: energy, water, taxes, carbon trading schemes

My business What's the effect of this on my business?

Effect on stakeholders How could this affect my stakeholders? How might they react? e.g.: customers, suppliers, lenders, investors, regulators

Figure 5.3   A complex cause and effect chain

Source: Peck, 2006.

Identification of global warming-based parameters via the Enterprise Risk Management-based perspective is accomplished in this section. We maintain that this work can be seen as the initial step for the cost–benefit-based risk analysis which is also the first step of the Enterprise Risk Management process.

Global warming is also both a strategic and financial management issue. The risk management-based approach can help companies to design and implement global warming strategies that build business value via identifying costs and benefits of global warming related to business objectives and activities. For this reason, business organizations should develop and establish their risk management strategies according to the impact of global warming. The complex global issue is analyzed from a risk management perspective in this chapter. The global warming impacts on the business organizations are called "risks." After that, identified risks are categorized into two main groups as costs or benefits. Future work is planned to weigh costs and benefits according to their impact on shareholder wealth and company activities. Cost–benefit analysis results will be presented in our future work.

The global warming-based sustainability costs and benefits are identified in two main categories of costs and benefits for aviation organizations. This will be useful for the risk analysis of climate change and global warming-based issues for aviation organizations. Also, the costs and benefits categories can be grouped within the aspects of the triple bottom line concept: economic, social, and environmental issues. These can be useful to the improvement of the climate change strategy and should be considered in the corporation's risk management framework.

Managers can list their cost and benefit factors separately in view of economic, social, and strategic issues; political and regulatory issues; and scientific and technical issues. This chapter deals with the determination of the fundamental context of cost and benefit-related parameters.

The research of Bob Willard, author of *The Sustainability Advantage*, shows more concrete benefits from the adoption of eco-friendly corporate policies: reduced manufacturing expenses, increased market share, a better talent pool, and higher productivity. All of this, according to Willard, can lead to a 66 percent increase in profit, on average, for small and medium-sized companies that adopt environmentally-minded practices (Taylor, 2006).

Identified cost and benefit factors are listed below. This list shows the effects of global warming on Corporate Sustainability via its costs and benefits. Managers will then continue to the next steps of the risk management process such as prioritization, assessment, handling, and so on. All of the global warming-based parameters are also risky issues since each of them requires an investment and corporate resources. These parameters should be analyzed in the risk management process, and then optimum risk-handling options should be put into practice by management. The following costs and benefits lists show the identified global warming-based risks for aviation business organizations:

Costs (includes social, financial, and environmental cost categories):

- investment in tackling climate change, noise, and air quality;
- new fuel saving initiatives;
- emissions trading scheme;
- impact of global warming on the world economy;
- additional impact on cost structure;
- additional vulnerability to energy prices and supply;
- ground infrastructure investment;
- green building investment;
- additional capital demands;
- major behavioral changes by customers;
- corporate preparedness;
- increased taxes on gas, utilities, and other forms of energy: booming energy costs;
- additional emerging carbon markets;
- bringing in new lines of reporting and accountability;
- new compliance costs;
- corporate social responsibilities-based investments;
- establishing an ISO 14001 Environmental Management system;
- growing sense of environmental awareness;
- impact on demand;
- fleet replacement/improvement and fleet planning;

- regulation-based compliance costs;
- taxes and internalized charges;
- negotiated agreements;
- voluntary action;
- probability of ticket prices rising;
- necessity of improving technology and air traffic management;
- developing fuel efficient flying patterns;
- new liabilities;
- climate change regulatory impact;
- commitment to buying the majority of energy from suppliers of renewable sources;
- potential future exposures (risk scenarios);
- potential adverse effect on the risk profile of the company and clients/customers;
- carbon liabilities;
- increasing legal and regulatory pressures and mounting public and shareholder activism;
- compliance with emissions regulations;
- strong threat of increasingly volatile weather conditions;
- resulting impact on insurance markets, business resources, and personnel;
- significant increase in unemployment;
- substantial productivity losses;
- risk of recession;
- threat of litigation;
- implementation of plans to reduce the production of CO_2 and other gases;
- Kyoto Protocol compliance implications.

Benefits (includes social, financial, and environmental benefit categories):

- new market opportunities;
- developing market for clean technologies;
- new careers and jobs;
- enhancement of the corporate brand/image, resulting in improved consumer perception and product marketing;
- capability of flying dynamic routes to optimize fuel efficiencies;

- sustainability advantages;
- more concrete benefits from the adoption of eco-friendly corporate policies;
- reduction of manufacturing expenses;
- increased market share;
- better talent pool;
- higher productivity;
- increase in profit via environmentally-minded practices;
- reduction of the material intensity of goods and services;
- reduction of the energy intensity of goods and services;
- enhancement of material recyclability;
- maximization of sustainable use of renewable resources;
- increase in the service intensity of products;
- social responsibility efforts;
- improved human relationships;
- better flow of control techniques (delays can be dealt with on the ground, with engines off, not in the air) from better maintenance, repair, and overhaul (cleaner aircraft, better fuel performance) to better air traffic management, so aircraft can use jet-streams to minimize fuel burn and "glide approaches" into airports;
- human resource development.

Aviation does not yet meet its full climate change responsibilities. However, blunt taxation that collects revenue without incentivizing sustainable behavior will not reduce the negative environmental impact. BAA believes that an emissions trading scheme is the solution to aviation's contribution to climate change (BAA, 2006a).

If ever there was a dynamic international risk area, global climate change certainly qualifies for this distinction. It raises a myriad of risk issues that will impact people, governments, industries, and businesses. At the 2002 World Economic Forum, Davos, Switzerland, business and government leaders described climate change as "the most urgent problem facing humanity" (Anderson, 2007).

According to Anderson's opinion, global climate change may be the leading risk area in sustainability risk management. Besides the traditional risks of property, liability, life, and health, global climate change produces a broad array of additional risks, including ethical, cultural, boycott, reputation, and regulatory risks (Anderson, 2007). In our opinion, global warming-based cost and benefit indicators should be included in risk identification and handling, in the Enterprise Risk Management process.

Global warming economics is the leading issue of strategic and financial risk management for companies. Global warming-based costs and benefits can't be compared directly for business organizations. The current global financial crisis creates threats for business organizations. Airlines and airport businesses require the implementation of sustainability strategies and risk management, integrating sustainability into their operating models, business strategies, and critical processes. The risk management-based holistic approach—which encompasses strategy, design, and execution—enables managers in the aviation industry to grow revenue, reduce costs, and manage risks, enhancing their brand and reputation. Global warming-based sustainability costs and benefits should be identified to effectively manage sustainability risks in the aviation business organization. This book presents the initial step of the risk management system for the aviation business organization via determination of the costs and benefits of global warming.

Global warming is driving a much more fundamental change in how managers and business leaders view the broad risk profile their firm presents to insurers, investors, employees, and any other stakeholders. Companies should be engaging risk management, financial, and legal professionals (William Gallagher Associates, 2009).

Aviation's carbon footprint is growing, and that is politically unacceptable for any industry. The challenge is to keep the many benefits of aviation—unprecedented global mobility that supports 32 million jobs and US$3.5 billion worth of economic activity—while eliminating its negative impact (Bisignani, 2007).

In this part, we have presented some of the important ways in which global warming impacts the aviation business via the risk management-based approach. This book supports that climate change risks and opportunities can be managed in a systematic and proactive manner. This study is the initial step of our risk management model to managing global warming-based risks for aviation businesses. Our planned future work is the development of a new systematic and proactive model to both understand and manage these risks across an entire aviation enterprise.

The risk management-based approach is important to meeting public expectations that companies will take a responsible approach in managing climate change/global warming-based issues. Managing these risks also involves many factors such as corporate governance, reputation management, strategic management, financial management, stakeholder management, resource planning, and Corporate Responsibility. For this reason, integration of risk management and other managerial approaches is of vital importance to Corporate Sustainability.

Climate change-based risks should be considered in view of both their cost and benefit items for corporations. Risk analysis is a critical step for enterprise-wide financial risk management. Basically, climate change triggers the following risk issues, and these must be managed in order to meet targets of Corporate Sustainability:

- litigation;
- reputational risks due to response on climate issues;
- compliance risks(including new compliance costs);
- competitive risks;
- stakeholder interest and demands: investors and consumer responses;
- loss of business resources;
- effective resource allocation;
- initiatives about corporate social responsibility.

Given the myriad of risks and opportunities due to climate change, corporate Board members should do more than just ask good questions. They should be directing management to develop and implement a corporate climate change strategy as a matter of good corporate governance. The three key components of a comprehensive climate change strategy are assessment, implementation, and disclosure. The first step in the assessment process is to create a Board committee with direct oversight responsibility that will prioritize the establishment and attainment of greenhouse gas reduction targets. Meeting such targets should be an explicit factor in executive compensation, and an interdepartmental team (reporting directly to the Chief Executive Officer (also known as CEO) should be formed. Such a team should also conduct a comprehensive assessment of the company's greenhouse gas "footprint" and assess the full spectrum of risks as well as opportunities to the business (Lubber, 2008). DuPont has adopted such a structure; its Board has overseen the company's climate change activities since 1994, and it includes an Environmental Policy Committee chaired by William Reilly, former head of the Environmental Protection Agency. DuPont's executive Climate Change Steering Team reports directly to the CEO, and environmental stewardship is reviewed as part of performance assessment. The second step is the implementation phase which should include a greenhouse gas emissions reduction plan with specific reduction targets and deadlines for its operations and products. Bank of America is currently implementing such a plan. The company has committed US$1.4 billion to achieve "green" Leadership in Energy and Environmental Design (LEED) certification for all new construction and is investing US$100 million in energy conservation in its bank buildings. The company has also announced a US$20 billion, ten-year initiative to support businesses that address climate change. Comprehensive public disclosure of company assessments and strategies for dealing with climate change is the third key component. Such disclosure allows investors, employees, and other stakeholder groups to engage in a meaningful way with the company and to help develop creative solutions to maximize shareholder value (Lubber, 2008).

A basic additional contribution of this study is that by examining the costs and benefits of global warming via the risk management-based approach, aviation organizations can better understand how this links to other corporate priorities and how they can consider other sustainability challenges they are facing.

Corporate Sustainability and Risk Management to the Airline Business and Management

The twenty-first century and its business environment are bringing new risks and impacts that threaten the very survival of every organization. There are also new challenges and opportunities for both continuity and risk managers. All companies have to take risks, and some risks can be mitigated with insurance. All companies operate in highly competitive markets and cannot grow or compete without taking risks. So trying to achieve the right balance between risk and reward is the optimum goal (Lane, 2007).

Effective risk management requires a business-wide approach known as Enterprise Risk Management in order to improve the success rate of achieving business objectives and reduce the erosion of critical sources of enterprise value. Enterprise Risk Management is deployed to advance the maturity of an organization's capabilities for managing the priority risks. It helps management to successfully enhance as well as protect enterprises in five main ways: Enterprise Risk Management informs strategic direction; helps improve business performance; optimizes the cost of managing risk; invigorates opportunity-seeking behavior; and assists in establishing sustainable competitive advantage. Effective risk management also enhances shareholder value. This approach draws out the risks, particularly those emanating from value-creating activities, which expand business complexity. The pursuit of these commonly adopted activities introduces business complexity and requires active risk management to ensure that Boards of organizations make informed decisions. While Enterprise Risk Management seeks to invigorate and give confidence to opportunity-seeking activity, its aim is to ensure Boards take actions with their eyes wide open, comprehensively appraising the risks associated with the growth and performance improvement activities planned (Chapman, 2007).

The aim of this section is to first explain the complexity of airline management and offer the new Corporate Sustainability Management (also known as CSM) model for effective and competitive airline business management. We assume that Corporate Sustainability Management is a part of the overall concept of business management and corporate strategy. Corporate Sustainability is placed within a holistic management model. The aim of the new model is to effectively support Corporate Sustainability efforts of airline companies since sustainability is a major risk for companies in the highly volatile and uncertain business environment. We also assume that sustainability risks will be a catalyst for innovation and opportunities.

The aviation industry has brought many benefits to society in both economic and social terms. The relative affordability and speed of air transport today have made international travel accessible to many people, and it has become an integral part of their lifestyle (Romanova, 2004). Few businesses are as important as the airline industry for the smooth and efficient working of a modern society. Air transport has come to play an irreplaceable role in service to commerce and to the travel needs of the millions of people who fly every day. It is a global, technologically advanced, and dynamic growth industry (Lazar, 2003).

Air transport forms a unique global network, linking people, countries, and cultures, and it plays a vital role in the further integration and development of Europe. It is increasingly accessible to a greater number of people who can now afford to travel by air for leisure and business purposes. Air transport is essential for world business, creating jobs and opening up new market opportunities by attracting businesses to locations in the developed and developing world. It moves products and services quickly over long distances enabling economic and social participation by outlying communities. Air transport is committed to meeting its customers' growing demand in a sustainable manner, maintaining an optimal balance between economic progress, social development, and environmental responsibility. The aviation industry has reduced its environmental impact in recent decades through the development of new technology and the adoption of specific operating methods. Aviation noise and emission levels are modest (when considering the long distances covered), and land usage for air transport is comparatively small. The industry also capitalizes on inter-modal air–rail opportunities to alleviate congestion (Collaborative Forum of Air Transport Stakeholders, 2003).

The air transport industry is large, important, and complex. It makes a massive contribution to the prosperity of Europe, both in terms of a globally competitive manufacturing sector providing goods and services, and also in terms of promoting the effective transfer of people and goods within Europe and globally (Air Transport Net, 2009). A dynamic industry such as international aviation requires the ability to cope with rapidly changing markets, institutional structures, and operational environments. The international aviation industry is an integral part of the modern, global economy, both influencing and being influenced by the pattern of economic development. It is an industry which has grown prodigiously over the past three decades and has had to cope with major economic and technological challenges. There is little evidence that this dynamism is subsiding, and given the industry's position in the national and international economy, it is vital that it be able to respond effectively to the demands of modern industry and of consumers (Michalski, 1996).

Air transport is an innovative, environmentally responsible industry that drives economic and social progress (Rochat, 2009):

- From an economic point of view, air transport is essential for world business and tourism. It creates jobs and facilitates the expansion of world trade by opening up new market opportunities. It also attracts businesses to locations in the developed and developing world, thereby satisfying the mobility requirements of a growing portion of the world's population — and moves products and services quickly over long distances enabling economic and social participation by outlying communities.
- From a social perspective, air transport forms a unique global transport network linking people, countries, and cultures safely and efficiently. It is increasingly accessible to a greater number of people who can now afford to travel by air for leisure and business purposes.
- In environmental terms, air transport has been able to reduce or contain its environmental impact by continually improving its fuel consumption, reducing noise, and introducing new, more sustainable technologies.

Air travel remains a large and growing industry. It facilitates economic growth, world trade, international investment, and tourism and is, therefore, central to the globalization taking place in many other industries. A number of factors are forcing airlines to become more efficient. In Europe, the EU has ruled that governments should not be allowed to subsidize their loss-making airlines. Elsewhere, too, governments' concerns over their own finances and recognition of the benefits of privatization have led to a gradual transfer of ownership of airlines from the State to the private sector. In order to appeal to prospective shareholders, the airlines have to become more efficient and competitive. Airlines' profitability is closely tied to economic growth and trade. Airlines have had to recognize the need for radical change to ensure their survival and prosperity. For airlines, the future will hold many challenges. Successful airlines will be those that continue to tackle their costs and improve their products, thereby securing a strong presence in the key world aviation markets (Stanford University, 2009).

The airline industry has gone through plenty of turbulence over the last few years. Following a period of crisis caused by an economic slowdown in the US and amplified by the attacks of 9/11, the SARS epidemic, and the war in Iraq, air traffic began growing again in 2004. The airline sector remains fragile, however, and a jump in oil prices or new terrorist attacks could set things back again (Montreal Economic Institute, 2006). Airlines are operated in an extremely dynamic, and often highly volatile, commercial environment. Both opportunities and risks are part of everyday business for the company. As with any company, airline companies have sustainability risks (social, environmental, operational, threats, strategic, and financial risks) that they have to deal with. Airline managers are responsible for optimal decision making regarding Corporate Sustainability Risks (also known as CSR) in their daily business. Perhaps a more important risk, though, is the simple fact that these companies are airlines. The key issues facing today's airlines are optimization, improved capacity, cost savings, and the ability to react quickly to changes. The portfolio of solutions for airline planning and control ranges from network planning, code share handling, and crew management to pricing, price distribution, and revenue management. The portfolio is rounded out by business intelligence services, marketing and sales solutions, and consulting (Lufthansa Systems, 2008).

Airlines are operated in an extremely dynamic, and often highly volatile, commercial environment. Both opportunities and risks are part of everyday business for these companies. Airlines have to develop their ability to recognize, successfully control, and manage risks early on in their enterprise-wide management. The airline industry is constantly undergoing change, and the ability to react and adjust swiftly is imperative. The need to improve safety, reliability, and customer appeal while offering competitive prices is an ever-present challenge. Meanwhile, airlines face the following pressures (SAP AG, 2005):

- Globalization and the trend toward mergers and alliances require the flexibility to adjust accordingly.
- World financial instability and eroding yields make it more important than ever to streamline processes, reduce redundancies, and simplify system architecture to lower costs.
- Because the industry is so competitive, airline operators must analyze every aspect of their business—and that requires fast, flexible, and focused access to information for sound decision making.
- Quality customer service differentiates one airline from the other and helps secure customer loyalty. Accurate customer data is essential for personalizing services and maximizing the benefit of marketing initiatives.

For a company to survive, we believe it is necessary to build a Corporate Sustainability Management system, taking into consideration social, environmental, economic, business, and strategic risks. This requires that employees understand everyday risk management without exception. It is also necessary to take measures for emergency management in the case of risk actualization and other measures based on business continuity planning which takes into consideration, for example, large-scale disasters (Nomura, 2003).

In the dynamic environment of the airline industry, active management of business risks and targeted identification and usage of opportunities count as part of daily commercial life for the Austrian Airlines Group. The Group's cross-department, value-oriented risk management system continuously records and analyzes the trend in factors including exchange rates, interest rates, fuel prices, the load factor, yields, and production costs. The management process was placed on a new footing in November 2006, and is now to be expanded further and developed into a Group-wide risk and opportunity management system. As an aviation company, Austrian Airlines acts in a high-risk, dynamic environment. Risks and opportunities are part of everyday business life for the company. For some time now, Austrian Airlines has been working to actively manage its business risks (Austrian Airlines Group, 2008).

The challenges, threats, and opportunities facing companies today in the area of sustainability are more complex and have greater potential impact than ever before (Frigo, 2007). The Corporate Sustainability model offers better ways to manage these challenges and opportunities. Today, many of the world's leading companies are taking significant steps not only to improve their sustainability performance but also to turn it into a central part of their offering and identity and drive their own processes of innovation (Grayson et al., 2008). Integrating Corporate Sustainability into the management system requires a systematic approach, commitment to leadership, and team work that enables the establishment, management, and implementation of a Corporate Sustainability strategy.

This new model can provide direction and guidance to help airline managers integrate Corporate Sustainability into their daily decisions and to better understand and manage corporate social responsibilities and corporate performance. A sustainability and risk management-based approach and risk culture are required in order to understand the context of Corporate Sustainability. Corporate Sustainability has to be a fundamental strategic, holistic, and entrepreneurial aim for managers. Related efforts must be realized within an integrated, systematic, and disciplined management system. We assume that the Corporate Sustainability Management model is the best and most effective way for airline management to achieve Corporate Sustainability objectives. For this reason, we have developed a new Corporate Sustainability model based on Kucuk Yilmaz and Yilmaz's book *Auto Wars* (2008). Sustainability is a term often used by corporations, politicians, and environmental groups to evaluate industrial processes, economic systems, and corporate policies (Phillips, 2008). In business terms, to focus on sustainability might be defined as acting with long-term consequences in mind and managing a business such that its processes or overall state can be maintained indefinitely. If economic Sustainable Development means developing corporate systems that will last indefinitely, the assumption is that these systems will have less impact on the environment than traditional, or less sustainable, systems. Sustainability is difficult to define or truly measure, since overall impacts and other variables exist that might never truly be known. However, a process can be defined as more or less sustainable as another, or as moving toward or away from sustainability (Phillips, 2008).

Thomas Dyllick and Kai Hockerts (2002) in *Beyond the Business Case for Corporate Sustainability* define Corporate Sustainability as, "meeting the needs of a firm's direct and indirect stakeholders (such as shareholders, employees, clients, pressure groups, communities, etc.) without compromising its ability to meet the needs of future stakeholders as well." The Australian Government defines Corporate Sustainability a little bit closer to the "Daly Rules." They see Corporate Sustainability as, "encompassing strategies and practices that aim to meet the needs of the stakeholders today, while seeking to protect, support, and enhance the human and natural resources that will be needed in the future" (Carewren, 2004). According to the Dow Jones Sustainability Indexes web site, Corporate Sustainability is a business approach that creates long-term shareholder value by embracing opportunities and managing risks deriving from economic, social, and environmental developments. Corporate Sustainability leaders achieve long-term shareholder value by gearing their strategies and management to harness the market's potential for sustainability products and services while at the same time successfully reducing and avoiding sustainability costs and risks. The quality of a company's strategy and management and its performance in dealing with opportunities and risks deriving from economic, social, and environmental developments can be quantified and used to identify and select leading companies for investment purposes (Dow Jones Sustainability Indexes, 2009).

These are clear indications that Corporate Sustainability Management is directly linked with Corporate Sustainability, and the model is highly supported as the best way to assist in Corporate Sustainability Management efforts. Corporate

Sustainability is an investable and inevitable concept. This is crucial in driving interest and investments in sustainability to the mutual benefit of companies and investors. As this benefit circle strengthens, it will have a positive effect on the societies and economies of both the developed and developing world.

Leading sustainability companies display high levels of competence in addressing global and industry challenges in a variety of areas (Dow Jones Sustainability Indexes, 2009):

- *Strategy*: integrating long-term economic, environmental, and social aspects in their business strategies while maintaining global competitiveness and brand reputation.
- *Financial*: meeting shareholders' demands for sound financial returns, long-term economic growth, open communication, and transparent financial accounting.
- *Customer and product*: fostering loyalty by investing in customer relationship management and product and service innovation that focuses on technologies and systems which use financial, natural, and social resources in an efficient, effective, and economic manner over the long term.
- *Governance and stakeholder*: setting the highest standards of corporate governance and stakeholder engagement, including corporate codes of conduct and public reporting.
- *Human*: managing human resources to maintain workforce capabilities and employee satisfaction through best-in-class organizational learning and knowledge management practices and remuneration and benefit programs.

Sustainability continues to grow as both a challenge and opportunity for businesses and their investors. The aim of this study is to contribute to the awareness of Enterprise Risk Management as a Corporate Sustainability tool for best practice. Companies should concentrate on their risks and opportunities in the business environment. These are important to managing a business in an entrepreneurial and sustainable manner in order to remain competitive in the long term, and are necessary to being a leader in quality. Anderson's paper, "Sustainability Risk Management as a Critical Component of Enterprise Risk Management: Global Warming-Climate Change Risks," focuses on one of the most important and discussed Corporate Sustainability Risk issues today. Anderson's paper shows how mitigation strategies can reduce these risks and, more importantly, how the incorporation of Enterprise Risk Management-based Corporate Sustainability Management strategies can produce substantial business opportunities (Anderson, 2007).

Corporate Sustainability-based risk management is the art and science of balancing risk and reward across functional areas within an organization for Corporate Sustainability (University of Toronto, 2008). By another definition, Corporate Sustainability-based risk management is the process of planning, organizing, leading, and controlling the activities of an organization in order to minimize the effects of risk on an organization's capital and earnings. Corporate Sustainability Management expands the process to include not just risks associated with accidental losses, but also financial, strategic, operational, and other risks. In recent years, external factors have fueled a heightened interest by organizations. Industry and government regulatory bodies, as well as investors, have begun to scrutinize companies' risk management policies and procedures. In an increasing number of industries, Boards of directors are required to review and report on the adequacy of risk management processes in the organizations they administer. Since they thrive on the business of risk, financial institutions are good examples of companies that can benefit from effective Corporate Sustainability Management. Their success depends on striking a balance between enhancing profits and managing risk (SearchCIO.com, 2009). Also, Corporate Sustainability Management supports a managerial approach to the achievement of business, strategic, operational, and financial objectives and the best handling of corporate risks.

In order to manage corporate risk in accordance with sustainability, companies must first be able to identify the obvious and perhaps less obvious risks they face. Risk assessment is a proven, effective method to identify the key risks, weigh their significance and develop actions to address them *before* an event or a series of catastrophic events happens. In order to obtain value, organizations must be able to balance growth and return goals with related risks through effective Corporate Sustainability Management. UHY Advisor's Enterprise Risk

Management approach is targeted to specific needs and can be tailored to include (UHY Advisors, 2008):

- aligning risk tolerance and strategy so management can set its objectives and develop mechanisms to manage the related risks;
- identifying and selecting from alternative risk responses such as risk avoidance, reduction, sharing, and acceptance;
- reducing operational surprises so that potential risks can be identified and associated losses minimized;
- facilitating effective responses to the interrelated impacts and integrated responses to multiple risks within an organization;
- identifying and proactively realizing opportunities;
- assessing capital needs and enhancing capital allocation.

The Corporate Sustainability Management model is the process of the basic risk management principles to all risks faced by an organization. Under Corporate Sustainability Management, social, environmental, economic, hazard, strategic, and operational risks are integrated into a single framework. Corporate Sustainability is becoming an important issue in the business environment. In this study, the new Corporate Sustainability Management model is highlighted as the innovative approach that airlines will use to remain competitive and to provide a good insight into their future performance plans. The Corporate Sustainability Management model takes into consideration Sustainable Development issues.

The introduction of new security provisions, combined with escalating fuel costs, consumer uncertainty, and static labor and aircraft costs are forcing radical adjustments and implementation of effective risk management in the airline business. This business climate requires the consideration of how to balance risk and opportunity, while integrating new business, processes and operations. Mismanaging risk can be very costly and risky, and it is impossible to avoid all risk. For these reasons, the only effective solution is Enterprise Risk Management (Protiviti, 2008).

The effective risk management model is also reviewed in this study. The level of effort to implement effective risk management is significant, and no two effective risk management solutions are alike. Companies have different objectives, strategies, structures,

PROTIVITI RISK MODEL FOR THE AIRLINE INDUSTRY			
ENVIRONMENTAL RISK	Competitor Customer wants Innovation Sensitivity	Shareholder Expectations Capital Availability Sovereign/Political Legal	Regulatory Industry Financial Markets Catastrophic Loss
PROCESS RISK	FINANCIAL **Price** Interest Rate Currency Equity Commodity Financial Instrument **Liquidity** Cash Flow Opportunity Cost Concentration **Credit** Default Concentration Settlement Collateral	EMPOWERMENT Leadership Authority/Limit Outsourcing Performance Incentives Change Readiness Communications	GOVERNANCE Organizational Culture Ethical Behavior Board Effectiveness Succession Planning
OPERATIONS	REPUTATION Image and Branding Stakeholder Relations Customer Satisfaction Human Resources Knowledge Capital Product Development Efficiency Capacity Scalability	INTEGRITY Management Fraud Employee Fraud Third-Party Fraud Illegal Acts Unauthorized Use Performance Gap Cycle Time Sourcing Channel Effectiveness Partnering	INFORMATION TECHNOLOGY Integrity Access Availability Infrastructure Compliance Business Interruption Product/Service Failure Environmental Health and Safety Trademark/Brand Erosion
INFORMATION FOR DECISION-MAKING RISK	STRATEGIC Environmental Scan Business Model Investment Portfolio Investment Valuation/ Evaluation Organization Structure Measurement (Strategy) Resource Allocation Planning Life Cycle	PUBLIC REPORTING Financial Reporting Evaluation Internal control Evaluation Executive Certification Taxation Pension Fund Regulatory Reporting	OPERATIONAL Budget and planning Product/Service Pricing Contract Commitment Measurement (Operations) Alignment Accounting Information

Figure 5.4   **Effective risk management model for the airline industry**

Source: Protiviti, Inc., 2008.

cultures, risk appetites, and financial resources. Thus, the specific approaches, processes, methodologies, systems, and metrics that define the solution will differ from company to company (Protiviti, 2008).

The sustainability-based management model is needed for the air transportation industry to survive. This industry has many and various risks. In actuality, the nature of aviation has a fundamental risk: flight. The Corporate Sustainability Management model is developed and improved according to the characteristics in the implementation process. This model offers a flexible basic process model.

In this part of the book, Protiviti's effective risk management model (see Figure 5.4) is given as a good model sample for the airline industry. This model's context may be useful for the understanding and implementation of the Corporate Sustainability Management model.

Protiviti's model for effective risk management is designed to help airline management move beyond traditional risk management to holistic risk management. Traditional risk management focuses on managing uncertainties around physical and financial assets. In comparison with Corporate Sustainability Management and effective risk management, risk may also be viewed as a positive (opportunity) since the objective of a risk management managerial approach and its system is not only to protect but also to create and enhance enterprise value (see Figure 5.5). With this approach, risk management is embedded in the company's strategy and is managed at the top of the organization (Protiviti, 2008).

The airline industry has more complicated and dynamic qualifications which requires implementing Corporate Sustainability Management (Protiviti, 2008). The new model can be a strong support for implementing a truly and holistically enterprise-wide approach across all of corporate operations. This approach cannot be fully implemented among corporations in other industries. According to the Oliver Wyman survey, one of the world's fastest growing airlines is facing significant challenges and new risks, due to the following (Oliver Wyman, 2007):

- increased competition;
- fuel price increases;
- post-merger integration issues;
- possible regulatory changes and market liberalization.

PROTECT AND ENHANCE VALUE	
Establish competitive Advantage	♣ Integrate Risk Management with Business Planning and Strategy Setting ♣ Implement More Robust Risk Assessment Process ♣ Improve Management of Common Risk Across Enterprise ♣ Improve Capital Deployment and Resource Allocation ♣ Configure Risk Taking with Core Competencies ♣ Protect Reputation and Brand Image
Optimize Risk Management Cost	♦ Align Risk Appetite and Strategy ♦ Properly Price Risks Inherent in Transactions ♦ Aggregate Risk Transfer and Acceptance Decisions ♦ Eliminate Redundant and Unnecessary Activities
Improve Business Performance	♠ Improve Change Readiness ♠ Reduce Operational Losses and Surprises ♠ Improve Regulatory Compliance and Risk Responses ♠ Anticipate and Communicate Uncertainties Inherent in Performance Goals ♠ Enhance Understanding of Risks Affecting Earnings and Capital ♠ Instill Confidence from Systematic Risk Evaluation Process

Figure 5.5   Protect and enhance value

Source: Protiviti, Inc., 2008.

Oliver Wyman (OW) used a comprehensive and analytic intensive approach to identify and down select the key external and internal risks facing the major Asian airlines. Based on internal interviews and expert judgment, we created a comprehensive view of potential key risk areas for the major Asian airlines. Fundamentals and aims of Corporate Sustainability Management were considered in developing the new model. Basically, the new model is offered as a Corporate Sustainability Management best practice. The new Corporate Sustainability model identifies 32 steps, which are designed as six key components and their sub-components (see Figure 5.6).

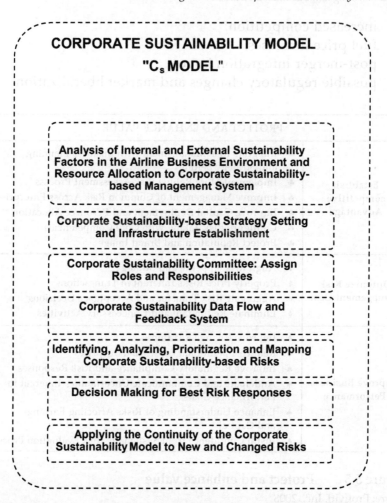

Figure 5.6   Corporate Sustainability model for airlines

The new model is shaped according to Sustainable Development, Corporate Sustainability fundamentals, and requirements and related efforts in the aviation industry. The Corporate Sustainability Management process consists of a series of steps that, when undertaken in sequence, enable continual improvement in decision making. Communication and consultation will be reflected in each step of the process. Monitoring and review is an essential and integral step in the risk management process.

Corporate Sustainability Management is an ongoing dynamic and flexible process journey. Implementing a fully integrated, holistic, and systematic Corporate Sustainability Management model and its components can provide significant value to the Corporate Sustainability and Sustainable Development of airlines. The following briefly illustrates both the main parts and the sub-components of the new model and its cyclical nature by process steps:

Step 1. Analysis of internal and external sustainability factors in the airline business environment and resource allocation to Corporate Sustainability-based management system:

   a. identification of airline's corporate goals and objectives;
   b. determination of external and internal pressures on airline (together with their risks);
   c. analysis of airline's internal audit structure, management systems, and information systems;
   d. establishment of airline's infrastructure, culture, and a common language for both Corporate Sustainability Management and risk management; Reviewing of corporate culture and level of risk awareness in the airline;
   e. analysis of stakeholder relations;
      - stakeholder identification: employees, shareholders, community, partners, regulators, and others;
      - stakeholder outreach: transparency, inclusiveness, conferences, web site, training, and governance;
      - marketing;
      - media relations;
   f. determination of airline resources and their allocation;
   g. determination of airline business strategy and its relationship with Corporate Sustainability;
   h. determination of airline corporate tolerances and appetite;
   i. reviewing of airline's corporate policies and procedure according to the sustainability;
   j. establishment of triple bottom line for Corporate Sustainability—economic, social, and environmental—as the conceptual commitment to a core sustainability theory and model;

k. supporting of sustainability by the current managerial approaches, applications, and functions: strategic management and planning, Sustainable Development, corporate governance, line management, portfolio management, value management, and so on.

Step 2. Corporate Sustainability-based strategy setting and infrastructure establishment:

a. definition of organizational Sustainability Strategy and integrating with the strategic planning;
b. establishment of high corporate level of sustainability and Sustainable Development awareness and risk perceptions;
c. determination of useful management guidelines and reports, best practices; decision making of which guidelines will be used in developing the company specific model;
d. development of a common risk language and terminology;
e. establishment of organizational capabilities according to the best practice;
f. research and development;
g. system design, funding, and staffing;
h. training and education on the fundamentals and concept of Corporate Sustainability and Sustainable Development;
i. establishment of Corporate Sustainability threats and opportunities profile.

Step 3. Corporate Sustainability Committee: assign roles and responsibilities:

a. establishment of the Corporate Sustainability Management function;
b. placement of the Corporate Sustainability Management Committee (CEO, CRO, CFO, CIO and so on) in the organization scheme;
c. assignment of roles and responsibilities;
d. establishment of the Corporate Sustainability Management philosophy: "In the company, everyone is a risk manager for Corporate Sustainability!"

Step 4. Corporate Sustainability data flow and feedback system:

a. establishment of a suitable Corporate Sustainability Management Information System (also known as CSMIS);
b. establishment of reporting format and line (top-down, across, down to top, external, and internal parties);
c. updating and improvement of the Corporate Sustainability Management and related systems;
d. providing of the effective and well-timed data flow and feedback line;
e. measurement and reporting: social capital, economic capital, natural capital, material flow analysis, energy flow analysis, internal environmental cost accounting, external environmental cost accounting, ecological foot-printing, social foot-printing, and stakeholder reporting.

Step 5. Identifying, analyzing, prioritization and mapping Corporate Sustainability-based risks within the social, environmental, and economic risks categories:

a. analysis and reviewing of the best sustainability, management, Sustainable Development, risk management frameworks, guidelines, and surveys;
b. determination of the sustainability factor identification and analysis tools, methods, and models;
c. identification, assessment, and prioritization of Corporate Sustainability factors (threats, opportunities);
d. analysis of key Corporate Sustainability factors and current capabilities;
e. determination of strategies and design capabilities;
f. classification of Corporate Sustainability factors according to the triple bottom line: social, economic, and environmental.

Step 6. Decision making for best risk responses:

a. mapping of Corporate Sustainability factors and selection of agreeable responses.

Step 7. Applying the continuity of the Corporate Sustainability model to new and changed risks:

a. establishment of continuous monitoring and review function for control of system efficiency and workable level in developed conditions;
b. providing for the continuity of both the Corporate Sustainability-based Enterprise Risk Management system and its development;
c. restart the Corporate Sustainability Management process loop again to address new and developing sustainability risks and risk sources.

To succeed in today's competitive environment, airline managers in all functions must have a good understanding of the airline business in its totality (International Air Transport Association, 2009). The Corporate Sustainability Management model provides a unique opportunity for managers to learn and practice a full range of airline management and planning skills and to understand the inter-related variables involved. Airline managers will gain a thorough understanding of the factors affecting airline success, sustainability, and profitability and will learn to think strategically about the business and how to turn key strategies into successful operating plans via Corporate Sustainability Management model implementation. They will also better understand the role of other departments and how to integrate and plan across departmental boundaries to achieve desired goals and planned results. Corporate Sustainability Management should be applied to airline business management and all air transportation companies since Corporate Sustainability Management is the fundamental part of the decision-making process, marketing, sales management, and corporate governance. Corporate Sustainability Management is an important element of competition and value creation since Corporate Sustainability Management is the fundamental sustainability component for airline management. The Corporate Sustainability Management model should be integrated with managerial issues to support the principle functions of airline management, as follows (SH and E, 2009):

- airline performance measures and financial audits;
- passenger and cargo market research and analysis;
- fleet planning;
- traffic forecasting and revenue analysis;
- scheduling and network optimization studies;
- reservations and distribution systems;
- reorganization and turn-around management;
- safety and security evaluation;
- airline marketing and competition strategy;
- cargo studies and management;
- corporate missions and objectives for Corporate Sustainability;
- business strategic planning;
- restructuring and reorganization strategies;
- mergers and acquisitions;
- key resources acquisitions.

Risk is a fundamental and inseparable aspect of business. Providing maximum shareholder value is possible if enterprise-wide risks are effectively and truly managed. Confronting opportunities involves many risks. Therefore, determining, measuring, and managing corporate risks are the most important factors for the achievement of Sustainable Development objectives in business management. Today's airline business is under pressure as a result of the development of the international markets, globalization, liberalization, commercialization, expectation of raised effectiveness and cost reduction, hardy legal regulations, rapid technological developments, and increasing competition. The cost of making mistakes is increasing day by day. The possibility of compensation to the faults is gradually reducing. Managers should establish the risk–profit balance. It has been shown that earning should be optimized by increasing output and decreasing operational costs and loss. Enterprise Risk Management is increasing corporate value by providing sustainable competitive advantages and cost optimization, increasing business performance, and focusing all value sources on the company (Kucuk Yilmaz, 2008b).

For best results in implementation of the Corporate Sustainability Management model, airline and risk managers must know all aspects of airline management issues. This section provides an overview of airline management decision-making processes with a focus on economic issues and their relationship to operations planning models and decision support tools. The application of the model includes demand, pricing, costs, and supply to airline markets and networks, and it also covers examination of the industry practice and emerging methods for fleet planning, route network design, scheduling, pricing, and revenue management.

This part aims to support Corporate Sustainability efforts in airline businesses via the new Corporate Sustainability Management model. This model may be tailored to meet the specific industry and airline business needs, objectives, and managerial tone.

The airline industry faces a number of risks in today's industry and business environment and its dynamics. Today, airline managers want to have company-specific models to achieve competitive advantages. This new Corporate Sustainability Management model will provide high potential for the integration of environmental and social aspects and objectives into the core management of companies. We assume this to be a huge step toward the best Corporate Sustainability Management system based on Enterprise Risk Management.

This model is aimed to both support current sustainability efforts in the airline business and contribute to airline management issues regarding Corporate Sustainability via this new Corporate Sustainability model. This model can change and improve according to the sector and company requirements. Corporate Sustainability and Sustainable Development is highly relevant to the airline business, a fundamental part of the air transportation system, which is recognized as an essential link to the global economy.

Corporate Sustainability Management, using the Corporate Sustainability Management model, is a necessary managerial approach and framework for optimal Corporate Sustainability Management and implementation of the sustainable competition strategy for airline businesses. Air transport and airlines already make an important and unique contribution to the development of our global society, but related efforts should be practiced more systematically with risk awareness in a timely and disciplined way. In order to meet the requirements of sustainability, specific tools are necessary. For this reason, managers should consider the sustainability model to achieve their sustainability targets in the airline business.

Risks from Global Warming to the Contemporary Business and Management

When it comes to assessing the *business risk* from global warming, for example, businesses need to assess two short-term risks and at least five longer-term risks (Pollard, 2008):

- regulation risk (risk of new carbon taxes and caps, and restrictions to supply and operations);
- reputation risk (risk of boycott for notorious emitters of global warming pollutants);
- risk of water shortages (related to glacial melt, evaporation, and droughts)—every business needs water and some use staggering amounts of it;
- risk of energy shortages (as oil supplies are depleted and become vastly more expensive and restricted);
- risk of pandemics (as infections spread beyond their normal tropical habitat to areas with no natural resistance, affecting humans and they animals they eat);
- risk of pestilence (as insects likewise spread beyond tropical areas and attack trees and agricultural plants with no natural resistance, wiping out crops and making food, paper, and wood unaffordable);
- risk of sea-level and sea-temperature rises (engulfing low-lying cities and growing areas, and affecting aquatic life).

A chart of the major real risks to a business (see Figure 5.7), at least in the longer term (20–50 years rather than ten) might look like this (Pollard, 2008):

The global warming business risk can also be broken down into the following (Pollard, 2008):

- risks that arise because of actions the company takes, or neglects to take, that contribute to global warming or reduce impact on global warming (for example, cost of reducing pollutants, and taxes paid on emissions);
- risks that arise because of the consequences of global warming on the company's operations (for example, water shortages).

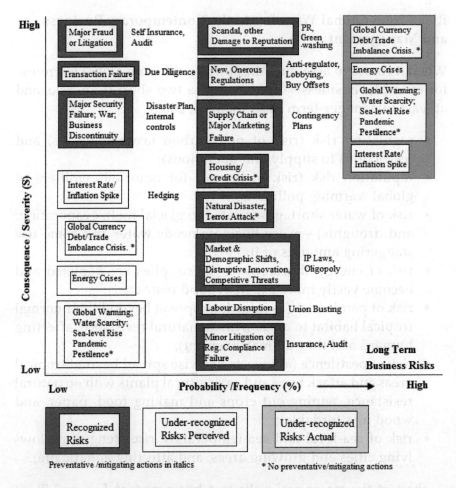

Figure 5.7   Long-term business risks

Source: Pollard, 2008, from http://blogs.salon.com/0002007/2008/03/11.html.

The risks that are not considered to be significant short term (less than two years) are in the upper-right corner, and as long as business is only concerned with the short term, these risks are perceived to be those in the lower-left corner and not worth being concerned about. Besides, most businesses perceive these as largely unpreventable and immitigable anyway, so their approach is to worry about them *if and when* they occur. Table 5.1 offers a brief summary of these 15 types of global warming business risks. "Global Warming-Based Business Risks" is adapted from Pollard (2008) "How to Save the World: Dave Pollard's Environmental Philosophy, Creative Works, Business Papers and Essays," and is used with the permission of Dave Pollard. Each of the stakeholders in the business—management, employees, customers, investors, suppliers, community members, and so on—could then use this risk chart to make decisions in their own areas of interest. Customers might be more interested in reputation (Risk #4), supply chain (Risk #6), and innovation (Risk #9), for example. Management could focus risk management decisions on the upper-right quadrant, short-term risks, while institutional investors could focus investment decisions on longer-term risks (Pollard, 2008).

Table 5.1 Type of risk: Global warming-based business risks

	Probability % = P%	Consequence $: C$
1. Major Fraud or Litigation Risk: A large-scale theft, governance or human error or litigation sufficient to threaten business continuity. (I/E)	P%: Low	C$: High
2. Major Transaction Failure Risk: Collapsed merger or acquisition or reorganization. (I)	P%: Low	C$: High
3. Major Security Failure Risk: A war, control breakdown, system failure, or industrial sabotage severely disrupting business operations, solvency, or continuity. (I/E)	P%: Low	C$: High
4. Reputation Risk: A scandal, massive boycott, product tampering, industrial accident, or other event that destroys customer confidence e.g. major product quality, service, or delivery problems. (I/E)	P%: Medium	C$: High
5. Regulatory Risk: Major new legislation that is prohibitively expensive to comply with. (E)	P%: Medium	C$: High
6. Major Supply Chain or Marketing Failure Risk: Loss of a major source of critical supply, embargo, or disastrous new product/market launch. (I/E)	P%: Medium	C$: Medium
7. Customer Credit Risk: An economic crisis severely hampering customers' liquidity, solvency, or ability to buy, or pay for what they've bought. (E)	P%: Medium	C$: Medium
8. Natural Disaster or Terror Attack Risk: A localized major destruction of infrastructure and human habitat. (E)	P%: Medium	C$: Varies
9. Competitive, Market, or Demographic Shift Risk: Innovation, new competitive threat, or major shift in customer or employee market e.g. skill/talent shortage. (E)	P%: Medium	C$: Varies
10. Labor Disruption Risk: Strike, embargo, loss of access to employee market, or sudden change in cost or availability of workers. (I/E)	P%: Medium	C$: Low

Table 5.1 Continued Type of risk: Global warming-based business risks

	Probability % = P%	Consequence $: C$
11. Minor Litigation or Regulatory Compliance Failure Risk: Small lawsuit or infraction of the law. (I)	**P%:** Medium	**C$:** Low
12. Global Currency, Debt, or Trade Crisis Risk: An economic recession or capital market crisis brought on by currency collapse, or unsustainable national debts, or trade imbalances. (E)	**P%:** Low/High	**C$:**Low/High*
13. Energy Supply Risk: Major shortage of energy supply or spike in energy price. (E)	**P%:** Low/High*	**C$:** Low/High*
14. Global Warming Risks: Chronic water scarcity, flooding of ports by rising sea levels, pandemic disease outbreaks in people and animals, insect plagues destroying crops and forests, droughts, uncontrolled forest fires, and other consequences of global warming. (E)	**P%:** Low/High*	**C$:** Low/High*
15. Interest Rate and Inflation Risk: Jump in interest and/or inflation rates sufficient to create a type 7 or 12 crisis. (E)	**P%:** Low/High*	**C$:**Low/High*

Notes: *Low in the current perception of business; high according to economists and scientists. (I) = Internal cause risks. (E) = External cause risks.

Source: Pollard, 2008.

Chapter 6
Modeling Human Factor-Based Risks in Aviation

Are human factor-based risks unmanageable in the airline business? We attempt to answer this question in this chapter by suggesting a human factor (also known as HF) risk management model for airlines containing a new full-set of risk shaping/influencing factors (RSF/RIF) taxonomy and a score formula. This model is expected to support corporate risk management and Human Resource Management (also known as HRM) efforts aimed at identifying and managing human factor-related issues and to provide a systematic process-based approach to airline management. Managers can provide holistic snapshots of their company's human resources by using this human factor-based risk management concept. We apply our theoretical model to the airline industry and more specifically:

- discuss the importance of human factors in airline management and operations;
- develop a human factor-based risk list for airlines;
- assess the cost of human-based risks on an airline's financial and operational performance; and
- develop a human factor-based risk analysis model for the airline business.

Human Factors in Aviation Management

Airlines, like other companies, face a multitude of diverse risks in their dynamic business environment. Risks are an expected part of business life and entrepreneurship. Risks, business systems, and their activities are generally interrelated with human factors either directly or indirectly. The human element impacts all managerial and operational systems and activities in a company. Therefore, managing human factors is an inseparable part of business management.

Our Human Factor Risk Management (also known as HFRM) model is structured by managing activities of human-based risks for businesses and provides a comprehensive and coherent framework for the evolution and management of human factors. The Human Factor Risk Management model continues to anticipate potential human factor-based risks and develops appropriate responses for various scenarios.

Our Human Factor Risk Management model can help provide a more precise understanding of risk factors associated with the human element and furnish insights on their appropriate identification and prioritization via score and management.

This chapter reviews both leading Enterprise Risk Management (also known as ERM) guidelines and Strategic Human Resource Management (also known as SHRM) literature in the development process of the Human Factor Risk Management model. These are reviewed in view of their context of human factor-based risks. A number of weaknesses in current literature and works on both Enterprise Risk Management and Human Resource Management have been identified. These weaknesses come mostly from a single acting approach to human factors, the absence of internal strategies, and lack of a systematic and holistic approach for managing human-based risks.

Strategic Human Resource Management and Enterprise Risk Management literature have generally focused on the risk source dimension of human factors thus having ignored or insufficiently focused on the dual role of human factors. In addition, human-based risk work did not use taxonomy and related risk scoring approaches. The Human Factor Risk Management model supports Strategic Human Resource Management and whole management efforts via consideration of the multidimensional nature of human factors. Our model is designed as a combination of holistic risk management (of financial, strategic, operational, and threat risks) and Strategic Human Resource Management.

The human element is both a critical aspect of aviation safety and airline management in view of an airline's financial and operational performance. Historically, safety in the aviation system was sought through enhanced systems, equipment design, and certification procedures. A technological plateau was achieved in the 1970s, yet incidents and accidents continued to occur. This directed the attention of the international community to the human component. The influence of human capabilities, and in particular limitations in safety of operations, has been evident for many years. However, little attention or interest has been directed to them (Aviation Watch, 2009).

Managing human factor-based risk within this complex environment involves the implementation of a proactive approach, a well-planned risk management process, and preventive measures, such as continuously improving processes, human factor analysis, and training. This leads to improved risk awareness, creating and maintaining risk culture, and consideration of the following elements (adapted from National Steering Committee on Patient Safety, 2004):

- Personnel (evaluate to ensure optimal numbers for workload, proper credentials, and staff physical/mental well-being).
- Equipment (evaluate to ensure that needed devices are present, functioning properly, monitored for safety, and regularly serviced with a plan for phased and emergency replacement).
- Environment (evaluate for physical designs that may inhibit or increase risks to those receiving or providing care).
- Administration (create an organizational culture of safety; evaluate and plan for effective policies and procedures— including a policy for reporting actual and potential risks to those receiving or providing care).

The commercial airline industry is an extremely competitive, safety-sensitive, high-technology service industry. People, employees, and customers—not products and machines—must be the arena of an organization's core competence. The implications are vast and pervasive, affecting no less than the organization's structure, strategy, culture, and numerous operational activities (Appelbaum and Fewster, 2002).

This chapter is organized into four main sections, including the preceding introduction. In the second section, we explain

Strategic Human Resource Management in the airline industry and key drivers of the Human Factor Risk Management model. Our methodology is provided in the third section. A visual model is used for developing the Human Factor Risk Management model which contains a full-set of RSF/RIF and a scoring formula. Finally, we conclude with a summary and the significance of our model, as well as a brief discussion of future research possibilities.

Strategic Human Resource Management and Drivers of the Human Factor Risk Management Model

Strategic Human Resource Management focuses on the relationship between an organization's strategy and the management of its human resources (Millmore et al., 2007). By combining the Human Resource Management function with business strategy, Strategic Human Resource Management reflects a more flexible arrangement and utilization of human resources to achieve set organizational goals and accordingly helps organizations gain a competitive advantage (Wei, 2006). The strategic perspective of human resource has grown out of researchers' desires to demonstrate the importance of human resource practices in organizational performance (Delery and Doty, 1996). The field of human resource strategy differs from traditional Human Resource Management research in two important ways (Becker and Huselid, 2006):

1. Strategic Human Resource Management focuses on organizational performance rather than individual performance.
2. Strategic Human Resource Management emphasizes the role of Human Resource Management systems as solutions to business problems rather than individual Human Resource Management practices.

With respect to Human Resource Management: increasing workforce diversity; the increasing size and complexity of companies; the absolute and relative rise in the labor costs of firms; the intensification and globalization of competition; the individualization of Human Resource Management issues;

structural developments in the labor market; and innovations in technology, have been the factors that have led to this increased acknowledgment of Human Resource Management-related issues. With respect to the airline industry: it is one of the fastest-growing industries in the world and has gained importance through the current era of globalization. Today, operations are being dealt with on a worldwide basis, and airline travel plays an increasing role in bridging geographical distance. According to the International Air Transport Association (IATA), the number of passengers traveling on scheduled flights has increased on average by over 6 percent annually for the last three decades. In comparison with 2003, international airline passenger traffic increased by over 15 percent in 2004, and in certain regions, such as Asia–Pacific, which includes China, passenger numbers increased by over 20 percent, showing that the industry is becoming ever more significant (Wilson, 2005).

The term "human factors" has grown increasingly popular as the commercial aviation industry has realized that human error, rather than mechanical failure, underlies most aviation accidents and incidents. If interpreted narrowly, a human factor is often considered synonymous with crew resource management (also known as CRM) or maintenance resource management (also known as MRM). However, it is much broader in both its knowledge base and scope. Human factors involves gathering information about human abilities, limitations, and other characteristics and applying it to tools, machines, systems, tasks, jobs, and environments to produce safe, comfortable, and effective human use. In aviation, human factors is dedicated to better understanding how humans can most safely and efficiently be integrated with the technology. That understanding is then translated into design, training, policies, or procedures to help humans perform better (Graeber, 2009).

Aviation is an excellent example in which a high-risk industry implements coordinated and comprehensive strategies to reduce preventable accidents. Also, the study of human factors engineering has led to an understanding that, although adverse events will occur in any human endeavor, they can be minimized through the design of equipment or tools, design of the tasks themselves, the environmental conditions of work, the training of staff, and the selection of workers. Airline regulators, plane manufacturers, and commercial airline carriers have combined human factors engineering with the knowledge that failures in communication and coordination among team members have led to tragic aviation accidents. Their collaboration has resulted in a wide variety of mandatory and voluntary processes that have dramatically improved passenger safety (National Steering Committee on Patient Safety, 2004):

- redundancy in key operating systems;
- simulator training to improve teamwork and prepare for sudden emergencies;
- restrictions on the number of consecutive hours worked;
- mandatory reporting of designated aviation accidents/ incidents;
- voluntary reporting of near misses;
- extensive use of information technology for the provision of flight information and weather conditions;
- comprehensive and objective investigation of accidents with reporting of the probable cause;
- procedural checklists with alarms for key equipment and/or human failures.

Human Factor Risk Management recognizes that people do not always understand, communicate, or perform consistently. Each individual brings to the workplace a unique background and technical ability, and has different needs and priorities (Committee of Sponsoring Organizations of the Tradeway Commission, 2004:5). Both sources and managers of risk and human resources have dual roles in corporate management systems and risk management. Human resources are one of the keys to success in corporate management systems. For this reason, the aforementioned dual roles (risk source and risk manager) require a different approach to both Human Resource Management and the corporate management systems. This is due to the fact that the human element has different, highly dynamic, and hardly controllable characteristics from other corporate sources.

The drivers for developing a new Human Factor Risk Management model are as follows:

- integration of Human Factor Risk Management into the organization as a part of achieving the overall goal of a managed corporate culture;
- increase the human factor contribution to company functions and activities;
- meet requirements for managing human factors;
- reduce costs arising from human performance limitations, and add value through improved human performance;
- meet demand of business owners and high level managers.

Desired outcomes from our Human Factor Risk Management model, taxonomy, and score formula are as follows:

- human factors will be considered as leading risk factors in the corporate management system and organization;
- human-based factors will be managed to achieve corporate objectives (for example, financial outcomes and operational performance);
- threats and opportunity-based awareness and responsibility will be increased amongst the managers and other personnel in the organization;
- human factors management will be considered an essential part of the business planning process.

The Human Factor Risk Management model intends to maximize the benefits of existing functions and activities in all departments via a human-centric approach. Expected additional benefits include:

- a strategy for Human Factor Risk Management across the organization;
- a generic framework which enables flexible and tailored approaches;
- a systematic managerial tool for the best management of human factor-based risks;
- a common language and culture for corporate risk management;

- a tool for increasing human-based opportunities and decrease human-based threats;
- a common approach for internal monitoring, control, and review;
- a strong managerial tool for continuous control of human factor-based risks.

Human Factor Risk Management Model

We use qualitative research methodology and visual modeling in setting up our model. Additionally, we use quantitative risk analysis methodology in order to aid in the assessment of the human factors. A new full-set of the RSF/RIF taxonomy has been determined and weighted by an Analytical Hierarchy Process (also known as AHP) and then results are used in the new score formula.

Faced with rapid change, organizations need to develop more focused and coherent approaches for managing people. The Airline Human Factor Risk Management (also known as AHFRM) model allows for the management of human risk (like any risk) to be a continuous process of identifying, analyzing, and mapping areas that have the potential to cause threats and can provide an opportunity in implementing system improvements. We developed a model that would allow human risk to be considered systematically and which would gain maximum advantage from tools and processes already in existence. Detailed information about our Human Factor Risk Management model elements and tools are given later in this book.

The Human Factor Risk Management model provides a generic framework for the establishment and implementation of the management process within organizations. A number of large companies have recognized the value in adopting some kind of a risk model. The proposed model is primarily a process for applying human factors tools and techniques in a coordinated and systematic way. The model has a number of elements that deal with and link management processes to Corporate Sustainability (also known as CS).

The model also takes into account work ethic, culture, and stakeholder expectations as organizational culture is affected

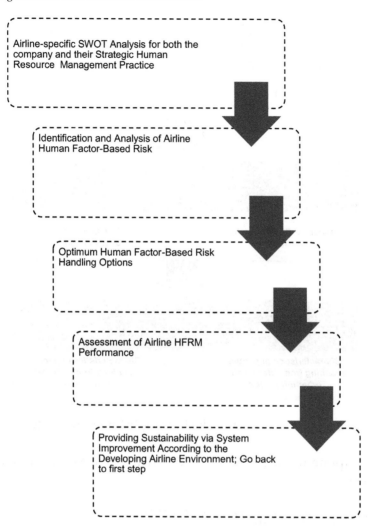

Figure 6.1   Airline Human Factor Risk Management model

by these concepts. This model can be applied in any industrial and business management segment. Our Human Factor Risk Management process includes a continuous monitoring, review, communication, and consultation system along with its five steps. These four aspects are integral to the entire Human Factor Risk Management process. Communication and consultation will be reflected in each step of the process. Figure 6.1 provides an overview of the model and its elements as a continuous loop.

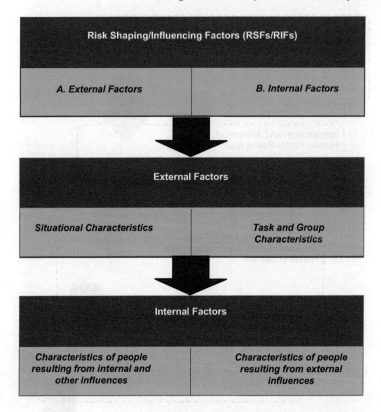

Figure 6.2   New full-set risk shaping/influencing factors

The components of the full-set RSFs/RIFs (see Figure 6.2) are as follows:

Risk shaping/influencing factors (RSFs/RIFs)

External factors
- Situational characteristics:
  - organizational structure;
  - organizational culture;
  - politic environment and conditions;
  - company life cycle;
  - system, policy, and procedures;
  - rewards and benefits;
  - tone at the top and shareholder's expectations (for example, company owner, board of directors);

- external environment forces (for example, external audit, requirements for corporate social responsibility, Sustainable Development);
- organizational targets;
- audit and internal control systems;
- workplace environment.
- Task and group characteristics:
  - communication and coordination;
  - feedback (knowledge of results);
  - intra and inter-group conflict and cohesion;
  - decision making.

Internal factors
- Characteristics of people resulting from internal and other influences:
  - training;
  - experience;
  - knowledge and skills;
  - past self efficacy;
  - current self efficacy;
  - verbal and written communication skills;
  - task knowledge;
  - social factors;
  - threats (of failure, loss of job).
- Characteristics of people resulting from external influences:
  - job satisfaction;
  - personality and intelligence variables;
  - achievement, motivation, and attitude;
  - emotional state;
  - attitudes based on influence of family and other outside persons and agencies;
  - individual control;
  - ethical values;
  - loyalty;
  - timeliness;
  - personnel management skills;
  - social responsibility;
  - reliability;
  - risk taking and confidence;

- past behavioral performance;
- current behavioral performance;
- creativity;
- comprehensive and integrative thinking;
- strength/endurance;
- analytical and problem-solving skills;
- response to crises and seizing opportunities on timely basis;
- physical/health condition;
- stress level;
- perceptional abilities;
- gender differences.

Our full-set RSF/RIF taxonomy is based on Performance Influencing/Shaping Factors (PIF/PSF) of Miller and Swain (1987) and Ya-Lih Lin and Sheue-Ling Hwang (1992). These are the most appropriate taxonomies when compared to others for our systematic approach of the Human Factor Risk Management model. All of the factors researched and collected from the above-mentioned sources are collated into a new full-set RSF/RIF taxonomy. After that, we omitted RSF/RIF items that had little relevance to human risks. Alternatively, items that were determined to have a bearing on human factors were included. Items involving the stressor factors were also removed because it was difficult to calculate risk score from the approach of human risk factors. These factors affecting and influencing human performance in business management can be classified into two main groups: external and internal RSF/RIF, four sub-group categories, with 45 items determined.

After the new full-set RSF/RIF taxonomy, the Analytical Hierarchy Process weights the impact score of the human factor. Weighted results (see Figure 6.3) are used in calculating the total score: Likelihood <multiplied by> Impact. Corporate high-level managers and human resources managers or selective jury members are responsible for this process. They report to present company management according to the score formula results. Impact levels of RSF/RIF are ranked by Saaty's Analytic Hierarchy Process.

Analytical Hierarchy Process results show that internal factors are highly influenced and shaped by human risk factors.

Name		Normalized by Cluster	Limiting
IMPACT SCORE		0.00000	0.000000
Characteristics of people resulting from external ~		0.27960	0.279604
Characteristics of people resulting from internal ~		0.34171	0.341707
Situational characteristics		0.25263	0.252634
Task and Group characteristics		0.12606	0.126055

Figure 6.3   Impact score results of risk shaping/influencing factors by Analytic Hierarchy Process

All of the RIFs are important to achieving organizational objectives and satisfactory human performance. Impact factor scores will be used to calculate risk likelihood as follows:

- Impact (Characteristics of people resulting from external influences) x 0.279604.
- Impact (Characteristics of people resulting from internal and other influences) x 0.341707.
- Impact (Situational characteristics) x 0.252634.
- Impact (Task and Group characteristics) x 0.126055.

Human Factor Score Formula

We developed a new formula to assess the human factor in view of likelihood, impact, and related factors. Our Human Factor Score Formula and its elements area as follows:

1. Likelihood Scale:
   $L = \{0 < L < 1\}$
   The likelihood calculation includes favoring conditions, adverse conditions, and uncertainty in this formula. These should be considered by managers in the calculation of the likelihood.

2. Impact Scale:
   $I = \{0 < I < 100\}$

3. Internal Factors:

Characteristics of people resulting from internal and other influences:

$$I_f = \frac{\sum\limits_{i=1}^{n} I_{fi} \times L_{I_{fi}}}{n} \times 0.34$$

Characteristics of people resulting from external influences:

$$E_f = \frac{\sum\limits_{i=1}^{n} E_{fi} \times L_{E_{fi}}}{n} \times 0.28$$

4. External Factors:

Situational characteristics:

$$S_f = \frac{\sum\limits_{i=1}^{n} S_{fi} \times L_{S_{fi}}}{n} \times 0.25$$

Task and group characteristics:

$$T_f = \frac{\sum\limits_{i=1}^{n} T_{fi} \times L_{T_{fi}}}{n} \times 0.13$$

5. Total Risk Score to Human Factor is:

R = If + Ef +Sf + Tf

Calculated rounded weighted rates of Impact by Analytic Hierarchy Process are:

- characteristics of people resulting from internal and other influences = 0.34;
- characteristics of people resulting from external influences = 0.28;
- situational characteristics = 0.25;
- task and group characteristics = 0.13.

Prioritization via the Human Factor Score Formula is a critical outcome of our model. Managers can use this formula in their human resources performance analysis. The calculation of the risk score includes internal and external factors. RSF/RIF and score formulas can be used for personnel performance assessments. For this reason, this model provides for a systematic approach, and the risk score formula is a support tool for human resources and its performance management. This formula and its result have great applicability and importance in assessing human resources in terms of current performance situations. A high score means that an employee provides advantages for a company. If an employee achieves a low score, this person should improve in terms of their job-related activities such as (depending on the applicability to the company) sales performance, training, marketing skills, and human relationships. Personnel empowerment should be one of the required fields.

If the results of the score calculation are analyzed in detail, the strengths and weaknesses of personnel can be seen clearly and understood by the management of a company that employs this system. This can create the opportunity to reinforce the strengths of evaluated personnel. Managers can then work on optimizing personnel capabilities in order to derive maximum benefit from personnel capabilities and skills. The most fundamental contribution of the Human Factor Risk Management model is the effective management of human-based threats and opportunities toward achieving corporate objectives. Thus, human-based threats can be minimized, and human-based opportunities can be maximized. Therefore, a company can be provided with reasonable assurance toward organizational and strategic objectives linked to Corporate Sustainability.

Like many airlines, Qantas has advanced systems for detecting and managing human risk in flight operations. The Qantas Human Factors Strategy provides a framework for applying Human Factor Risk Management principles in any operational area. The model uses a Safety Management Systems (also known as SMS) approach to manage human performance limitations. The Human Factors Strategy is intended to maximize the benefits of existing practice while outlining a common approach for human factors management across the Qantas group. The proposed solution is primarily a framework for applying human factors tools and techniques in a coordinated and systematic way. The model has a number of elements concerned with risk management processes as part of normal operations, as well as "triggers" for when particular human factors attention is required. For example, following an event or incident, there could be the acquisition of new equipment or the need to manage change. The model also takes into account that human behaviors do not occur within a vacuum but are influenced by an organization's safety culture which should also be subject to periodic measurement, assessment, and improvement. The model can be applied generically across all the operational businesses and has sufficient flexibility to cope with customized tools and processes within each element (Raggett, 2006:2).

Our Human Factor Risk Management model can be useful to airlines in obtaining a clearer view and recognizing human factors in all aspects and is the beginning to improving the management of human risk for optimization of airlines operations and performance. Human Factor Risk Management is a major contributor to the success of any organization. Human factors should be an important piece of Enterprise Risk Management in airlines and aviation operations. A Human Factor Risk Management model-based framework that allows systematic evaluation of human factors research and interventions could contribute to minimizing human-based threats and optimizing aviation operations performance. Our Human Factor Risk Management framework is designed to support airline operators in focusing their efforts on human factors issues that may negatively affect the performance of aviation operations.

In this chapter, we have offered a new Human Factor Risk Management model. We developed a fresh full-set of human factor-based RDF/RIF taxonomy for use in the Human Factor Risk Management process. We calculated the impact weighting of the obtained RSF/RIF items that we evaluated through an Analytical Hierarchy Process technique. Impact weighted scores were used in the score formula for prioritization of human factor-based risks. The proposed full-set RSF/RIF taxonomy and score formula is used in our Human Factor Risk Management model. An appropriate analysis/assessment framework must be developed in order to use the taxonomy in other human resource areas.

This chapter presents a model for managing human factors in airline operations via a well-grounded, proactive, and systematic process-based approach. The Airline Human Factor Risk Management model is a very helpful tool for airline managers in assessing and managing their human resources; therefore, this model is offered as a managerial tool. The Likelihood and Impact elements of our formula may improve employee performance. An effective Airline Human Factor Risk Management model can provide a sustainable competitive advantage, critical to the success of the airline.

Our research aims to contribute to the fields of Corporate Sustainability Management (also known as CSM), risk management, airline management, human factors management, and Human Resource Management. Since the processes of the model are capable of dealing with all kinds of feedback and dependence when modeling a complex decision environment, we advocate that this Human Factor Risk Management model, full-set RSF/RIF taxonomy, and formula are useful and workable. The Human Factor Risk Management model deals with the complexity of human factors and provides insights into managing human factor-based risks.

Chapter 7
Risk Management, Change Management, and Effectiveness in Aviation Operations

This chapter focuses on providing a theoretical answer to the question, "How can an air carrier effectively implement a Safety Management System (also known as SMS) in its operations?" The core assumptions of this chapter are that:

A. the value of a well-structured Safety Management System in enhancing air carrier operational safety is axiomatic; and
B. risk management is an integral part of Safety Management Systems in aviation to provide effective aviation operations.

We present a road map for change management, risk management, and their utility and application in transforming a non-Safety Management System compliant system to a Safety Management System one using change management principles.

Safety Issues in the Aviation Industry

Safety is cornerstone in any aviation operation and expected by customers, governments, and the public in general. The Civil Aviation Authorities' primary goal is to safeguard, proactively, the safety of aviation operations. Commonly perceived as lack of accidents (ICAO defines an airplane accident as, "an occurrence associated with the operation of an airplane that takes place between the time any person boards the airplane with the intention of flight and such time as all such persons have disembarked, and in which 1) the airplane sustains substantial damage; 2) death or serious injury results from being in or upon the airplane, direct contact with the airplane or anything attached thereto, or direct exposure to jet blast") or incidents, aviation safety is primarily achieved by an organization through compliance with prescribed standards. Airlines are subject to strict regulatory oversight by their national authorities which prevents them from deviating from safe operating standards. Furthermore, airlines and their suppliers are constantly audited by regulatory agencies, manufacturers, and other airlines, often following international standards such as IATA's Operational Safety Audit Program (IOSA).

Likewise, regulatory agencies themselves are overseen by ICAO's Universal Safety Oversight Program (USOAP). As a result of technological developments (notably Traffic Collision Avoidance Systems and Ground Proximity Warning Systems) as well as standardization initiatives, such as ICAO's Standards and Recommended Practices (SARPS) and other regulatory oversight, the airline industry has achieved considerable safety improvements since the 1960s. During these last decades, international aviation has witnessed an improvement in the rate of civil aviation accidents (Boeing Commercial Airplanes, 2005).

Despite this, operators are still susceptible to error which is not always preventable through regulatory oversight. Air carriers are still responsible for following safe operational practices to prevent accidents or incidents and are mandated by their national authorities to monitor their internal processes constantly to ensure that deviations are adequately addressed. For instance, complying with prescribed maintenance standards could, theoretically, maintain the probability of an accident due to mechanical failure at 1E-9 (one event per 100 million opportunities). This is the acceptable level of safety risk for an individual catastrophic failure, as defined by national authorities during aircraft certification.

Air carriers are required to manage their operations adequately to ensure that their service, transporting passengers or cargo, is delivered in an efficient manner in order to satisfy stakeholder expectations. (Stakeholders are the general public in addition to regulatory authorities.) An airline can be perceived as an intricate network of departments, employees, contractors, and regulators interacting with each other. To conduct a safe operation, an airline's management needs to understand the complexities associated with its operations and to develop, implement, and monitor control systems that will ensure compliance with safety standards. Moreover, the management of safety requires the organization to manage hazards particular to its operations proactively. Safety management has been recognized as a key aspect of an airline's operation and is now a regulatory requirement in many countries around the world. It is now recognized that the implementation of a Safety Management System (for national authorities, a draft Safety Management System manual has been released by ICAO (Doc 9859) is a contributor to further reductions in aircraft accidents and incidents.

Is a Safety Management System a panacea or just another buzzword that will be replaced with something new in a few years? How can an operator effectively implement an effective Safety Management System in its operations? In this book, we consider the value of a well-structured Safety Management System in enhancing operational safety as an axiom and consider the Safety Management System to be nothing new. The Safety Management System is deeply rooted in organizational behavior theory, and we propose that aviation operators, through the use of change management, can successfully transform existing systems into Safety Management System compliant systems. Therefore, our argument focuses on how change management can be used as an effective technique in implementing a Safety Management System in an operation that is accustomed to a non-Safety Management System type system of regulatory compliance. Thus, we describe what change management is and how it can be utilized in a Safety Management System transformation. By extension, though not a focus of this theoretical book, our argument presupposes that an adequate management of safety is an indicator of the overall performance of an organization and, as such, a quality to be desired.

Airlines, employees, and regulators all proceed with different concepts of risk, based on the perceptions of their people, their experience, public pressure, and any number of other "environmental" factors. If differing risk strategies and views exist, then there are inevitable disagreements, any of which drag the operating process down. If the three actors can come to agreement on the ideas of risk, then the operating process can go smoothly and efficiently (SMS Project Team of The Air Line Pilots Association, International, 2006). The objective of a Safety Management System is to provide a structured management system to control risk in operations. Effective safety management must be based on characteristics of an operator's processes that affect safety (Federal Aviation Administration, 2006).

First, we briefly discuss organizational culture, define what a Safety Management System is, and then proceed to define change management and propose ways the concept applies to the implementation of a Safety Management System in an airline environment. In our discussion of organizational culture, we propose that the stronger the culture is in an organization, the more effectively the organization addresses change. By extension, the more effectively the organization addresses change, the more successful it can be in implementing a new Safety Management System in its operations and the less it will need the deployment of radical change management techniques.

Review of Literature on Culture

Definitions of organizational culture vary and typically depend on the academic discipline from which they originate. Business schools have the tendency to define organizational culture as a phenomenon that can be managed. Sociologists and anthropologists stress the uniqueness of individual organizations. Organizational psychologists with an empirical background believe that organizational culture can be broken down into its component parts and then studied part by part.

This chapter defines organizational culture as the values, beliefs, assumptions, rituals, symbols, and behavior that define an organized group, especially in relationship to other organized groups, and closely follows the business school definition. The visible part of organizational culture consists of observable behaviors and recognizable manifestations, for example, members' uniforms, symbols and logos, organizational routines and rituals, and printed documents. The deep layer of culture consists of the values, beliefs, and the subconscious assumptions that provide the logic, which guides the members' behaviors.

The management of safety in the aerospace industry has been linked to organizational culture. In fact, the proactive management of safety, including Safety Management System initiatives, depends on the establishment of a hazard reporting culture (Reason, 1997). The important aspect of organizational culture vis-à-vis aviation safety outcomes is the underlying or deep culture. The visible aspect of culture is only procedural and is based on an organizational symbology. For instance, an employee who is dissatisfied with his organization and not performing his duties to high standards will still wear the company uniform to work. Therefore, in this scenario, the values, beliefs, and subconscious assumptions of the employee, vis-à-vis his organization, are sub-optimal and yet his appearance will seem normal.

The cultural strength of an organization has been defined by researchers in organizational management, sociology, and anthropology in a variety of ways. It has been defined as coherence, homogeneity, stability and intensity, congruence, and internalized control. Cultural strength relates to whom and how many accept the dominant values, how strongly these values are held, and how long the values have been dominant (Marshall, 1998). The underlying concept of cultural strength is the way in which employees accept these values, which is to say that employees must substantively believe in their organizational culture in order for the culture to be successful.

To believe in one's company's organizational culture substantively, an employee must be convinced of the superiority of this culture, and this culture must conform to his personality and national culture. However, this is complicated for organizations that exist in multicultural states (this is really not a major problem because in culturally diverse states the relevance of a national culture is evident, going beyond cultural or ethnic diversity and unifying people under one national framework; the US is a good example of such a case) and companies that rely on expatriate personnel, thereby, bringing a multitude of people from diametrically different cultures, ethnicities, and nations under one organizational rubric. Does cultural strength actually have an impact on organizational performance? Using an operationalization of cultural strength (cultural strength was measured based on the consistency rather than the content of employee responses to survey items on organizational culture), two longitudinal studies have shown that a strong culture is predictive of organizational performance as measured by short-term profits and growth in assets (Gordon and DiTomaso, 1992).

Defining Safety Management Systems

Effective safety management emphasizes the importance of managing safety in a systematic, proactive, and explicit manner. Systematic means that safety management activities are conducted in accordance with a predetermined and well-documented plan and applied in a consistent manner throughout the organization. The existence of an integrated and strong company culture is an essential enabler in achieving this consistency. A strong and uniform company culture comes together with high morale amongst employees and good interdepartmental links and communication systems throughout an organization. Proactivity means adopting an approach which emphasizes prevention through the identification of hazards and the introduction of risk mitigation measures before the risk-bearing event occurs and adversely affects safety performance. If this type of organizational practice already exists in a company culture that emphasizes incident and accident prevention, rather than a reactive culture that focuses on solving problems after they occur, then a Safety Management System becomes easier to implement. Finally, what is explicit in a Safety Management System system is the fact that all safety management activities should be well documented in a clear manner. In addition, they should be visible both to inter-as well as intra-organizational stakeholders and performed independently from other management activities. Safety becomes a uniform focus for the organization, rather than an afterthought, and responsibility for its management is delegated to a specific organizational unit which is, at the same time, pervasive in the practices of the organization as a whole.

Essential practices that are associated with safety management include hazard identification and the closing of gaps in defending an existing system. This practice is related to the principle of proactive management in that quality assurance is a dynamic process that is achieved through the use of some sort of an ever-evolving and improving total quality management system. Additionally, effective safety management is multidisciplinary; it involves several departments within the organization. More specifically, even though the organization's safety department has core competency vis-à-vis safety and in promulgating a safety culture throughout the organization, the know-how of technical experts in a variety of other areas is equally valuable. These experts are involved in the day-to-day practice of safety and should be allowed to offer input in the proactive solution of potential hazards. This approach requires that an appropriate and systematic application of a variety of techniques and activities are utilized in an array of situations, and this is done in a way that fits the specific problem. Thus, for example, if the problem is one of a human resource process, the appropriate expert with a disciplinary competence who is best suited to take a lead in identifying and solving a specific gap is called upon to contribute to the solution.

An effective Safety Management System is built across three defining cornerstone characteristics. First, a comprehensive corporate approach to safety has to be assured, which sets the tone for the management of safety, builds upon the safety culture of the organization, embraces the organization's safety policies, objectives and goals, and ensures that senior management is fully committed to safety. Second, effective organizational tools to deliver safety standards must exist. These tools are needed to deliver the necessary activities and processes to advance safety. They are also important in arranging organizational matters in order to fulfill safety policies, objectives, and goals. They establish standards and allocate resources as well as focus on hazards and their potential effects on safety-critical activities. Finally, a formal system for safety oversight is needed to confirm the organization's continuing fulfillment of its corporate safety policy, objectives, goals, and standards. It is important, along the parameters of this discussion, that it is understood that the scope of the Safety Management System be appropriate to the size and complexity of the operation. Therefore, a one size and scope fits all approach is not commensurable with an effective Safety Management System.

Moving to Safety Management Systems as a Restructuring Exercise: What is Change Management?

Restructuring implies change. So, how is change at an airline that is moving to a Safety Management System system managed? This study focuses on the theory of change as it relates to any organization. In this effort, we present definitions of change, models of the organization, an outline of the change process, and a diagnostic model for identifying where change should take place. Further study will have to be conducted where the theory and concepts of change are applied to a specific airline case study, which includes recommendations for managing the change process.

All organizations by definition take inputs from the external environment, transform those inputs internally through their existing organizational processes, and then produce outputs which again are directed at the external environment. As such, organizations can be considered open systems, and thus are susceptible to developments in their business environment since they are part of that environment. When an organization's internal structure and functions are organized such that they can exploit the external environment to their advantage, then an organization can be considered to be operating effectively. However, the external environment is in most cases more dynamic and fluid than that of a typical organization. Changes in the external environment can happen so quickly that, almost overnight, organizations can find themselves unable to deal effectively with the situation. If an organization wishes to survive, it too must change. The ability of managers to guide and influence the outcome of changes is change management. These abovementioned statements are particularly true in the case of Safety Management System implementation by air carriers. The inability of an airline to transition itself effectively under a new Safety Management System, especially if it is a new regulatory standard or widely acceptable industry practice, will have a negative impact on its efficiency.

Types of Change

As mentioned earlier, change is initiated in the external environment, and this requires firms to change in order to remain effective. In the case of a Safety Management System, its acceptance as a good global safety practice through ICAO and IATA has been instrumental in its broader acceptance. The external environment with respect to any firm or collection of firms in a similar industry can be characterized by the amount of change that is occurring over time in the environment. Broadly speaking, the external environment can be considered to be in either equilibrium or disequilibrium. Equilibrium in the airline industry would be considered the era of regulation which implies there would be only small incremental changes in the way a firm operates. On the other hand, the external environment can be characterized by a period of disequilibrium which is often triggered by a destabilizing event, or set of events, that change the basic dynamics or relationships in a particular industry. The destabilizing event can be triggered from one of the industry participants (as it attempts to gain a competitive advantage), or it can come from outside the industry (fears of terrorism, for example) (Hayes, 2002). The events of September 11, 2001, provide us with an example of an external destabilizing agent for the airline industry.

Thus, two types of change can be considered to affect the organization: incremental and discontinuous. Incremental change is a type of change associated with those periods when the industry is in equilibrium and the focus of change for the organization is to do things better, through continuous change, adaptation, and modification (Hayes, 2002). In contemporary language this type of change is often referred to as continuous improvement.

On the other hand, discontinuous change is change that occurs in periods of disequilibrium (Hayes, 2002). This type of change is sometimes called transformational change as the organization that undergoes such change must completely break with its past and find new ways to operate. In addition to new operational methods, an organization facing transformational change must also create and define a completely new set of strategies since previous core competencies may have been undermined due to changes in the external environment. In essence this type of change requires the organizations to do things differently rather than doing things better. It may even mean doing completely different things (Hayes, 2002) as can be the case with a Safety Management System.

In addition to the concept of incremental and discontinuous change, two other categories of change can be defined, both of which incorporate the element of time. First, there is anticipatory change which is initiated by a firm without a clear external demand. This type of change might be undertaken by a firm in order to gain a competitive advantage in the market place or to prepare for a likely future event. Anticipatory change happens before an event in the external environment. Second, there is reactive change which is a firm's response to a clear and present danger that already exists at present in the external environment. Movement toward the design and implementation of a Safety Management System for an airline can be attributable to either anticipatory or reactive change and depends on how the airline in question brings it about. For example, if a Safety Management System is mandated by a national regulatory authority as the new regulatory standard, an airline that has not taken steps to change its existing system to a Safety Management System-type system must react to the new regulatory standard. On the other hand, an airline that starts using a Safety Management System system in anticipation of regulatory change or in order to self-generate more efficiency in its safety management operations is said to engage in anticipatory change. Efficiency here is defined as the internal ability to do more with less or the same with less while maintaining or improving safety outcomes.

Combining the concepts of equilibrium together with that of time, a change matrix for organizations can be constructed as follows (see Figure 7.1).

Defining a change matrix, as above, provides a useful tool that enables us to make preliminary diagnoses of the type of change facing an organization. As will be illustrated later, knowing

	Incremental	Discontinuous
Anticipatory	Tuning	Re-orientation
Reactive	Adaptation	Re-creation

Figure 7.1   Types of organizational change
Source: Hayes, J. (2002).

the type of change facing an organization will greatly assist in directing resources and time to the appropriate places within the organization.

Tuning is simply a change that is undertaken when there is no immediate requirement for change. Essentially, this type of change is associated with fine-tuning an existing strategy. *Adaptation* is similar to tuning but is undertaken due to the presence of some external factor. This type of change essentially means "doing things better." *Re-orientation* is a wholesale change undertaken by an organization in anticipation of some future event. The aim of this type of change is to ensure that the organization remains aligned with the external environment. Finally, *re-creation* is a fundamental realignment of the firm due to events currently taking place in the environment. Both *re-orientation* and *re-creation* require the organization to dramatically change all of its elements. This includes a change in strategies (corporate and business) and thus implies that old core competencies may need to be abandoned in order that new, more effective competencies are developed. Safety Management System implementation in a non-Safety Management System environment falls under any of the abovementioned categories. The magnitude and type of change that are required depend on the degree to which an air carrier's existing system is already aligned with specific Safety Management System requirements. By this we mean how close the air carrier's existing system is to a Safety Management System compliant system from an organizational or safety culture strength perspective.

Why Do Organizations Need to Change?

Thus far, basic definitions of change have been described and defined. What has not been discussed, however, is why organizations need to change. From the preceding discussion, it is probably obvious to the reader that an organization's ability to navigate change is directly related to its organizational effectiveness and performance.

Decline typically occurs when an organization fails to give proper regard to changes in its external environment. Hall (2002) discusses decline in regard to four dialectic and interrelated phases. In the first stage, which is termed "Blinded," organizations are unable to recognize internal and external changes that may affect their long-term survival. In the second stage, which is termed "Inaction," organizations fail to respond to a need for change despite signs of worsening performance. In the third stage, which is termed "Faulty Action," the organization takes actions, but these actions are inappropriate. In the fourth stage, which is termed "Crisis," after failing to deal with the problems facing it, the organization finds itself in crisis. Finally, failure to respond to the crisis results in the eventual death or dissolution of the organization.

While the abovementioned discussion makes the process of decline obvious, another point is worth mentioning. It seems intuitive that an organization in decline should respond to the change it faces, which has put it in a position of vulnerability, in an appropriate manner rather than over or under react. For example, adequate identification of threats in the external environment may prompt the organization to make small incremental changes (*tuning*), rather than large-scale transformational changes (*recreation*).

The Change Process

The change process is a dynamic and fluid one. Generally, change can be categorized into three basic stages. The first stage is the unfreezing process where the organization leaves or alters its existing levels of behavior. The second stage involves moving to a new behavioral level. The third stage is refreezing at this new level. Refreezing means that, new behaviors have supplanted old ones, resulting in a new set of behaviors for the organization. For example, the management of safety requires the organization to manage hazards particular to its operations proactively. If proactive management does exist, an airline that wants to move in this direction can "unfreeze" current processes which prevent it from doing so (for example, unwillingness to speak up if a mistake is detected for fear of management or colleague retaliation), then, through a training program, realign the behavioral pattern of its employees (moving to a new behavioral level), and finally refreeze the organizational process once adequate evidence is presented that behavior modification has taken place.

Finally, we should note that this is a continuous process and that refreezing does not mean that the organization is locked into a new behavior but rather that new modes of operation have been learned and integrated into the organization. It is like a dialectic process where continuous change and adaptation are not just necessary but inevitable if the organization is to survive.

The most critical steps of the change process are the diagnosis stage and the transition to the implementation phase. The diagnosis phase is important as the organization must determine where organizational performance is being adversely affected and needs to be changed. The implementation plan then sets out to correct or modify the defects noted in the diagnosis and represents a crucial step toward re-establishing organizational effectiveness.

With this in mind, Hayes (2002) presents a process view of change. Hayes (2002) has identified a change process to be used in change management situations. This process is not a one-time event. Rather, the model requires continual implementation in a loop like manner. Qualifying the model in this manner looks similar to a conventional risk management process. However, this change process is a sort of a serial process while risk management is not. The change process by Hayes (2002) has seven serial steps as follows:

A. external change: opportunities and threats;
B. recognize need for change;
C. start of change process;

    D. diagnosis: present and future states;
    E. plan and prepare for implementation;
    F. implement change;
    G. review.

Note that this model reflects on and extends the three-stage model for change presented earlier. The first of the three steps of the process view essentially represents the unfreezing stage as the organization first observes changes in its external environment, translates this perception into a need, and thus begins the change process. The diagnosis and implementation planning represent the movement from the previous state to the new state. The implementation and review stages of the process model represent the beginning of refreezing where new behaviors are absorbed into the organization.

Diagnosing Where to Change

There are several models available in order to diagnose change. One of them, the Burke-Litwin model is very useful as it describes 12 interrelated change elements (dimensions) of an organization. According to this model, in its original manifestation, the change process is depicted via a flow diagram. At the top of the diagram is the external environment, and this represents the inputs for an organization. At the bottom of the diagram is the performance of the individual and organization and as such represents the output. The area in between represents how an organization turns inputs into outputs and thus represents the key activities and elements of an organization. Furthermore, the model is organized in a vertical fashion to indicate the relative impact that one element has over another element in the organization. For example, the organizational culture will affect both the work unit climate and individual needs and values. While the work unit climate can affect the organizational culture, this model posits that organizational culture has a much greater weight or force on the work unit climate than vice versa.

    We believe that, whereas the Burke-Litwin model provides an effective strategy to manage organizational change, its effectiveness is subject to how well each of the 12 dimensions identified by it are explored and put to use. Furthermore, the other most critical aspect in its effectiveness, is how well management and staff collaborate to achieve the new strategies and goals as proposed in the change process.

Here is a brief description of each of the 12 dimensions identified by the Burke-Litwin change model. According to Thakur (2010) and tied to the description of the dimensions, and for the model to be put into practical use, it is important to address the following key factors and questions seeking answers:

1. *External environment*: the key external factors that have an impact on the organization must be identified and their direct and indirect impact on the organization should be clearly established.
2. *Mission and strategy*: the vision, mission, and the strategy of the organization, as defined by the top management, should be examined in terms of the employees' point of view about them.
3. *Leadership*: a study of the leadership structure of the organization should be carried out, which clearly identifies the chief role models in the organization.
4. *Organizational culture*: an organizational culture study should seek information on the explicit as well as the implied rules, regulations, customs, principles, and values that influence the organizational behavior.
5. *Structure*: the study of structure should not be confined to hierarchical structure; rather it should be a function-based structure *focusing on the responsibility*, authority, communication, decision making, and control structure that exists between the people of the organization.
6. *Systems*: systems includes all types of policies and procedures with regards to both the people and the operations of the organization.
7. *Management practices*: this would entail a study of how well the mangers conform to the organization's strategy when dealing with employees and the resources.
8. *Work unit climate*: it is a collective study of how the employees think, feel, and what do they expect. The kind of

relationships the employees share with their team members and members of other teams is also an important aspect of work unit climate.

9. *Tasks and skills*: this involves understanding *what a specific job position demands and the kind of kind of skills* and knowledge that an employee must have in order to fulfill the task responsibilities of that job position. It's important to see how well jobs and employees have been matched.

10. *Individual values and needs*: this dimension seeks to explore the employee's opinion about their work so as to identify the quality factors that will result in job enrichment and better job satisfaction.

11. *Motivation level*: *identifying the motivation level of the employees* will make it easier to determine how willingly they would put in their efforts to achieve organizational goals. This would also involve identifying motivational triggers.

12. *Individual and overall performance*: this dimension takes into account the level of performance, on individual and organizational levels, in key areas like productivity, quality, efficiency, budget, customer satisfaction, and so on.

What makes this model most interesting for diagnosing change, however, is the fact that it inherently distinguishes between transformational change and transactional change. Earlier in this book, change was broadly categorized as either "incremental" or "discontinuous." An organization faced with the former need only modify itself in order to do things better (transactional change) while the latter required the organization to drastically remodel itself (transformational change).

As transactional change is focused on minor "tuning," change efforts need to be directed at the structures, management practices, and systems which affect the work climate unit that in turn affects motivation and performance of both the individual and organization (Hayes, 2002).

On the other hand, it is clear that when an organization is confronted with transformational change, efforts for change must be directed higher up in the organization. In other words, this type of radical change calls for a reworking of the organization's mission and strategy, its leadership, and its organizational culture. As the model implies, changes at this relatively high level will be transmitted through the lower levels and thus may well cause incremental change to occur as well.

Improving the Safety Management System as a Supporting and Integrating Exercise: The Risk Management-Based Approach?

The efficient and effective management of any aviation organization, regardless of the nature of its functions or its size, requires the management of basic and traditional business processes: financing, budgeting, communicating, allocating resources, and so forth. In recent years, managing safety has been added to the list of basic and traditional business processes. Managing safety risk should now be as much a part of running an aviation organization as managing any of the traditional business processes. The term *safety risk management* conveys the notion that the management of safety is a business process that must be considered at the same level and along the same lines as any other business process (Galotti, Rao, and Maurino, 2008: 1).

The aviation industry is both complex and unique. The demands on employees are great and, in many cases, the requirements are not accurately communicated to upper management. Passengers and regulators both demand an increased level of safety. This is emphasized in recent legislative requirements for airlines to implement a systematic approach to safety management or a Safety Management System. The core requirement for a Safety Management System is an effective method of identifying and controlling risk.

The concept is described by ICAO: "The risks and costs in commercial aviation necessitate a rational process for decision-making. Daily, operators and managers make decisions in real time, weighing the probability and severity of any adverse consequences implied by the risk against the expected gain of taking the risk. This process is known as risk management" (Southern California Safety Institute, 2009).

Risk management is a system-based approach that focuses on the identification of hazards involved in each aspect of the operation, whether it involves aircraft flight operations, cockpit procedures, aircraft maintenance, turn-around, ticketing, scheduling, or baggage handling. As an integral and required part of a Safety Management System, Operational Risk Management formalizes this approach by implementing a logic-driven process to analyze the degree of risk associated with identified hazards, recommending risk-based solutions, and monitoring the effectiveness of these solutions (Southern California Safety Institute, 2009).

Figure 7.2 shows how the safety risk management and safety assurance processes are integrated in the Safety Management System. The safety risk management process provides for initial identification of hazards and assessment of risk. Organizational risk controls are developed, and, once they are determined to be capable of bringing the risk to an acceptable level, they are employed operationally. The safety assurance function takes over at this point to ensure that the risk controls are being practiced and they continue to achieve their intended objectives. This system also provides for assessment of the need for new controls because of changes in the operational environment (Federal Aviation Administration, 2006).

In order to conduct efficient and effective aviation operations and to be aware of the safety-based risk factors, operators should have risk and change management-based safety systems. Operators in the aviation sector must improve and maintain a high level of safety by proactive risk management and holistic change management integration into Safety Management Systems in order to minimize accidents in airline operations.

This theoretical study shows that Safety Management System is a concept that has existed in academic literature for quite some time. Furthermore, its application in the aviation industry in transforming existing safety compliance systems is tied to the application of change management and risk management principles to administer the Safety Management System procedures. We assume that the existence of strong organizational cultures would make change management and risk management in establishing Safety Management System systems entertain higher likelihoods of success. The most critical steps of the change process for an airline that moves from a conventional system of safety compliance to a Safety Management System are the diagnosis stage and the transition to the implementation

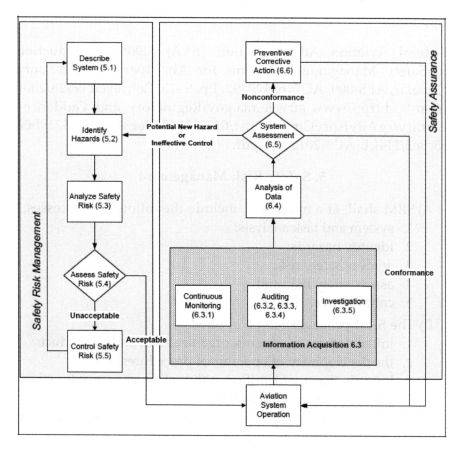

Figure 7.2   Safety risk management and safety assurance processes

Source: Federal Aviation Administration (FAA) (2006).

phase. The diagnosis phase is important as the organization must determine where organizational performance is being adversely affected and needs to be changed. The implementation plan then sets out to correct or modify the defects noted in the diagnosis and represents a crucial step toward re-establishing organizational effectiveness. Empirical research through case studies of Safety Management System implementation will be necessary to test the hypotheses presented in this chapter.

Appendix

Federal Aviation Administration (FAA) (2006). Introduction to Safety Management Systems for Air Operators. Advisory Circular, AFS-800, AC No: 120–92. Pp. 9–15. Retrieved 08/28/2009 from http://www.airweb.faa.gov/Regulatory_and_Guidance_Library/rgAdvisoryCircular.nsf/0/6485143d5ec81aae8625719b00 55c9e5/$FILE/AC%20120-92.pdf.

5. Safety Risk Management

A) SRM shall, at a minimum, include the following processes:
  1. system and task analysis;
  2. identify hazards;
  3. analyze safety risk;
  4. assess safety risk; and
  5. control safety risk.

B) The SRM process shall be applied to:
  1. initial designs of systems, organizations, and/or products;
  2. the development of operational procedures;
  3. hazards that are identified in the safety assurance functions (described in Section 6); and
  4. planned changes to the operational processes to identify hazards associated with those changes.

C) The organization shall establish feedback loops between assurance functions described in Section 6 to evaluate the effectiveness of safety risk controls.

D) The organization shall define acceptable and unacceptable levels of safety risk (or safety risk objectives):
  1. descriptions shall be established for:
     a) severity levels, and
     b) likelihood levels;
  2. the organization shall define levels of management that can make safety risk acceptance decisions;
  3. the organization shall define acceptable risk for hazards that will exist in the short term while safety risk control/ mitigation plans are developed and executed.

E) The following shall not be implemented until the safety risk of each identified hazard is determined to be acceptable in:
1. new system designs;
2. changes to existing system designs;
3. new operations/procedures; and
4. modified operations/procedures.

F) The SRM process shall not preclude the organization from taking interim immediate action to mitigate existing safety risk.

5.1 System and Task Analysis

A) System and task descriptions shall be developed to the level of detail necessary to identify hazards.

B) System and task analyses should consider the following:
1. the system's interactions with other systems in the air transportation system (for example, airports, air traffic control);
2. the system's functions for each area listed in paragraph 4.1 A);
3. employee tasks required to accomplish the functions in 5.1 B) 2);
4. required human factors considerations of the system (for example, cognitive, ergonomic, environmental, occupational health and safety) for:
   a) operations, and
   b) maintenance;
5. hardware components of the system;
6. software components of the system;
7. related procedures that define guidance for the operation and use of the system;
8. ambient environment;
9. operational environment;
10. maintenance environment;
11. contracted and purchased products and services;
12. the interactions between items in Section 5.1.B., 2–10 above; and
13. any assumptions made about:
    a) the system,

b) system interactions, and

c) existing safety risk controls.

5.2 Identify Hazards

A) Hazards shall be:
1. identified for the entire scope of the system that is being evaluated as defined in the system description; and
2. documented.

B) Hazard information shall be:
1. tracked; and
2. managed through the entire SRM process.

5.3 Analyze Safety Risk

The safety risk analysis process shall include:

A) Existing safety risk controls;

B) Triggering mechanisms; and;

C) Safety risk of reasonably likely outcomes from the existence of a hazard, to include estimation of the:
1. likelihood; and
2. severity.

5.4 Assess Safety Risk

A) Each hazard shall be assessed for its safety risk acceptability using the safety risk objectives described in Section 5D.

B) The organization shall define levels of management that can make safety risk acceptance decisions.

5.5 Control Safety Risk

A) Safety control/mitigation plans shall be defined for each hazard with unacceptable risk.

B) Safety risk controls shall be:
1. clearly described;
2. evaluated to ensure that the requirements have been met;
3. ready to be used in the operational environment for which they are intended; and
4. documented.

C) Substitute risk shall be evaluated in the creation of safety risk controls/mitigations.

6. Safety Assurance and Internal Evaluation
6.1 General Requirements

The organization shall monitor their systems and operations to:

A) Identify new hazards;

B) Measure the effectiveness of safety risk controls; and

C) Ensure compliance with regulatory requirements.

6.2 System Description

The safety assurance function shall be based upon a comprehensive system description as described in Section 5.1.

6.3 Information Acquisition

The organization shall collect the data necessary to demonstrate the effectiveness of the organization's:

A) Operational processes; and

B) The SMS.

6.3.1 Continuous Monitoring

A) The organization shall monitor operational data (for example, duty logs, crew reports, work cards, process sheets, or reports from the employee safety feedback system specified to:
   1. assess conformity with safety risk controls;
   2. measure the effectiveness of safety risk controls;
   3. assess system performance; and
   4. identify hazards.

B) The organization shall monitor products and services received from subcontractors.

6.3.2 *Internal Audits by Operational Departments*

A) Line management of operational departments shall ensure that regular internal audits of safety-related functions of the organization's operational processes (production system) are conducted. This obligation shall extend to any subcontractors that they may use to accomplish those functions.

B) Line management shall ensure that regular audits are conducted to:
1. determine conformity with safety risk controls; and
2. assess performance of safety risk controls.

C) Planning of the audit program shall take into account:
1. safety significance of the processes to be audited; and
2. the results of previous audits.

D) The audit program shall include:
1. definition of the audit:
   a) criteria,
   b) scope,
   c) frequency, and
   d) methods.
2. the processes used to select the auditors;
3. the requirement that individuals shall not audit their own work;
4. documented procedures, which include:
   a) the responsibilities, and
   b) requirements for:
      (1) planning audits
      (2) conducting audits
      (3) reporting results
      (4) maintaining records
5. audits of contractors and vendors.

6.3.3 *Internal Evaluation*

A) The organization shall conduct internal evaluations of the operational processes and the Safety Management System at planned intervals to determine that the Safety Management System conforms to requirements.

B) Planning of the evaluation program shall take into account:
1. safety significance of processes to be audited; and
2. the results of previous audits.

C) The evaluation program shall include:
1. definition of the evaluation:
   a) criteria,
   b) scope,
   c) frequency, and
   d) methods.
2. the processes used to select the auditors;
3. the requirement that auditors shall not audit their own work;
4. documented procedures, which include:
   a) the responsibilities, and
   b) requirements for:
      (1) planning audits
      (2) conducting audits
      (3) reporting results
      (4) maintaining records
5. audits of contractors and vendors.

D) The program shall be under the direction of the management official described in Section 4.5.

E) The program shall include an evaluation of the program required described in Section 6.3.2.

F) The person or organization performing evaluations of operational departments must be functionally independent of the department being evaluated.

6.3.4 External Auditing of the Safety Management System

The organization shall include the results of oversight organization audits in the analyses conducted as described in Section 6.4.

6.3.5 Investigation

A) The organization shall collect data on:
1. incidents; and
2. accidents.

B) The organization shall establish procedures to:
1. investigate accidents;

2. investigate incidents; and
3. investigate instances of potential regulatory non-compliance.

6.3.6 Employee Reporting and Feedback System

A) The organization shall establish and maintain a confidential employee safety reporting and feedback system as in Section 7.1.5).

B) Employees shall be encouraged to use the safety reporting and feedback system without reprisal as in Section 4.2 B) 5).

C) Data from the safety reporting and feedback system shall be monitored to identify emerging hazards.

D) Data collected in the safety reporting and feedback system shall be included in analyses described in Section 6.4.

6.4 Analysis of Data

A) The organization shall analyze the data described in Section 6.3 to demonstrate the effectiveness of:
   1. risk controls in the organization's operational processes; and
   2. the Safety Management System.

B) Through data analysis, the organization shall evaluate where improvements can be made to the organization's:
   1. operational processes; and
   2. the Safety Management System.

6.5 System Assessment

A) The organization shall assess the performance of:
   1. safety-related functions of operational processes against their requirements; and
   2. the Safety Management System against its requirements.

B) System assessments shall result in a finding of:
   1. conformity with existing safety risk control(s)/Safety Management System requirement(s) (including regulatory requirements);
   2. non-conformity with existing safety risk control(s)/Safety Management System requirement(s) (including regulatory requirements); and
   3. new hazard(s) found.

C) The SRM process will be utilized if the assessment indicates:
  1. the identification of new hazards; or
  2. the need for system changes.

D) The organization shall maintain records of assessments in accordance with the requirements of Section 4.9.

6.6 Preventive/Corrective Action

A) The organization shall develop, prioritize, and implement, as appropriate:
  1. corrective actions for identified nonconformities with risk controls; and
  2. preventive actions for identified potential non-conformities with risk controls actions.

B) Safety lessons learned shall be considered in the development of:
  1. corrective actions; and
  2. preventive actions.

C) The organization shall take necessary corrective action based on the findings of investigations.

D) The organization shall prioritize and implement corrective action(s) in a timely manner.

E) The organization shall prioritize and implement preventive action(s) in a timely manner.

F) Records shall be kept of the disposition and status of corrective and preventive actions per established record retention policy.

6.7 Management Reviews

A) Top management will conduct regular reviews of the Safety Management System, including:
  1. the outputs of SRM (Section 5);
  2. the outputs of safety assurance (Section 6); and
  3. lessons learned (Section 7.5).

B) Management reviews shall include assessing the need for changes to the organization's:
  1. operational processes; and
  2. Safety Management System.

6.8 Continual Improvement

The organization shall continuously improve the effectiveness of the Safety Management System and of safety risk controls through the use of the safety and quality policies, objectives, audit and evaluation results, analysis of data, corrective and preventive actions, and management reviews.

Chapter 8
The Integration of Sustainability Risk into Airport Business and Management

Airport Sustainability is important in view of an urban context. Airports need to grow in a sustainable way to maintain their operations. This includes the minimization of the adverse environmental and social impact and maximization of the socio-economic benefits for their stakeholders. Let us not forget that the key stakeholders for any airport are the communities that it serves defined both geographically and functionally. Optimization of economic, social, and environmental objectives is the main challenge for airport operators. It is a kind of risk management. Airport operators can gain reasonable assurance in achieving their optimization objective via Enterprise Sustainability Risk Management (also known as ESRM).

Airports in Istanbul generate substantial benefits for the community and economy in Turkey. Airports, especially, create great employment opportunities for both developed and undeveloped countries. For this reason, implementation of sustainability practice in airports is of critical importance for Istanbul.

Corporate Sustainability is the major challenge for companies in today's global environment. All modes of transportation are of critical importance for urban sustainability and also national Sustainable Development. From this point of view, Airport Sustainability is a highly important topic under world transportation. Airports are vital national resources. They serve a key role in the transportation of people and goods and in regional, national, and international commerce (Berry, Gillhespy and Rogers, 2008). This chapter aims to illustrate the current situation of Airport Sustainability as practiced in Turkey across the triple bottom line (also known as TBL) of economic, social, and environmental issues.

Sustainability Issue in Civil Aviation Management

Sustainability is an important topic in civil aviation management since this sector is developing with increased acceleration. Also, costs increase significantly with the increased number of airplanes, fuel consumption, and political factors. Aviation can be viewed as having improved sustainability if there is a balance: if it demonstrates an overall reduction in adverse environmental-socio-economic impacts and/or an increase in positive environmental-socio-economic impacts. It should be kept in mind, however, that because of its reliance on scarce resources, even if current equipment, technology, and techniques are fully optimized, this will not make European air transport sustainable in the longer term without a major step change in technology or the supporting framework. The "sustainability" concept is often simplistically portrayed as follows in Figure 8.1 by Eurocontrol (Eurocontrol, 2010):

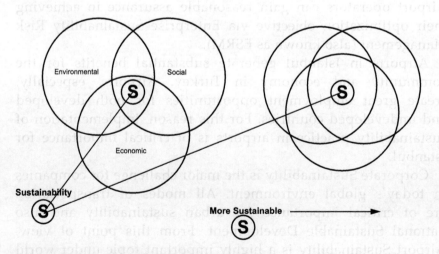

Figure 8.1   Sustainability concept
Source: Eurocontrol, 2010.

Airport Sustainability is a business strategy. It has both immediate and long-term benefits that can be measured and when persistently managed, should be rewarded. Airport Sustainability, in effect, is a holistic approach to managing an airport so as to ensure the integrity of the Economic viability, Operational efficiency, Natural resource conservation, and Social responsibility (EONS) of the airport. Aviation industry research and sources validate that environmental and energy-based sustainability initiatives are already being implemented and practiced in response to the aviation/airport industry's financial pressures as well as to the expectations or mandates of regulatory agencies (Airports Council International—North America, 2010).

Sustainability for airports involves developing a planning approach to responsibly address the economic, social, and environmental concerns of stakeholders. A pragmatic approach to sustainability yields a careful balance among these concerns while maintaining focus on the mission of the airport. Inherently, this balance is specific to each airport and community because each airport has unique environs, and impacts may be perceived differently by the surrounding communities (Jacobs Consultancy, 2008):

- Economic aspects refer to the continued business viability of the airport, the tangible assets in facility capital investments, and aviation's direct and indirect economic benefit to the region.
- Social aspects refer to the surrounding community and aviation's contribution to practices that promote social and cultural enrichment.
- Environmental aspects are the natural resources that are used or affected as a result of airport operations and potential impacts on the ecosystem in which the airport is located.

The principles of sustainability have reached mainstream acceptance and the aviation industry is rapidly embracing new concepts and techniques to maintain economic security, minimize natural resources depletion, and enhance the communities served. Generally, sustainability can be thought of as taking action to meet current requirements without compromising the ability for future generations to meet future needs (Jacobs Consultancy, 2008).

Sustainability is on the brink of become a main issue to the aviation industry. Aviation sustainability practices include industry-wide, organizational, economic, social, and environmental issues. The aviation industry is a leader in the use of advanced technologies and susceptible to environmental impacts. For this reasons, the aviation sector is monitored closely by environmentalist and green organizations. Airport operators are under the influence of both the external impacts and/or internal dynamics to the airports' stakeholders, Sustainable Development should be handled as both a natural part of their business and corporate social responsibility. These responsibilities are listed as follows (see Figure 8.2) (Burr, 2007):

- respect the right of people to live in a healthy and good environment;
- protect and use natural resources with awareness of responsibility;
- publish information about responsible use of natural resources and environmental quality, and share this information with the public;
- develop standards to protect the environment;
- comply with related laws and regulations.

According to Eurocontrol (2010), aviation brings several sustainability-related benefits and costs including the following:

- Benefits:
    - freedom of mobility;
    - leisure;
    - improvement to health through poverty reduction;
    - cultural enrichment and diversity;
    - employment;
    - technology transfer;
    - major direct, secondary, and indirect economic improvement;
    - global business links;
    - military security; and
    - positive globalization effects.

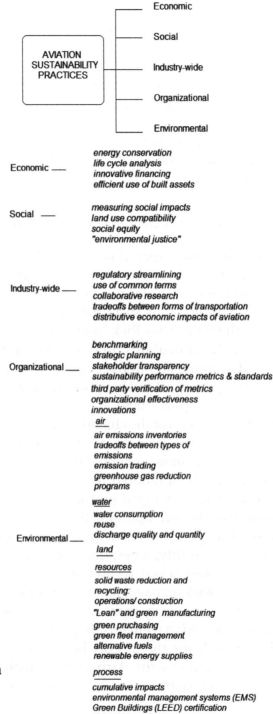

**Figure 8.2
Concept of aviation
sustainability
practices**

Source: Burr, 2007.

- It also provides costs including:
  - finite resource depletion;
  - noise;
  - atmospheric emissions (air quality, ozone depletion, acid rain, and climate change);
  - water and land pollution;
  - waste products;
  - negative globalization effects;
  - associated adverse health impacts; and
  - accidents.

Airport Sustainability Risk Management Process

Sustainability means operating and developing the airport in a way that minimizes the airport's environmental negative impacts and maximizes the socio-economic benefits for the local community, region, and nation. Our sustainability approach in this article is built into the Enterprise Risk Management (also known as ERM) framework. The aim of this process is to support set strategy and policies, determine and deliver appropriate plans and solutions, and to manage airport business safely and responsibly (adapted from Gatwick Airport, 2009).

The consequences of the changing function of airports in social, economic, and ecological regards requires the implementation of sustainability risk management. The Enterprise Risk Management framework has been tailored to the aviation industry. This new process has been developed for the purpose of managing Airport Sustainability. In our opinion, this should be considered as a business strategy. This strategy can support the core benefits of economic viability, operational efficiency, natural resource conservation, and social responsibility in airport business and management. Risk management related to sustainability is a basic part of strategic management and organization. Contemporary Business and Management requires a risk management-based approach for the airport business. The steps of the risk management process for Airport Sustainability are organized into four main groups with sub-steps as follows:

1. Strategy setting and strategic planning:
   a. embedding sustainability (social, environmental, and economic concept) policy and/or program in airport operations;
   b. aiming to achieve best practice in related operations of Airport Sustainability;
   c. aiming to achieve industry-leading policy or program;
   d. setting long-term planning horizon.
2. Risk assessment:
   a. establishment of the goals and targets;
   b. risk assessment;
   c. setting mechanism for continuous performance improvements;
   d. alignment of performance goals with strategic planning/corporate-level goals and targets.
3. Performance monitoring and reporting:
   a. performance reporting to stakeholders and general public;
   b. emplacement of the feedback loops;
   c. continuous surveying of the stakeholders.
4. Incentives and awareness:
   a. training in sustainability, management, and risk management;
   b. support innovative approaches;
   c. support sustainability risk-based corporate culture.

Sustainability embraces business practices that promote the continual improvement of a healthy environment, economy, and community. Airport Sustainability is best achieved through deliberate coordination and optimization of cross-functional practices and business decisions. However, there continue to be challenges for the industry in the areas of planning and development. Often, sustainability does not drive the priority for strategic decisions and as a result, planning horizons are not long enough to effectively integrate sustainability into the airport's business model. As a result, airports and their partners are confronted with meeting capacity demands which adds to the existing cost structure and holistically evaluating the payback for "greening" a project or program. Regulatory compliance can also affect the airport's desire to progress in the areas of innovation and improvement. It is not unusual for airports to become conditioned to seek recognition for merely meeting compliance—which can hinder a holistic viewpoint (Salt Lake City Department of Airports, 2010).

Sustainable outcomes are characterized by four complementary dimensions. These dimensions (EONS) are accepted and promoted within the aviation industry as enabling a holistic approach to Airport Sustainability. Incorporating the sustainability dimensions into Salt Lake City Department of Airports' (SLCDA) business practices, policies, and programs ensures consideration of these across the business functions of the airport organization (Salt Lake City Department of Airports, 2010):

1. Economic viability:
   a. provides positive return on investment within a reasonable timeframe;
   b. creates strategic opportunities for future development or funding;
   c. promotes innovation and continuous improvement of the organization.
2. Operational efficiency:
   a. improves operational outcomes through documented policies, guidelines, and procedures;
   b. reduces costs while preserving social, economic, or conservation benefits;
   c. improves workforce effectiveness through the use of tools and technology.
3. Natural resource conservation:
   a. minimizes waste through effective management;
   b. conserves resources through process change and innovative practices;
   c. focuses on preserving nature within an economic framework.
4. Social responsibility:
   a. improves and manages the environmental qualities that promote healthy living;
   b. focuses on social awareness and responsibility within the community;
   c. considers community needs and practical initiatives.

Best Practices: Sustainability Implementations in Istanbul's Airports[1]

According to The Airport Cooperative Research Program (ACRP) Synthesis 10 (Berry, Gillhespy and Rogers, 2008), environmental practices commonly in place at airports include measuring and monitoring water conservation, water quality, climate change, air quality, land use, biodiversity, environmentally sustainable materials, waste, noise and aesthetics, energy, and green buildings. Economic sustainability practices commonly in place at airports include local hiring and purchasing, contributing to the community, quantifying the value of sustainability practices, contributing to research and development, and incentivizing sustainable behavior. Social concerns at airports include public awareness and education, stakeholder relationships, employee practices and procedures, sustainable transportation, alleviating road congestion, accessibility, local culture and heritage, indoor environmental quality, employee well-being, and passenger well-being. The ACRP Synthesis 10 focuses on the following topics and subtopics developed by the research team (Berry, Gillhespy and Rogers, 2008):

- organizational governance of airports with respect to implementation of sustainability practices;
- existing and future barriers to implementing sustainability practices in airports;
- existing and future drivers for implementing sustainability practices at airports;
- environmental sustainability performance of airports, especially:
  - water quality
  - climate change
  - air quality
  - land use
  - biodiversity
  - materials
  - waste

---

1   In this chapter, best practices samples were extracted from the research which was performed by Torum and Kucuk Yilmaz (2009).

- noise and aesthetics
- energy
- green buildings.
- social sustainability performance of airports, especially:
  - public awareness and education
  - stakeholder relationships
  - employee practices and procedures
  - sustainable transportation
  - alleviating road congestion
  - accessibility
  - local culture and heritage
  - indoor environmental quality
  - employee well-being
  - passenger well-being.
- economic sustainability performance of airports, especially:
  - local hiring
  - local purchasing
  - contribution to the community
  - quantifying sustainability
  - contribution to research and development
  - incentives for sustainable behavior.

This next part includes best practices for Airport Sustainability implementation according to the ACRP survey as follows:

- general information: TAV Airports Holding and Istanbul Sabiha Gökçen International Airport Investment Development and Operation Inc. (ISG);
- existing sustainability initiatives;
- environmental sustainability:
  - managing environmental sustainability
  - implementation of environmental sustainability initiatives.
- economic sustainability:
  - managing economic sustainability
  - implementation of economic sustainability initiatives.
- social sustainability:
  - managing social sustainability
  - implementation of social sustainability initiatives.
- other initiatives and barriers;
- future sustainability priorities.

The sustainability-based matters are taken into consideration by all people and companies active in the aviation and airport operation sector. The environment also tops the agenda of authorities such as IATA and Airports Council International (TAV Airports Holding, 2009).

As sustainability becomes a bigger issue for the aviation industry, it is important to understand what motivates airport operators to improve their economic, social, and environmental performance. Changes in behavior can be attributed to external influences or internal changes in an organization (Berry, Gillhespy and Rogers, 2008).

Which company is the best in the industry? Which one has the best sales organization, the best customer service department, the leanest manufacturing operation? Which one is setting the standard? And what is that standard? How did that company become the best? And what do other companies have to do to equal it? That's what benchmarking is all about. It's a critical component in terms of monitoring a company's success in attaining strategic objectives, and it assists in the assessment of operations issues that support those objectives. Benchmarking is the process of comparing the business processes and performance metrics including cost, cycle time, productivity, or quality to another that is widely considered to be an industry standard benchmark or best practice (http://en.wikipedia.org/wiki/Benchmarking, 2010). There is no single benchmarking process that has been universally adopted.

This part presents best practices samples from both the TAV Airports Holding and ISG separately. Also, a benchmarking table is prepared to show differences and similarities between these airport operator's practices for sustainability.

Sustainability Management in TAV Airports Holding

TAV Airports Holding is the leading airport operator in Turkey in regard to business volume with a market share of 48 percent as per the General Directorate of State Airports Authority of Turkey (DHMI) 2009 passenger statistics including transfer passengers. In regard to its structure, TAV Airports Holding Company is comprised of 12 companies. The Company seeks to build on its record of horizontal expansion in the industry by successfully leveraging its economies of scope and track record in both the region, as well as in the emerging markets of Eastern Europe, North Africa, and in the Caucasus region (TAV Investor Relations, 2010).

In Turkey, TAV Airports Holding operates Istanbul Atatürk Airport (one of the busiest in Europe), Ankara Esenboğa Domestic and International Terminals, Izmir Adnan Menderes Airport International Terminal and Antalya Gazipasa Airport. They also operate the Tbilisi and Batumi Airports in the Republic of Georgia, the Monastir Habib Bourguiba International Airport and the Enfidha Zine Abidine Ben Ali Airport in Tunisia as well as Skopje Alexander the Great Airport and Ohrid St Paul the Apostle International Airport in The Former Yugoslav Republic of Macedonia (TAV Investor Relations, 2010).

TAV Airports operates in other branches of airport operations as well, such as duty free sales, food and beverage services, ground handling services, information technologies, security and operation services. TAV Airports facilitates 375,000 flights for approximately 300 airline companies and 42 million passengers on average per year. As per 2009 figures, 57 percent of TAV Airport's consolidated revenues consisted of non-aviation revenues. TAV Airports Holding generated 609 million euro consolidated revenues (turnover) according to 2009 financial tables prepared in compliance with the International Financial Reporting Standards (IFRS). The company shares are listed in the Istanbul Stock Exchange since February 23, 2007, under the name of "TAVHL" ((TAV Investor Relations, 2010).

In the 12 years since its inception, TAV has established itself in both the airport construction and operation business segments. As stated in company documents, such as the "TAV Investor Relations," in order to keep in step with its growth and investment opportunities, the Company reorganized its businesses in 2006 into TAV Airports Holding Company and TAV Construction, respectively. This was followed by the initial public offering (IPO) of TAV Airports Holding Company in 2006.

According to TAV management, the Company has adopted the principle of taking into consideration not only the present day of the airports but also the future generations that the airports will cater to, positioning itself among the pioneers in supporting the concept of green airports that is gaining momentum rapidly throughout the world. In short, TAV Airports is determined to expend its best efforts to pass on to future generations a fast and safe, as well as clean, mode of transportation (TAV Airports Holding, 2009).

Both the General Manager of TAV İstanbul and Vice General Manager have the responsibility for sustainability initiatives at their airport. Drivers for their sustainability practices are identified by TAV Airports Holding as follows (Torum and Kucuk Yilmaz, 2009):

- state/regional regulations;
- Corporate Responsibility;
- stakeholder concerns/relations;
- airport policy;
- economic incentives, for example, rebates.

The identified reasons behind failed or slow implementation of sustainability practices at Istanbul airports by airport operators is one of the important results of this survey. The following are barriers to the implementation of sustainability practices at TAV airports:

- either lack of national regulations and laws about sustainability in triple bottom line concept or insufficient application of these laws and regulations nationwide;
- lack of funding;
- undeveloped societal awareness in the country about sustainability/Sustainable Development issues.

TAV Airports Holding does not publicly report on performance for any of the following issues:

- protection of the environment, including conservation of natural resources;
- social progress that recognizes the needs of all stakeholders;
- maintenance of high and stable levels of economic growth and employment;

TAV organization provides training for staff on the following issues:

- social progress that recognizes the needs of all stakeholders;
- approaches including conservation of resources;
- maintenance of high and stable levels of economic growth and employment;
- other: personal (human resource) development and branch training about civil aviation.

Existing sustainability initiatives are listed by TAV Airports Holding managers as follows:

- airport policy;
- international regulations, for example, European Union directives, International Aviation Authority policies;
- stakeholder concerns/relations;
- customers;
- Aviation Industry Association, for example, position papers.

Implementation of environmental sustainability initiatives

Airports now act very conscientiously to minimize environmental impact and even expend efforts to make contributions. To offer a few examples, the factors taken into serious consideration by airport operators include measures such as renewable energy systems, utilization of environmentally friendly maintenance, repair and cleaning materials, acceleration of replacing ground service vehicles powered by diesel or gasoline fired internal combustion engines with electric vehicles, utilization of terminal and service building designs that do not significantly impact the topographical structure and that take into consideration the natural wind flows and surface structure, and heavier utilization of plants that are important for wildlife in landscaping (TAV Airports Holding, 2009).

TAV implements environmental/sustainability performance monitoring using an Environmental Management System (EMS) which is ISO14001 certified. TAV Holding has planned initiatives for an Eco-Management and Audit Scheme (EMAS) and a Sustainability Management System. TAV airport is conserving water through both actual and planned initiatives in the following fields.

Potable water efficiency is increasing, and irrigation water demand is decreasing in TAV airports. Also, there are planned initiatives such as collecting and reusing greywater (that is, wastewater from kitchen, laundry and bathroom basins). Waste waters from TAV facilities are purified and then discharged by a treatment facility. Also, TAV has planned projects for advance purification to use purified water in TAV facilities again.

TAV managers are seeking to reduce its impact upon the global climate through planned initiatives as follows:

- demonstrate industry leadership, for example, partnerships, research, and a voluntary low emissions program;
- reduce emissions from aircraft on ground, for example, reducing taxiing and engines on standby;
- reduce emissions from airport ground vehicles, for example, purchasing electric luggage or food trucks.

Reducing emissions from passenger surface access traffic, for example, by subsidizing public transit for passengers, is not applicable to TAV. Also, reducing emissions from aircraft in the air, for example, influencing the descent or stacking patterns, is not applicable in the current situation.

TAV Airports displays a particular sensitivity to the environment. As part of the "Trigeneration Project" implemented at the İstanbul Atatürk Airport, the company is increasing its contribution to the environment through facilities that are self-sufficient in energy and air conditioning needs. This project reduces CO_2 emissions by 40 percent because of the use of natural gas in electricity generation, compared to fossil fuel-fired electricity generation plants. TAV Airports is also studying the feasibility of solar energy. The Company's airports and terminals in Tunisia, Antalya Gazipaşa, and İzmir that can most benefit from solar energy stand out as suitable platforms, as facilities that can be used as test cases for the company's solar energy initiatives (TAV Airports Holding, 2009).

Correspondence to airport operators has been sent by the Directorate General of Civil Aviation (DGCA) of Turkey regarding emissions of both airplanes which approach the terminal crossover and vehicles which are used in baggage handling areas.

Electrical hybrid vehicles have been placed on the agendas of various platforms including the Green Airport Project which is under the leadership of the DGCA in Turkey (2009).

In accordance with the Green Airport Project, the DGCA initiated necessary work to systematically decrease the existing or future damage of airport establishments on the environment and human health and to eliminate them if appropriate.

First, in the terminal luggage areas of Atatürk, Adana, Adnan Menderes, Antalya, Dalaman, Esenboğa, Milas Bodrum, and Trabzon Airports where the traffic is dense, instructions were given to the ground handling services to utilize electric power-operated vehicles for moving the luggage instead of those operating on fuel oil and to accomplish 50 percent of the conversion by the end of 2009 and the remainder by the end of 2010.

Under the DGCA's Green Airport Project, airports whose airline operators and service providers comply with the specified requirements will be called "Green Airports." In return, the DGCA shall provide the complying organizations and establishments with a reduction in service tariff as an incentive and reward for their sensibility.

Also, as a result of intensive studies over the last three years, followed up on by the Directorate General, the works performed by the Directorate General of State Airports Administration were put into practice with regard to ambient noise. Within this context, it has been stated that noise rating, noise mapping, action plans, and relevant precautions will be performed by the Directorate General of State Airports Administration (Directorate General of Civil Aviation, 2009).

TAV Airports is maintaining and improving air quality through initiatives to both monitor and manage air quality. TAV Airports Holding also has planned initiatives to demonstrate industry leadership. Air temperature, moisture, and exhaust merits are monitored in both offices and common areas in terminals. Also, chimney exhaust merits (SO_2, carbon monoxide) and air quality of baggage handling areas is monitored.

TAV Airports is ensuring sustainable use of land through avoidance and/or remediation of contaminated land. They are utilizing long-term strategic sustainable land-use planning, for example, maximizing brownfield and minimizing greenfield development. Countryside initiatives are being handled by airports to protect the environment from trash and other waste and to keep the natural landscape green.

With waste water treatment facilities installed at the airports and terminals it operates, TAV Airports employs practices such as returning treated water to sewage systems and using the treated water in irrigation. With a pilot project initiated at the Tbilisi International Airport, the company prevents de-icing fluid applied to the body and wing surfaces of the aircraft in the winter months from mixing into the sewage system by collecting it through channels other than rain water channels. This practice prevents negative environmental impacts (TAV Airports Holding, 2009).

Furthermore, the company is accelerating its efforts in replacing vehicles and construction equipment powered by diesel or gasoline-fired internal combustion engines with electric vehicles and construction equipment. With these initiatives, TAV Airports undoubtedly will be among the world's pioneers in environmentally friendly airport operations (TAV Airports Holding, 2009).

TAV does not yet have any initiatives to enhance biodiversity and the conservation of wildlife.

TAV Airports actively select sustainable materials for use in their airports such as:

- renewable resources, for example, timber instead of concrete;
- environmentally-sensitive materials, for example, biodegradable and non-toxic;
- socially-responsible materials, for example, fair trade and organic.

TAV Airports implement waste management initiatives to reduce, reuse, or recycle waste from administrative areas, for example, paper recycling, and to reduce, reuse, or recycle waste from terminal areas, for example, prohibiting food outlets from using disposable plates/cutlery. To gain value from waste, for example, composting, waste to energy.

While liquid and solid waste materials were negligently dumped into the nearest stream or shore before, now great efforts are undertaken for the recycling of these wastes and the laws and regulations on this issue are getting stricter by the day. Solutions are designed for the recycling and re-usage of the water used, and these solutions are turned into concrete projects, especially in Middle Eastern countries (TAV Airports Holding, 2009).

TAV Airports Holding is reducing and mitigating aesthetic and/ or noise impacts through initiatives to reduce noise from ground borne planes, for example: altering taxiing/takeoff patterns and installing triple glazing, and to reduce negative aesthetic impacts for neighboring properties or key viewpoints.

Discontented with only these measures, airport operators force aircraft and engine manufacturers to develop more environmentally friendly airplanes, helicopters, and similar aircraft. For example, while the noise level of a typical jet engine during takeoff was around 170 to 185 decibels in the 1970s, today some airports fine individuals or companies whose airplanes exceed the noise level of 90 decibels during takeoff. Furthermore, as emission (exhaust and similar gases) standards become more strict, airplanes that leave behind a black cloud of smoke can only be found in museums or salvage yards (TAV Airports Holding, 2009).

TAV is reducing energy use through initiatives to:

- improve energy efficiency, for example, by installing efficient lighting/equipment;
- utilize low-carbon energy sources, for example, LPG and bio-fuels;
- implement green building principles, for example, insulation.

Lighting in the airport terminals is provided by energy efficient lamps. The lighting system is controlled by auto-motion with daylight sensitivity. Energy source facilities with low-carbon emissions (for example, LPG and bio fuel) are being constructed. TAV Airports Holding has conducted research on zero-carbon energy sources such as solar terminal heating and photovoltaic solar cells.

Having acquired a "Self-Producer License" from the Energy Market Regulatory Authority (EPDK) in February 2008, TAV

Istanbul is implementing a "Trigeneration Project" in order to generate the electricity of the İstanbul Atatürk Airport. Once the project is completed, İstanbul Atatürk Airport will be generating its own electricity and air-conditioning energy. While generating electricity with this project, the heat recaptured will be used for terminal air-conditioning. These measures will provide a 25 percent savings in energy costs. Expected to have an installed capacity of 9.9 MW, the plant will generate 100 percent of the airport's electricity consumption, as well as 40 percent of its heating and 35 percent of its cooling needs. As a result, Atatürk Airport will have lower costs and more efficient energy usage (TAV Airports Holding, 2009).

TAV is seeking to achieve green building certification for existing buildings, renovations and retrofits, and new construction. TAV is also working in collaboration with the Istanbul Technical University's Department of Architecture on green building concepts.

Managing economic sustainability

TAV is trying to maximize economic sustainability through initiatives to support local hiring and purchasing by their airports. They are purchasing goods or services from businesses who adopt environmentally friendly practices.

TAV Airports Holding is trying to improve their community-related contributions. They are providing monetary or in-kind support to various groups such as academic institutions, charitable organizations, and community organizations. To improve the corporate-based approach and create awareness, TAV has given sponsorship and/or financial contributions to various non-governmental organizations.

TAV is working on quantifying the value of sustainability initiatives by:

- considering life-cycle costs;
- quantifying monetary savings, for example, reduced energy bills from implementing energy initiatives;
- undertaking strategic long-term planning with sustainability scenarios in mind, for example, insurance costs due to climate change impacts;

- reducing water cost;
- reducing energy cost.

These measures are being tracked by TAV for cost control, cost minimization, and optimization when using natural resources.

Contributing to research and development is important to TAV. They are investing in or supporting research, development, and innovation which contribute toward both protection of the environment, including conservation of natural resources, and social progress that recognizes the needs of all stakeholders.

The incentivizing of sustainable behavior from a TAV Holding-wide perspective is important to TAV Airports Holding managers. For this reason, TAV Airports Holding is providing incentives to encourage adoption of sustainable behavior by:

- airport operations staff, for example, awareness and training on environmental issues such as water and energy;
- tenants and their employees, for example, incentivizing public transport use;
- passengers, for example, encouraging separation and recycling of waste;
- personnel, for example, training in various fields at the TAV Academy.

Managing social sustainability

TAV Airports Holding defines social responsibility as "... the voluntary contribution by companies to create a better society and future" (TAV Airports Holding, 2010:126). In this respect, the Company tries to act with a sense of corporate social responsibility in such areas as the environment, culture, the arts, and education. TAV Airports invests in all branches of the arts in Turkey; from literature and music to theatre, photography and sculpture, supporting many arts organizations. According to company documents, TAV Airports considers one of its fundamental objectives that of meeting its responsibilities regarding Sustainable Development in full (TAV Airports Holding, 2010:126).

In view of Entity Risk Management, the stakeholder relationships concept is one of the fundamental focuses of Contemporary Business and Management. For this reason, TAV

Airports is maintaining and enhancing relationships with the following stakeholders:

- airlines;
- tenants;
- employees of the airport operator;
- employees of airlines/tenants.

TAV Airports supports sustainable transportation through initiatives to:

- enhance pedestrian access, for example, safe, accessible footpaths and zebra crossings;
- support public transport, for example, shuttle bus and rail links;
- implement clean transport technologies, for example, converting vehicles to alternative fuels.

TAV Airports helps to alleviate road congestion through initiatives to both reduce car travel by employees working at the airport, for example, by charging for parking; and by passengers using the airport, for example, by creating high-occupancy lanes.

TAV Airports is trying to maximize accessibility for all passengers to and within airport terminals through initiatives to enhance services for physically impaired persons, for example, accessible restroom facilities, ramps, and signage for the visually impaired, and for families, for example, access for baby carriages and strollers. TAV also provides baby carriages and strollers for their customers, and highchairs in their airport restaurants for families.

In view of social contribution, TAV is trying to create and/or enhance local identity, culture, and heritage through initiatives such as native landscaping and public art which reflects local history, in order to acknowledge and celebrate both indigenous and local historical sites. Various organizations arrange for exhibition space in TAV's international terminal.

TAV Airports provided sponsorship support for the 5th World Water Forum, held at the Sütlüce Congress and Cultural Center, March, 16–22, which hosted participants including heads of State and international non-governmental organizations (TAV Airports Holding, 2010:126).

Indoor environmental quality is high through initiatives in TAV Airports. Terminal comfort in the areas of ventilation, lighting, vibration control, and odor control are provided in the airports. Lighting, ventilation, and public address systems are controlled by modern technology and automation. Ventilation and odor control are used in the restrooms.

TAV Airports provides a variety of facilities to enhance employee well-being such as:

- accessible open and/or green space;
- essential services, for example, banks, shops, post office, places of worship, and meditation rooms;
- support facilities, for example, childcare and Internet access;
- leisure or recreation facilities, for example, sport facilities or social spaces.

Facilities to enhance the well-being of passengers are provided but on a more limited basis in the interest of security precautions. There are essential and support services for passengers such as banks, shops, post office, places of worship, meditation rooms, childcare, sleeping facilities, showers, and Internet access. There are also leisure or recreation facilities, for example, wellness or spa facilities for passengers.

TAV Airports has determined that their future sustainability-based priorities (using the triple bottom line concept: economic, social, and environmental) over the next five years will be as follows:

- energy;
- waste;
- emission (noise, air quality, magnetic pollution, pollution of frequency).

Operations carried out at the airports inevitably closely impact the environment where they are located. The environmental problems arise particularly as a result of the expansion of airports that are located outside of cities, as well as the expansion of the cities they serve. As a result of the airports being located near the cities, they become integrated with the cities' own environmental problems and create environmental impacts. Operational activities carried out at the airports that have environmental impacts are listed below (TAV Airports Holding, 2009):

- landing, takeoff and maneuvering of aircraft;
- operation of all motor vehicles and construction equipment serving the airports;
- chemicals used for clearing the aircraft and runways of snow and ice;
- storage needs and leakage risk of fuel, oils, and similar chemicals used in aircraft;
- construction work performed for the maintenance, repair, modification and expansion of airport terminals, runways, aprons and taxi routes;
- chemicals and work needed for the maintenance, repair and cleaning of the terminals, operation buildings, vehicles and construction equipment, airplanes and other aircraft.

The headings listed above have environmental impacts not just because of the emissions of chemicals, gases such as smoke and steam, liquids and solid wastes; but also because of noise, light, population density, and even the change in topographical structure. It is undoubtedly true that an airport forever changes the environment where it is built. Wildlife, vegetation cover, and the like will never be as they were before. However, this change need not be harmful, destroy the environment, or negatively impact nature, as it is usually perceived. Many more environmental projects have been undertaken in the last ten years of the twentieth century and the first nine years of the twenty-first century. Airplanes emit nearly a quarter less of the noise now than previously, and according to some sources, exhaust gas emissions have been reduced by almost 45 percent. Aircraft and aircraft engine manufacturers conscientiously fulfill their duties (TAV Airports Holding, 2009).

TAV Airports Holding, according to statements in its management documents, expands maximum effort to be sensitive to its social responsibilities in its operations (TAV Investor Relations, 2010). It strives to comply with all regulations regarding the environment, consumer and public health, as well as ethics rules, and directs and supports its subsidiaries to behave in the same manner. Furthermore, the Company's terminal operating subsidiaries aim to conduct their operations in compliance with environmental legislation, directives and guidelines of international aviation organizations such as the International Civil Aviation Organization (ICAO), European Civil Aviation Conference (ECAC), Eurocontrol and the International Air Transport Association (IATA), as well as the Equator Principles of the World Bank (TAV Investor Relations, 2010).

Due to the nature of their operations, the Company and its subsidiaries are not legally obligated, within the scope of Turkish Environment Law and its related legislation, to produce environmental impact assessment reports. Nevertheless, the Company's relevant subsidiaries prepare environmental reports and Environmental Management plans during both the construction and operation phases of terminals and comply with updated Environmental Management plans. Furthermore, the Company's subsidiaries have international quality control plans for their operation areas and quality control audits are conducted in compliance with international standards (TAV Investor Relations, 2010).

Sustainability Management in İstanbul Sabiha Gökçen (ISG) International Airport Investment Development and Operation, Inc.

Istanbul Sabiha Gökçen International Airport Investment Development and Operation Inc. (ISG), a company founded in partnership by Limak Holding (LIMAK), GMR Infrastructure Limited (GMR), and Malaysia Airports Holdings Berhad (MAHB), has 20 years operation rights, as of May 1, 2008, of Istanbul Sabiha Gökçen International Airport, including the management of the terminal buildings, car park, ground handling, cargo, and aircraft refueling operations, and the airport hotel. In addition to the 1.932 billion euros paid for the operational rights, ISG will further invest a minimum 336 million euros in Istanbul Sabiha Gökçen. The new terminal building, the first step and an important part of these investments, which will support airport's rapid growth and bring the annual passenger capacity of Istanbul Sabiha Gökçen's to 25 million, was built with a modern design with international norms and standards, as well as an environment-friendly structure and was put into service on October 31, 2009. The features and the services that are provided that the new terminal building and its complementary structures provide include (http://www.sabihagokcen.aero/about_isg):

- 112 check-in and 24 Common Use Self Service (CUSS) check-in kiosks;
- 20 passport counters each for incoming and outgoing passengers;
- 5,000 m² food court for cafés and restaurants belonging to the leading food and beverage brands;
- 4,500 m² duty free shopping area run by SETUR and occupying a space of 3,300 m² and 1,200 m² in the departures and arrivals halls respectively. Other than the usual duty free shopping items, such as local/foreign drinks, tobacco and cosmetics, ready-wear, textile accessories and electronics is offered for sale;
- 3 apron viewing lounges and VIP halls;
- a two-storey VIP building with terminal connection;
- 400 m² conference center;
- A four-storey car park with a capacity of about 4,718 vehicles and 72 buses (3,836 indoors and 882 + 72 bus outdoors);
- a three-storey airport hotel with 128 rooms, adjacent to the terminal and with separate entrances at air and ground sides;
- multi-aircraft parking system, allowing synchronized service to eight aircraft with large fuselages (IATA code E) or 16 middle-sized fuselage aircrafts (IATA code C);
- Explosives Detection Systems (EDS) baggage screening.

Sustainability-based initiatives at ISG

ISG has a specialized department and accountability managers for sustainability initiatives at their airport. The technical service manager and environmental engineer in their operations department have been designated to be the responsible person in ISG (Torum and Kucuk Yilmaz, 2009).

ISG Airports Holding managers ranked the top five drivers (with 1 being the highest) of their sustainability practices as follows:

1. State/regional regulations;
2. Corporate Responsibility;
3. stakeholder concerns/relations;
4. airport policy;
5. economic incentives (for example, rebates).

The identified reasons behind failed or slow implementation of sustainability practices at Istanbul airports by airport operators is one of the important findings of the survey by Torum and Kucuk Yilmaz (2009). The following are the barriers to implementation of sustainability practices at ISG Airport:

- either lack of national laws and regulations regarding sustainability reflecting the triple bottom line concept or insufficient application of these laws and regulations nationwide;
- lack of funding;
- undeveloped societal awareness in the country regarding sustainability/Sustainable Development issues.

ISG Airports Holding does not report publicly on performance for any of the following issues:

- protection of the environment, including conservation of natural resources;
- social progress that recognizes the needs of all stakeholders;
- maintenance of high and stable levels of economic growth and employment.

The ISG organization does or does not provide training for staff on the following issues:

- social progress that recognizes the needs of all stakeholders: non-applicable;
- approaches including conservation of resources: in place;
- maintenance of high and stable levels of economic growth and employment: in place.

The drivers of existing sustainability initiatives are:

- international regulations, for example, European Union directives and International Aviation Authority policies;
- Corporate Responsibility;
- airport policy;
- global approaches;
- city/local regulations.

Implementation of environmental sustainability initiatives

ISG implements their environmental/sustainability performance monitoring using an uncertified Environmental Management System.

ISG Airport is conserving water through initiatives associated with increasing potable water efficiency and collecting and reusing greywater, for example, wastewater from kitchen, laundry, and bathroom basins.

ISG Airport is seeking to reduce its impact upon the global climate through planned initiatives to:

- demonstrate industry leadership, for example, through partnerships, research, and a voluntary low emissions program;
- reduce emissions from aircraft in the air, for example, by influencing descent or stacking patterns;
- reduce emissions from airport ground vehicles, for example, by purchasing electric luggage or food trucks;
- reduce emissions from passenger surface access traffic, for example, by subsidizing public transit for passengers.

ISG Airport is maintaining and improving air quality through planned initiatives to both monitor and manage air quality.

ISG Airport is ensuring sustainable use of land through planned initiatives to both avoid and/or remediate contaminated land through long-term strategic sustainable land use planning, for example, by minimizing brownfield and maximizing greenfield development.

ISG has partnerships with non-governmental organizations or wildlife organizations. ISG has also planned initiatives to enhance biodiversity and conserve wildlife through implementing programs within the airport boundaries, for example, by setting aside areas for nature conservation and programs for bird control which use non-lethal techniques.

They are actively selecting sustainable materials such as socially-responsible materials, for example, from fair trade and organic producers. There are also planned initiatives such as using environmentally sensitive materials, for example, biodegradable and non-toxic.

ISG Airport is implementing waste management initiatives to reduce, reuse, or recycle waste from administrative areas, for example, through paper recycling. There are also planned initiatives by ISG such as to reduce, reuse, or recycle waste from terminal areas, for example, by prohibiting food outlets from using disposable plates and cutlery.

ISG is trying to reduce and mitigate aesthetic and/or noise impacts through planned initiatives to use noise reduction materials in their buildings.

They are reducing energy use through planned initiatives to improve energy efficiency, for example, by installing efficient lighting and equipment; utilizing low-carbon energy sources such as LPG and bio-fuels; and by implementing green building principles, for example, using insulation.

Today, utilization of zero-carbon energy sources such as photovoltaic, solar thermal heating is non-applicable for ISG.

ISG is seeking to achieve green building certification for both existing and new buildings.

Implementing economic sustainability initiatives

ISG is trying to maximize economic sustainability through initiatives to support local hiring and purchasing by the organization or airport. Also, they are purchasing goods or services from businesses who adopt environmentally friendly practices.

In the area of community contributions, ISG is providing monetary or in-kind support to charitable organizations.

ISG has been implementing a variety of both actual and planned initiatives, quantifying the value of sustainability by:

- considering life-cycle costs: planned;
- quantifying monetary savings, for example, reduced energy bills from implementing energy initiatives: in place;
- undertaking strategic long-term planning with sustainability scenarios in mind, for example, insurance costs due to climate change impacts: in place;
- reducing water costs: in place;
- reducing energy costs: in place.

According the survey results by Torum and Kucuk Yilmaz (2009), ISG airport is planning to invest in or support research, development, and innovation which contribute toward protection of the environment, including conservation of natural resources, and social progress that recognizes the needs of all stakeholders.

ISG is attempting to incentivize sustainable behavior in their organization. For this, they are providing incentives to encourage adoption of sustainable behavior by the staff of the airport operator through, for example, awareness and training on environmental issues such as water and energy; and by passengers, for example, by encouraging separation and recycling of waste. Also, they have planned incentives for tenants and their employees, for example, to encourage the use of public transportation (Torum and Kucuk Yilmaz, 2009).

Implementing social sustainability initiatives

ISG is trying to raise public awareness and to educate others on the maintenance of high and stable levels of economic growth and employment. They are planning some initiatives to help protect the environment, including conservation of natural resources and social progress that recognizes the needs of all stakeholders.

ISG is maintaining and enhancing their relationships or is planning to do so with the following stakeholders:

- community/neighborhood groups: planned;
- airlines: planned;
- federal/national government: planned;
- local government: planned;
- tenants: in place;

- employees employed by the airport operator: in place;
- employees employed by airlines/tenants: planned.

ISG Airport is supporting sustainable transportation through both current and planned initiatives to:

- enhance pedestrian access, for example, by providing safe, accessible footpaths and zebra crossings: planned;
- support public transport, for example, by providing a shuttle bus and rail-link: planned and in place;
- implement clean transport technologies, for example, by converting vehicles to alternative fuels: planned.

They are helping to alleviate road congestion through planned initiatives to reduce car travel by both employees working at the airport (for example, by charging for parking) and passengers using the airport (for example, by creating high-occupancy lanes).

ISG is attempting to maximize accessibility for all passengers to and within their airport terminals through initiatives to enhance services for physically-impaired persons for example, accessible restroom facilities, ramps, and signage for the visually impaired and for families, for example, by providing access for baby carriages and strollers.

They are trying to enhance local identity, culture, and heritage through initiatives to acknowledge and celebrate local historical sites.

ISG has initiatives to manage indoor environmental quality. These initiatives include: lighting, ventilation, noise, thermal comfort, and odor control.

ISG Airport provides a variety of facilities to enhance employee well-being such as:

- accessible open and/or green space: in place;
- essential services, for example, banks, shops, post office, places of worship, and meditation rooms: in place;
- support facilities, for example, childcare and Internet access: in place;
- leisure or recreation facilities, for example, sport facilities or social spaces: planned.

Likewise, they provide a variety of facilities to enhance passenger well-being such as:

- accessible open and/or green space: in place;
- essential services, for example, banks, shops, post office, places of worship, and meditation rooms: in place;
- support facilities, for example, childcare and Internet access: in place;
- leisure or recreation facilities, for example, sport facilities or social spaces: planned.

Barriers to ISG's Sustainability Initiatives include a lack of three elements: time, funding, and technology.

ISG's environmental policy is a top priority over the next five years.

For ISG, the top five drivers of their future sustainability initiatives are:

1. international regulations, for example, European Union directives, and International Aviation Authority policies;
2. Corporate Responsibility;
3. airport policy;
4. global trends, for example, climate change;
5. city/local regulations.

The goal of this comparison is to achieve a better understanding of current sustainability practices in airports in Istanbul, Turkey; to understand the barriers to and drivers behind these practices; and to identify areas for improvement for airport operators.

Sustainability can best be implemented in airport planning by integrating appropriate elements of sustainability throughout the process, thereby connecting all planning elements and results. It is vital that the operational impacts of development alternatives are considered at the planning stage. Our future work will focus on or will include reputation and stakeholder-based Entity Risk Management to support Corporate Sustainability. We aim to develop a related model with this future work.

Table 8.1 Main benchmarking sustainability-based initiatives in TAV Airport Holding and Istanbul Sabiha Gökçen International Airport Investment Development and Operation, Inc. (ISG)

	TAV Airport Holding	Istanbul Sabiha Gökçen International Airport Investment Development and Operation, Inc. (ISG)
Basic sustainability-based initiatives	Basically, ENVIRONMENTAL-based initiatives are both implemented and planned by airports. Policy and programs embedded in airport operations and close to reflecting best practices. Risks assessment in systematic process. Goals and targets are established. Performance is monitored but is not reported external to the organization. Performance Monitoring and Reporting: Continuous monitoring of performance against goals and targets that are both updated and improved regularly. Performance is reported internally within the organization. Also performance goals are aligned with strategic planning/corporate-level goals and targets. Annually, results are reported externally to stakeholders and general public. Incentives and awareness: Feedback loops are in place. Continuous surveying of stakeholders. Performance goals incentivized.	ISG implements environmental/sustainability performance monitoring using uncertified Environmental Management System (EMS). Policy and program will develop over next five years.

Table 8.1 continued Main benchmarking sustainability-based initiatives in TAV Airport Holding and Istanbul Sabiha Gökçen International Airport Investment Development and Operation, Inc. (ISG)

		TAV Airport Holding	Istanbul Sabiha Gökçen International Airport Investment Development and Operation, Inc. (ISG)
Implementation of economic sustainability initiatives	The extent to which the airport manages ECONOMIC sustainability.	TAV airport is trying to maximize economic sustainability through initiatives to support local hiring and purchasing by their airport. TAV is trying to improve their community-related contributions. They are providing monetary or in-kind support to the various groups such as academic institutions, charitable organizations, and community organizations. TAV airport is working on quantifying the value of sustainability initiatives by: Considering life-cycle costs; Quantifying monetary savings e.g. reduced energy bills from implementing energy initiatives; Undertaking strategic long-term planning with sustainability scenarios in mind e.g. insurance costs due to climate change impacts; Reducing water costs; Reducing energy costs.	ISG is trying to maximize economic sustainability through initiatives to support local hiring and purchasing by organization or airport. Also, they are purchasing goods and services from businesses who adopt environmentally-friendly practices. In the area of community contributions, ISG is providing monetary or in-kind support to charitable organizations. ISG has been implementing a variety of both actual and planned initiatives to quantify the value of sustainability. Actual initiatives are: Actual: Quantifying monetary savings e.g. reduced energy bills from implementing energy initiatives; Actual: Undertaking strategic long-term planning with sustainability scenarios in mind e.g. insurance costs due to climate change impacts; Actual: Reducing water costs; Actual: Reducing energy costs.
Implementation of social sustainability initiatives	The extent is airport managing SOCIAL sustainability.	Considering corporate citizenship and corporate social responsibility-based issues and planning-related initiatives.	Considering corporate citizenship and corporate social responsibility-based issues and planning-related initiatives.

Table 8.1 continued **Main benchmarking sustainability-based initiatives in TAV Airport Holding and Istanbul Sabiha Gökçen International Airport Investment Development and Operation, Inc. (ISG)**

		TAV Airport Holding	Istanbul Sabiha Gökçen International Airport Investment Development and Operation, Inc. (ISG)
Barriers to sustainability initiatives		Either lack of national regulations and laws on sustainability reflecting the triple bottom line concept or insufficient application of these laws and regulations nationwide. Funding undeveloped societal awareness in the country about sustainability/ Sustainable Development issues.	Time, lack of funding technology.
Corporate Sustainability Risk management	This management approach includes the triple bottom line concept: economic, social, and environmental.	Current improvement initiatives focus on environmental sustainability, but risk management has become an agenda topic.	ISG has an environmental management system. Social initiatives are increasing. ISG is newer than TAV. Related initiatives are increasing day by day.

Concluding Remarks

Sustainability is a key concept in the current business environment which is subject to impacts of global warming. Enterprise Risk Management (also known as ERM) is a new business management approach to Corporate Sustainability that aims to create long-term shareholder value by embracing opportunities and managing risks deriving from economic, social, and environmental developments (Flatz, 2004).

Enterprise Sustainability Risk Management (also known as ESRM) has become an increasingly important issue in the global economic environment. We assume that risk management is a core business process. However, there is still little guidance on how companies should best manage their Corporate Sustainability (also known as CS) risks.

Sustainable companies, together with academics and professional consultants, have produced Corporate Sustainability Management (also known as CSM) systems which, although varying in shape and detail between different industries, generally involve categorizing, analyzing, and prioritizing risks under the following headings:

- strategic;
- operational;
- financial;
- threat;
- environmental;
- social;
- compliance.

Risk is the probability that "favorable impact" or "adverse impact" may occur and impact corporate objectives. The Enterprise Sustainability Risk Management framework is the process of identifying potential negative outcomes and managing them while realizing potential opportunities.

Global warming risk must be managed effectively since its consequences threaten the sustainability of our world. While this is understandable, a broader view is necessary to manage this risk in both the short and long term. Global warming is and will have serious impact on the environment, agriculture, human health, eco-system, and on society as a whole. Mark Twain's remark, "... everybody talks about the weather, but nobody ever does anything about it ..." appears apropos to the discussion of sustainability. For years we have heard so much about the causes of climate change that we have missed the fact that there are simple, practical solutions that can slow this growing problem (Union of Concerned Scientists, 2009).

Holistic and systematic risk management: the Enterprise Sustainability Risk Management approach provides an effective solution to Sustainable Development and the issue of business risks which includes climate change-based risks, too. The Enterprise Sustainability Risk Management model is viewed as a new approach to the best prioritization and management of holistic business risks. The context of the Enterprise Sustainability Risk Management model can change a reactive culture and current mentality regarding global warming and risk management issues since the model presents a proactive and systematic approach. The abovementioned are basic contributions of this study to exiting literature, however, our study can support the "think global act local" motto since our model can be tailored to any affected nation, region, or organization. For this reason, our model can produce effective results to reflect its specific implementation field. Finally, this model and score formula can be used in global warming-related risk management via local and regional priority setting.

This book's aim is to support current risk management efforts for Corporate Sustainability in the context of the business organization. Also, we view it as a contribution to risk management literature in regard to Sustainable Development and global warming.

This book focuses on constructing a theoretical model for Enterprise Sustainability Risk Management and aims to improve awareness in the following areas:

- corporate risks as both threats and opportunities;
- Enterprise Sustainability Risk Management;
- climate change and global warming;
- risk culture;
- basic philosophy of the "think global, act local" mentality.

The linkage between Enterprise Risk Management and sustainability management is an emerging field of research. The Enterprise Sustainability Risk Management framework model serves as a starting point to develop a company-specific model. Corporate Sustainability is a business approach that creates long-term shareholder value, improves performance by removing waste, and manages risk. It considers the interrelationship of economic, social, and environmental issues (Bureau Veritas, 2009).

Enterprise Sustainability Risk Management is the holistic risk management-based approach to Corporate Sustainability. Both Enterprise Risk Management and Corporate Sustainability Risk Management present the basic framework and processes used by companies to manage risks and seize opportunities related to the achievement of their objectives.

According to Bill Connell FCMA (Fellow Chartered Management Accountant) (2006), former Director of a FTSE 100 company, Chair of the Professional Accountants in Business Committee of IFAC (International Federation of Accountants) and CIMA (Chartered Institute of Management Accountants) Council member, "10 years ago 90 percent of the value of a business was on its balance sheet. Today only 30 percent of the value of a business is on its balance sheet (Fortune 500 analysis). If the value of your enterprise is more than the value on your balance sheet; you need enterprise risk management!" (Connell, 2006).

Businesses need Enterprise Sustainability Risk Management and as such, this book is designed as a starting point for the improvement of current risk management systems to be implemented by companies globally. Managers can consider this book as a practical handbook to set their sustainability risk management cultures and systems, and academics can use it as a reference point as a well as a course resource.

In our view, sustainability is about "Being Realistic and Asking for the Impossible." Managers in contemporary business need Corporate Sustainability-based Entity Risk Management practices as tolls to achieve their "impossibilities" within the framework of a globally-warmed business world which is their reality. Furthermore, risk management is by nature innovative. It aims to seize opportunities and meet demands of stakeholders and to manage corporate reputation via implementation of Enterprise Risk Management practices. Managers need risk assessment scenarios as tools to set their risk management strategies in the way of Corporate Sustainability.

References

Aeronautics and Space Engineering Board (ASEB) (2002). *For Greener Skies: Reducing Environmental Impacts of Aviation, Findings and Recommendations*. Washington, DC: National Academy Press (pp.47–50). Retrieved 08/26/2009 from http://www.nap.edu/openbook.php?record_id=10353&page=41.

Air Transport Net (AirTN) (2009). Home page. Retrieved 08/26/2009 from http://www.airtn.eu/.

Airline Business (2006). Riskprofile. (Airline Risk Management Survey 2005), Reed Business Information Ltd. Retrieved 08/27/2009 from http://www.flightglobal.com/articles/2006/04/26/206198/risk-profile.html.

Airports Council International—North America (2010). Airport Sustainability, A Holistic Approach to Effective Airport Management. Retrieved 01/18/2010 from http://www.sustainableaviation.org/pdfs/ACC%20-20Sustainability%20White%20Paper.pdf.

Altria Corporate Services, Inc. (2004). Stakeholder Engagement Planning Overview. Retrieved 08/26/2009 from http://www.forumstrategies.com/content/pdf/stakeholder_engagement.pdf.

Anderson, D.R. (2005). *Corporate Survival: The Critical Importance of Sustainability Risk Management*, New York: iUniverse, Inc.

Anderson, D.R. (2007). Sustainability risk management as a critical component of enterprise risk management: global warming—climate change risks, *The Geneva Papers on Risk and Insurance, Issues and Practice*, Special Competition Edition, 4–32. Retrieved 05/23/2011 from http://research3.bus.wisc.edu/file.php/127/SUSTAINABILITY_RISK_MANAGEMENT_IIS_article.pdf.

Appelbaum, S.H.; Fewster, B.M. (2002). Global aviation human resource management: contemporary recruitment and selection and diversity and equal opportunity practices, *Equal Opportunities International*, 21(7), 15. Retrieved 05/23/2011 from http://www.deepdyve.com/lp/emerald-publishing/global-aviation-human-resource-management-contemporary-recruitment-and-WPFts5EqIo.

Atkinson, G.; Hett, T.; Newcombe, J. (1999). Measuring "Corporate Sustainability". CSERGE Working Paper GEC 99-01. Retrieved 08/26/2009 from http://www.uea.ac.uk/env/cserge/pub/wp/gec/gec_1999_01.pdf.

Australian Broadcasting Corporation (2008). Risk Management Increases as Credit Crisis Continues. Broadcast: 13/10/2008. Reporter: Michael

Troy. Retrieved 08/28/2009 from http://ussc.edu.au/s/media/media/08/10/081013_LatelineBusiness_Chinoy.pdf.

Australian Government Department of the Environment, Water, Heritage and the Arts (2009). Corporate Sustainability. Business and Industry Sustainability. Retrieved 08/26/2009 from http://www.environment.gov.au/settlements/industry/.

Austrian Airlines Group (2006). Risk and Opportunity Management, Corporate Management and Control, Austrian Airlines Gropu Annual Report 2006, p.25. Retrieved 05/23/2011 from http://www.austrianairlines.ag/InvestorRelations/FinancialReports/~/media/Austrian%20Airlines/Corporate%20Site/Investor%20Relations/Other%20Formats/2006/GB%202006%20engl%20Korr-S.ashx#selected.

Aviation Environment Federation (AEF) (2009). What Are an Airport's Impacts? A–Z of Aviation and The Environment Planning Guide. Retrieved 08/26/2009 from http://www.aef.org.uk/uploads/PlanningGuide2.pdf.

Aviation Watch (2009). System Safety and Human Factors. Retrieved 08/26/2009 from http://www.aviationwatch.co.uk/#fn3.

Azapagic, A. (2003). Systems approach to corporate sustainability: a general management framework, Process Safety and Environmental Protection, 81(5), 303–316.

BAA (2006a). Aviation and Climate Change. Issue Brief, Publications. Retrieved 04/14/2009 from http://www.baa.com/assets//B2CPortal/Static%20Files/05AviationClimChange.pdf.

Banerjee, S.B. (2002), Organisational strategies for sustainable development: developing a research agenda for the new millennium, *Australian Journal of Management*, 27, 105.

Banerjee, S.B. (2004). Teaching Sustainability: A Critical Perspective, The Academy of Management Conference, New Orleans, August 2004, p.6.

Bansal, P. (2005). Evolving sustainably: a longitudinal study of corporate sustainable development, *Strategic Management Journal*, 26, s.197–218.

Becker, B.E.; Huselid, M.A. (2006). Strategic human resources management: Where do we go from here? *Journal of Management*, Southern Management Association, 32(6), pp.898–925.

Benson, B.W.; Davidson, W.N. (2009). The Relation between Stakeholder Management between Stakeholder Management, Firm Value, and CEO Compensation: A Test of Enlightened Value Maximization (November 12, 2009). Financial Management, Forthcoming. Available at SSRN: http://ssrn.com/abstract=1208403.

Berry, F., Gillhespy, S., and Rogers, J. (2008). ACRP Synthesis 10: Airport Sustainability Practices, Transportation Research Board of the National Academies, Washington, DC, 2008.

Bisignani, G. (2006). Remarks. AirServices Australia, Regional ANSP Conference, Brisbane. Retrieved 08/26/2009 from http://www.iata.org/pressroom/speeches/2006-08-18-01.htm.

Bisignani, G. (2007). Aviation and Global Warming. *The International Herald Tribune*, September 20, 2007. Retrieved 08/08/2009 from http://www.iht.com/articles/2007/09/20/news/edbisi.php?page=1.

Boeing Commercial Airplanes (2005). Statistical Summary of Commercial Jet Airplane Accidents Worldwide Operations 1959–2004, Boeing Commercial Airplanes, May 2005. Retrieved 08/26/2009 from http://www.aermalignani.org/pdf/boeing.pdf.

Boiral, O. (2006). Global warming: Should companies adopt a proactive strategy? *Long Range Planning*, 39(3), 315–330.

Bono de, E. (1996).*Going Beyond Competition, Sur/Petition* (Turkish Edition, Ceviren: Oya Ozel), Remzi Kitabevi, Istanbul, Turkey, 1996, Second Edition: 2000, p.20.

Bouma, E. (2007). Sustainable Development and Corporate Responsibility, Seminar on Good Corporate and Social Governance in Promoting ASEAN's Regional Integration, ASEAN Foundationi Indonesia. Retrieved 02/03/2010 from http://www.aseanfoundation.org/seminar/gcsg/papers/Elmar%20Bouma%20Presentation.pdf.

BSDglobal (2009). The Sustainable Development Journey. Retrieved 09/01/2009 from http://www.bsdglobal.com/sd_journey.asp.

Bureau Veritas (2009). Corporate Sustainability: A Proactive Approach to Brand Protection. Retrieved 08/26/2009 from http://www.bureauveritas.com/wps/wcm/connect/bv_com/Group/Home/bv_com_serviceSheetDetails?serviceSheetID=9306&siteID=1&industryID=-1&serviceCategoryID=-1&preciseObjectID=-1&divisionID=1&businessScopeID=-1.

Burke, W.W.; Litwin, G.H. (1992). The Burke-Litwin model, "A casual model of organizational performance and change", *Journal of Management*, 18(3), 532–545.; Di Pofi, J.A. (2002), Organizational diagnostics: integrating qualitative and quantitative methodology, *Journal of Organizational Change Management*, 15(2), 156–168.

Burr, S. (2007). Aviation Sustainability Update, UC Symposium on Aviation Noise and Air Quality, March 4, 2007, Port of Seattle. Retrieved 11/09/2009 from http://airquality.ucdavis.edu/pages/events/2007/aviation_presentations/Stewart.pdf.

Campbell, I.; King, J.; Kelly, G.; Connor, R.O.; Morgan, C. (2005). Dublin Airport and the Challenge of Sustainable Airport Growth: The Development of Sustainable Development Indicators for Dublin Airport. Queens University Belfast, December 2005. Retrieved 08/26/2009 from www.qub.ac.uk/ep/online/evp822/group6/index.htm.

Carewren, J. (2004). Corporate sustainability and corporate social responsibility—Do companies know the difference? EzineArticles. Retrieved 04/18/2009 from http://ezinearticles.com/?Corporate-Sustainability-and-Corporate-Social-Responsibility---Do-Companies-Know-the-Difference?&id=911059.

Chapman, R. (2007). Managing risk to enhance shareholder value, business continuity and risk management. IT Adviser, *The Magazine of the National Computing Centre*, 48 (March/April), 6–8. Retrieved 08/26/2009 from http://www.businesscontinuityexpo.co.uk/files/it_advisor_mar_april_2007.pdf.

Collaborative Forum of Air Transport Stakeholders (2003). Fast Facts. February 2003. Retrieved 08/26/2009 from http://www.eraa.org/intranet/documents/14/427/061005fastfacts.pdf.

Committee of Sponsoring Organizations of the Tradeway Commission (COSO) (2004). COSO's ERM-integrated Framework (draft version). Retrieved 08/26/2009 from http://www.erm.coso.org.

Committee of Sponsoring Organizations of the Treadway Commission (COSO) (2004). Enterprise Risk Management—Integrated Framework, Executive Summary. Retrieved 02/03/2010 from http://www.coso.org/Publications/ERM/COSO_ERM_ExecutiveSummary.pdf.

Connell, B. (2006), Enterprise Risk Management, Looking at Risk in Strategy, The 17th International World Accountants Congress, November 13–16, 2006, Istanbul, Turkey, Retrieved 05/23/2011 from http://www.tmud.org.tr/Icerik.aspx?KatID=6&YaziID=25; WCOA Enterprise Risk—Bill Connell Nov 06.

De Leo, G.A.; Rizzi, L.; Caizzi, A.; Gatto, M. (2001). Carbon emissions: The economic benefits of the Kyoto Protocol. Brief Communications, *Nature*, 413(6855), pp.478–479.

Delery, J.; Doty, D. (1996). Mode of theorizing in strategic human resource management: tests of universalistic, contingency, and configuration performance predictions, *Academy of Management Journal*, 39, 802–835.

DeLoach, J. (2004). The new risk imperative—an enterprise-wide approach. *Handbook of Business Strategy*. Emerald Group Publishing Limited, 5(1), 29–34. Retrieved 04/16/2009 from http://www.emeraldinsight.com/Insight/viewPDF.jsp?contentType=Article&Filename=html/Output/Published/EmeraldFullTextArticle/Pdf/2890050104.pdf.

Deloitte (2007a). Creating the "Wholly Sustainable Enterprise": A Practical Guide to Driving Shareholder Value through Enterprise Sustainability. Deloitte Development LLC., p.3, 9. http://www.deloitte.com/dtt/cda/doc/content/Creating/the wholly/20sustainable/enterprise(1).pdf.

Deloitte (2007b). Sustainability: Balancing Opportunity and Risk in the Consumer Products Industry. Retrieved 08/26/2009 from http://www.deloitte.com/dtt/cda/doc/content/us_cb_sustainability-study_june2007opt.pdf section 1:3.

Deloitte (2009). Risk Management, Stakeholder Management and Alternative Resolution. Retrieved 02/03/2010 from http://www.deloitte.com/view/en_ZA/za/services/audit/deloitteaudit/article/4f3fbf2733101210VgnVCM100000ba42f00aRCRD.htm.

Dervitsiotis, K.N. (1998). The challenge of managing organizational change: exploring the relationship of re-engineering, developing learning organizations and total quality management, *Total Quality Management*, 9(1), 109–122(14).

Directorate General of Civil Aviation (2009). Project of Green Airport. Retrieved 07/07/2010 from http://web.shgm.gov.tr/dgca.php?page=projects&id=4.

Dow Jones Sustainability Indexes (DJSI) (2009). Corporate Sustainability. Retrieved 08/26/2009 from http://www.sustainability-indexes.com/07_htmle/sustainability/corpsustainability.html.

Dow Jones Sustainability Indexes (DJSI) (2010). Corporate Sustainability. Retrieved March 30, 2010 from http://www.sustainability-indexes.com/07_htmle/sustainability/corpsustainability.html.

Drucker, P.F. (1999). *Management: Tasks, Responsibilities, Practices.* Oxford: Butterworth-Heinemann Ltd, Classic Collection.

Dunphy, D.; Griffiths, A.; Benn, S. (2002). *Organizational Change for Corporate Sustainability.* New York, NY: Routledge, Taylor and Francis Group.

Dyllick, T.; Hockerts, K. (2002). Beyond the Business Case for Corporate Sustainability. Business Strategy and the Environment. Retrieved 08/26/2009 from http://www.iwoe.unisg.ch/org/iwo/web.nsf/0/af0f51dab5ad967ec12569f2003c7416/$FILE/Dyllick+Hockerts%20-%20Beyond%20the%20Business%20Case%20-%20BSE%20Vers%202.0.pdf.

Economics Help (2009). Economics of Global Warming. Retrieved 08/26/2009 from http://www.economicshelp.org/2008/01/economics-of-global-warming.html.

Economist Intelligence Unit (2008). Doing Good: Business and the Sustainability Challenge, Economist Intelligence Unit Report, *The Economist*, February 2008. Retrieved 05/23/2011 from http://graphics.eiu.com/upload/Sustainability_allsponsors.pdf, p.18.

Esquer-Peralta, J. (2006). The Sustainability Performance Criteria. Sustainability Management Systems (SMS): Sustainable development in relation to different kinds of management systems. 10th Canadian Pollution Prevention Rountable. Halifax, Canada, June 14, 2006. Retrieved 09/02/2009 from http://www.c2p2online.com/documents/Javier_Esquer-Peralta.pdf, p.14.

Eurocontrol—European Organisation for the Safety of Air Navigation (2010). Aviation and Sustainability. Retrieved 07/07/2010 from http://www.eurocontrol.int/environment/public/standard_page/aviation_sustainability.html.

Experimental Aircraft Association (EAA) (2009). Aviation and Climate Change: The Views of Aviation Industry Stakeholders. Retrieved 08/26/2009 from http://www.eaa.org/news/2009/env_principles_full.pdf.

Farber, D.A.; Hemmersbaugh, P.A. (1993). The Shadow of the Future: Discount Rates, Later Generations, and the Environment, *Vanderbilt Law Review*, 46(2), 267–304.

Federal Aviation Administration (2006). Introduction to Safety Management Systems for Air Operators. Advisory Circular, AFS-800, AC No: 120–92. Retrieved 08/28/2009 from http://www.airweb.faa.gov/Regulatory_and_Guidance_Library/rgAdvisoryCircular.nsf/0/6485143d5ec81aae8625719b0055c9e5/$FILE/AC%20120-92.pdf.

Flatz, A. (2004). The Case for Sustainability from an Investors Perspective.

European Commission Enterprise Directorate-General, Seminar on The Business Case for CSR. Brussels, June 17, 2004, p.9. Retrieved 26/08/2009 from http://ec.europa.eu/enterprise/csr/documents/business_case/flatz.pdf.

Frederick W.C. (1994). From CSR1 to CSR2. *Business and Society*, 33(2), 150–164.

Friends of the Earth (2009). Aviation and Global Climate Change. Reports, p.7. Retrieved 08/28/2009 from http://www.foe.co.uk/resource/reports/aviation_climate_change.pdf.

Frigo, M.L. (2007). Corporate Sustainability. Strategic Finance. December 2007. Retrieved 08/28/2009 from http://www.allbusiness.com/management/risk-management/8895596-1.html.

Galotti, V.; Rao, A.; Maurino, D. (2008). Implementation of Safety Management Systems (SMS) in States. Article, SARPS and Guidance Material, Library, the United Kingdom Flight Safety Committee, p.1. Retrieved 08/28/2009 from http://www.ukfsc.co.uk/files/SMS%20Material/SARPS%20Guidance%20Material%20Oct%202008/Journal_SMS%20implementation.pdf.

Gatwick Airport (2009). Managing Sustainability at Gatwick Airport, Sustainability Performance Report 2008, July 2009. Retrieved 01/18/2010 from http://www.gatwickairport.com/assets//Internet/Gatwick/Gatwick%20downloads/Static%20files/LGW_Sustainability_FINAL09.pdf.

Geddes, P. (1915). *Cities in Evolution: An Introduction to the Town Planning Movement and to the Study of Civics*. London: Williams.

Geddes, P. (1915). The original phrase "Think Global, Act Local" first appears in the book "Cities in Evolution" (1915) by Scots town planner and social activist. www.wikipedia.org.

Gilding, P.; Hogarth, M.; Reed, D. (2002). Single Bottom Line Sustainability, Ecos Corporation, August 2002. Retrieved 08/27/2009 from http://www.nzbcsd.org.nz/_attachments/Single_Bottom_Line_Sustainability.pdf.

Glendon, A.I.; Clarke, S.; McKenna, E.F. (2006). *Human Safety and Risk Management*. Sydney: CRC Press.

Global Risk Alliance Pty Ltd.; NSW Department of State and Regional Development (2005). Details of Risk Management Process. Risk Management Guide for Small Business. Retrieved 23/05/2011 from http://www.proboards.nl/data_docs/NSW-Risk_management_guide_small_business.pdf.

Gordon, G.G.; DiTomaso, N. (1992). Predicting corporate performance from organizational culture. *Journal of Management Studies*, Vl:29(6), 783–798.

Goulder, L.H.; Pizer, W.A. (2006). The Economics of Climate Change, NBER Working Paper No. 11923, January 2006, Resources for the Future. Retrieved 05/23/2011 from http://www.nber.org/papers/w11923.pdf.

Graeber, C. (2009). The Role of Human Factors in Improving Aviation Safety. Aero Magazine, Boeing Commercial Airplanes Group, No. 8. Retrieved 08/28/2009 from http://www.boeing.com/commercial/aeromagazine/aero_08/human_textonly.htm.

Gray, P.C.R.; Wiedemann, P.M. (1999). Risk management and sustainable development: mutual lessons from approaches to the use of indicators, *Journal of Risk Research*, 2(3), 201–218.

Gray, P.C.R.; Wiedemann, P.M. (1996). Risk and Sustainability: Mutual Lessons from Approaches to the Use of Indicators. Arbeiten Zur Risiko-Kommunication, Heft 61, Jülich, September 1996. Retrieved 05/23/2011 from http://www2.fz-juelich.de/inb/inb-mut//publikationen/hefte/heft_61.pdf.

Grayling, T.; Bishop, S. (2001). Sustainable Aviation 2030. Institute for Public Policy Research, London. Retrieved 08/28/2009 from http://www.ippr. org.uk/uploadedFiles/projects/s_a_2030_discuss.pdf.

Grayson, D.; Jin, Z.; Lemon, M.; Rodriguez, M.A.; Slaughter, S.; Tay, S. (2008). A New Mindset for Corporate Responsibility. Retrieved 08/28/2009 from http://www.biggerthinking.com/docs/en/a_new_mindset_white_paper.pdf.

Gremouti, J. (2007). Developing a total supply chain carbon strategy. L.E.K. Consulting LLC, Publications, Executive Insights. IX,(4). Retrieved 08/28/2009 from www.lek.com/sites/default/files/Volume_IX_Issue_4. pdf.

Hahn, T.; Scheermesser, M. (2006). Approaches to corporate sustainability among German companies, *Corporate Social Responsibility and Environmental Management*, 13, 150–165. Published online in Wiley InterScience (www.interscience.wiley.com). DOI: 10.1002/csr.100.

Hall, R. (2002). *Organizations: Structures, Processes, and Outcomes* (8th edition). New Jersey, NJ: Prentice-Hall.

Hayes, J. (2002). *The Theory and Practice of Change Management*. Basingstoke: Palgrave.

Hillman, A. and Keim, G. (2001). Shareholder value, stakeholder management, and social issues: whats the bottom line? Strategic Management Journal, 22(2), 125–139.

Hoffman, A.J. (2002). Examining the rhetoric: the strategic implications of climate change policy, *Corporate Environmental Strategy*, 9(4), 329–337.

Hoffman, A.J. (Lead Author); Michael Toffel (Topic Editor) (2007). "Business strategy and climate change." In: *Encyclopedia of Earth*. Eds. Cutler J. Cleveland (Washington, DC: Environmental Information Coalition, National Council for Science and the Environment). (First published in the *Encyclopedia of Earth*, May 19, 2007; Last revised September 27, 2007; Retrieved August 27, 2009). Retrieved 08/28/2009 from http://www. eoearth.org/article/Business_strategy_and_climate_change.

HRH The Prince of Wales Accounting for Sustainability Project (2007). Accounting for Sustainability. Retrieved 05/23/2011 from http://www. accountingforsustainability.org/files/pdf/The%20Accounting%20 for%20Sustainability%20Report.pdf.

Hutton, R.B.; Cox, D.B.; Clouse, M.L.; Gaensbaur, J.; Banks, B.D. (2006), The Role of Sustainable Development in Risk Assessment and Management for Multinational Corporations, Presented at Multinational Enterprise and Sustainable Development: Strategic Tool for Competitiveness, A Research Colloquium, hosted by The Georgia Tech Center for International Business Education and Research, The ICN Business School (Nancy, France) and Groupe de Recherche en Gestion (Nancy-Metz, France) October 20, 2006. Retrieved 05/23/2011 from http://www.ciber.gatech.edu/papers/workingpaper/2007/013-07-08.pdf.

Intergovernmental Panel on Climate Change (IPCC) (1999). Executive Summary: Aviation and the Global Atmosphere. IPCC Special Reports. Retrieved 27/08/2009 from http://www.grida.no/publications/other/ipcc_sr/?src=/Climate/ipcc/aviation/149.htm.

International Air Transport Association (IATA) (2009). Airline Management Integration: Air Mercury. Retrieved 08/25/2009 from www.iata.org/training/courses/talg03.

International Civil Aviation Organization (ICAO) (2001). Aviation and Sustainable Development. Background Paper No. 9, Environmental Problems Associated with Aviation—A Brief Overview, p.3. Retrieved 27/08/2009 from http://www.un.org/esa/sustdev/csd/csd9_bp9.pdf.

International Coalition for Sustainable Aviation (ICSA) (2003). Aviation and its Impacts on the Global Atmosphere, A Position Paper of the International Coalition for Sustainable Aviation, December 2003. Retrieved 27/08/2009 from http://www.transportenvironment.org/Publications/prep_hand_out/lid:278.

International Federation of Accountants (IFAC) (2009). IFAC Sustainability Framework, Integration with Risk Management. Retrieved 02/03/2010 from http://web.ifac.org/sustainability-framework/bsp-intergration-with-risk-management.

International Federation of Accountants (IFAC) (2010). Integration with Risk Management, Sustainability Framework. Retrieved 03/31/2010 from http://web.ifac.org/sustainability-framework/bsp-intergration-with-risk-management.

International Institute for Sustainable Development (2007). The Sustainable Development Journey, 2007. Retrieved 27/08/2009 from http://www.bsdglobal.com/sd_journey.asp.

Istanbul Sabiha Gökçen International Airport Investment Development and Operation Inc. (ISG) (2009). About ISG. Retrieved 28/07/2010 from http://www.sabihagokcen.aero/about_isg.

Jacobs Consultancy (2008). Planning for Aviation Sustainability. Retrieved 07/07/2010 from http://www.jacobs-consultancy.com/pdfs/publications/planning_for_aviation.pdf.

Johnson, J. (2004). *MBA 251 Sustainable Enterprise*. MBA course Curriculum, UNC's Kenan-Flagler Business School. Retrieved 5/23/2011 from http://www.docstoc.com/docs/9931394/Sustainable-Enterprise.

Katsoulakos, P; Katsoulakos, Y. (2006). A Multi-dimensional View of Corporate Responsibility. The 4CR strategic approach to corporate responsibility. 4CR Working Papers. 4CR Part A. 4CR A1.5, July 12, 2006. Retrieved 09/02/2009 from www.csrquest.net/uploadfiles/4CR%20A1.5.doc.

Kelly, B. (2007). The SEA Sustainable Enterprise Model, Chatham-Kent Bio-Sustainability Workshop, November 29–30.

Knickerbocker, B. (2007). Could global warming cause war? *Christian Science Monitor*, p.2, April 19, 2007.Retrieved 27/08/2009 from http://proquest. umi.com/pqdweb?did=1256568491&sid=3&Fmt=3&clientId=417&RQT= 309&VName=PQD.

Kucuk Yilmaz, A. (2008a). The corporate sustainability model for airline business, *European Journal of Scientific Research*, 22(3), 304–317.

Kucuk Yilmaz, A. (2008b). The enterprise risk management model for corporate sustainability and selection of the best ERM operator in the Turkish automotive distributor company: ANP based approach, *European Journal of Economics, Finance And Administrative Sciences*, March, 10, 213–232.

Kucuk Yilmaz, A.; Yilmaz, M. (2008). *Auto Wars*. Germany: Verlag Dr. Muller.

Kuo, L. (2005). A Quantitative Exploration of the Correlations and Effects between Sustainability and Profitability, Master's Thesis, Executive Master of Business Administration, pp.4–9. Retrieved March 30, 2010 from http://thesis.lib.ncu.edu.tw/ETD-db/ETD-search/view_ etd?URN=92431010.

Lane, L. (2007). Risk and reward—Getting the right balance, business continuity and risk management, ITadviser, March/April. Retrieved 08/27/2009 from http://www.businesscontinuityexpo.co.uk/files/it_ advisor_mar_april_2007.pdf.

Laszlo, C. (2008). *Sustainable Value: How the World's Leading Companies Are Doing Well by Doing Good*. Stanford, CA: Unilever Stanford Business Books.

Lazar, F. (2003). A Vital Industry in Search of New Policies: Air Transport in Canada. Behind the Headlines. Retrieved 27/08/2009 from http://goliath. ecnext.com/coms2/gi_0199-162100/A-vital-industry-in-search.html.

Limak (2009). İstanbul Sabiha Gökçen International Airport, Retrieved 05/23/2011 from http://www.limak.com.tr/index.php?lang=en&pid=620.

Lin, Y-L.; Hwang, S-L. (1992). The application of the log linear model to quantify human errors, *Reliability Engineering and System Safety*, 37(2), 157–165.

Liyanage, J.P. (2006). "Strategies For Sustainability Risk Management Through Active 'Bap' (Business-Asset-Process) Performance Integration", WCEAM 2006 Paper 015, p.1, Proceedings of the 1st World Congress on Engineering Asset Management (WCEAM) July 11–14, 2006. Retrieved 08/27/2009 from http://www.springerlink.com/content/ k113241rn00811w5/fulltext.pdf?page=1.

Llewellyn, J.; Chaix, C. (2007). The Business of Climate Change II. Lehman Brothers. Retrieved 27/08/2009 from http://graduateinstitute. ch/webdav/site/international_economics/users/ana-cristina/public/ TheBusinessOfClimateChangeII.pdf.

Lubber, M.S. (2008). Climate Change and the Dangers of Undisclosed Risk. Finance. pp.179–181. Retrieved 27/08/2009 from http://www. climateactionprogramme.org/books/2008/ca/p179-181.pdf.

Lufthansa Systems (2008). Airline Management Solutions. Retrieved 27/08/2009 from http://www.lhsystems.com/solutions/airline-solutions/airline-management-solutions/index.htm.

Maeda, S.; Hibiki, S. (2008). Research Trends of Sustainability Science on the Global Warming Problems—Issues on the Japan Contribution in the IPCC 4th Assessment Report, Quarterly Review, No.28, July 2008, pp.35–55.

Marsden, C.; Jörg ADR_OF (1998). Toward an understanding of corporate citizenship and how to influence it, *Citizenship Studies*, 2(2), 329–352.

Marsh, Inc. (2009). Climate Change Risks. Marsh, Inc., Features and Articles, Risk Reports. Retrieved 27/08/2009 from http://global.marsh.com/risk/climate/climate/index.php.

Marshall, G. (1998). Weber, Max. A Dictionary of Sociology. 1998. Retrieved 27/08/2009 from Encyclopedia.com: http://www.encyclopedia.com/doc/1O88-WeberMax.html.

Martens, F. (2005). Enterprise Risk Management to the Rescue, *News and Trend*, CA Magazine, Print Version, March 2005. Retrieved 05/23/2011 from http://www.camagazine.com/archives/print-edition/2005/march/upfront/news-and-trends/camagazine17476.aspx.

McKitrick, R. (2000). Submission to the Joint Standing Committee on Treaties: Inquiry into The Kyoto Protocol, Parliament of Australia. Retrieved 08/27/2009 from http://www.uoguelph.ca/~rmckitri/research/australia.pdf.

Metcalf, M. (2010). Why Enterprise Risk Management is Business Critical. Retrieved 03/01/2010 from http://www.youtube.com/watch?v=Kxbe2SHHea8.

MicroAgility (2009). Sustainability: A Long-Term Strategy to Succeed in the Interdependent World, MicroAgility, Inc., p.4. Retrieved 3/31/2010 from http://microagility.com/docs/Sustainability.pdf.

Miller, D.P. and Swain, A.D. (1987). *Human Error and Human Reliability. Handbook of Human Factors*. New York: Wiley.

Millmore, M.; Lewis, P.; Saunders, M.; Thornhill, A.; Morrow, T. (2007). *Strategic Human Resource Management: Contemporary Issues*. Harlow: FT/ Prentice Hall, p.37.

Montreal Economic Institute (2006). How to Make the Canadian Airline Industry More Competitive. Economic Note. Retrieved 08/26/2009 from http://www.iedm.org/uploaded/pdf/nov06_en.pdf.

National Steering Committee on Patient Safety (2004). Building a Safer System: A National Integrated Strategy for Improving Patient Safety in Canadian Health Care, pp.5–6.

Nemli, E. (2004). The *Sustainable Development: Social and Environmental Approaches of the Companies*. Istanbul: Filiz Publishing House.

Nieuwlands, H. (2006). *Sustainability and Internal Auditing*, IIA Research Foundation, 2006.

Nieuwlands, H. (2007). Retrieved 08/27/2009 from http://www.riskmanagementmagazine.com.au/articles/4C/0C04CD4C.asp?Type=125&Category=1239.

Nomura, K. (2003). Managing Risks in Airline Industry. *Japan and the World Economy*, 15(4), 469–479.

Nordhaus, W. (2007). The Challenge of Global Warming: Economic Models and Environmental Policy, William Nordhaus, p.253. Retrieved 08/26/2009 from http://nordhaus.econ.yale.edu/dice_mss_072407_all.pdf, October 2008.

Oliver Wyman (2007). The Upside: How to Turn Big Threats into Growth Breakthroughs. MMC Riyadh Seminar. Retrieved 08/26/2009 from http://www.me.marsh.com/research/sa/OLIVER%20WYMAN.pdf.

Organisation for Economic Co-operation and Development (OECD) (2001). *The DAC Guidelines Strategies for Sustainable Development*, OECD Publications Service, France, p.27.

Parekh, S. (2008). The crisis and emancipation of the modern corporate executive: how the Bhagavad Gita reinforces Edward Freeman's stakeholder theory, *The Michigan Journal of Business*, 1 (January), p.12.

Peck, B. (2006). Global Warming—Impact on Financial Services. AON, ADR '06 in Oz, International Financial Ombudsman's Conference. Retrieved 02/08/2007 from http://www.conferenceworld.com.au/resources/other/Bill%20Peck.pdf.

Perrini, F.; Tencati, A. (2006). Sustainability and stakeholder management: the need for new corporate performance evaluation and reporting systems, *Business Strategy and the Environment Business Strategy Environment*, 15(5), 296–308. Published online in Wiley InterScience (www.interscience.wiley.com), John Wiley and Sons, Ltd and ERP Environment.

Phillips, T. (2008). What is sustainability? Newsletter SBiotech/Biomedical. Retrieved 08/27/2009 from http://biotech.about.com/od/faq/f/sustainability.htm.

Pleumarom, A. (2007). Tourism Feels the Heat of Global Warming. Tourism Investigation and Monitoring Team. Retrieved 08/27/2009 from http://www.dev-zone.org/cgi-bin/knowledge/jump.cgi?ID=13571.

Pollard, D. (2008). How to Save the World, Dave Pollard's Environmental Philosophy, Creative Works, Business Papers and Essays. Retrieved 08/27/2009 from http://blogs.salon.com/0002007/2008/03/11.html.

PricewaterhouseCoopers (2008a). The Sustainability Agenda: Industry Perspectives, p.4. Retrieved 03/30/2010 from http://www.pwc.com/en_GX/gx/sustainability/sustainability_agenda.pdf.

PricewaterhouseCoopers (2009). Developing an Enterprise Risk Management Program, Relevante Internal Audit Symposium, January 22, 2009.

Protiviti, Inc. (2008). Mitigating Risk in the Airline Industry with an ERM Approach. Retrieved 07/23/2009 from http://www.protiviti.fr/downloads/PRO/pro-us/industry_brochures/Protiviti_Airline_POV.pdf.

Raggett, L. (2006). A New Human Factors Risk Management Program for Qantas, ess2006: Evolving System Safety—The 7th International Symposium of the Australian Aviation Psychology Association. November 9–12, 2006, Manly Pacific Hotel, Sydney, Australia. Retrieved 08/27/2009 from www.aavpa.org/seminars/ess2006/pdf/pdf%20papers/Raggett.pdf, p.2.

Reason, J. (1997). *Managing the Risks of Organizational Accidents*. Aldershot, UK: Ashgate.

Rochat, P. (2009). Air Transport—A Global Approach to Sustainability. Retrieved 08/27/2009 from http://www.airport-int.com/categories/environment/air-transport-a-global-approach-to-sustainability.asp.

Roche (2009). Corporate Sustainability Committee Charter. Retrieved 08/27/2009 from http://www.roche.com/corporate_sustainability_charter.pdf.

Romanova, I. (2004). Air Transport in the UK: Current Trends and Future Scenarios. Retrieved 08/27/2009 from http://www.hausarbeiten.de/faecher/vorschau/36306.html.

Rossouw, G.J. (2005). Business ethics and corporate governance in Africa, *Business and Society*, 44(1), 94–106.

Rowland (2008). Corporate Sustainability 2008, Conference Program. Retrieved 07/31/2008 from http://www.rowland.com.au/site/Portals/0/Corporate_Sustainability_2008_Program.pdf.

Sage, A.P. (1998). Risk Management for Sustainable Development, IEEE *Xplore* Digital Library IEEE, 5, 4815–4819. Retrieved 08/27/2009 from http://ieeexplore.ieee.org/stamp/stamp.jsp?tp=&arnumber=727614&isnumber=15682.

Salt Lake City Department of Airports (2010). Airport Sustainability Program Assessment, Carter and Burgess, Inc. Retrieved 01/18/2010 from http://www.slcairport.com/cmsdocuments/sustainability.pdf.

Salzmann, O.; Steger, U.; Ionescu-Somers, A. (2005). Quantifying economic effects of corporate sustainability initiatives—Activities and Drivers, IMD 2005-28, November, 2005, p.3. Retrieved 08/27/2009 from http://www.imd.ch/research/publications/upload/CSM_Salzmann_Steger_Ionescu_Somers_WP_2005_28_Level_1.pdf.

Sanchez, T. (2008). Dow Jones Sustainability Group Index. Retrieved 12/11/2008 from p.3. http://www.oecd.org/dataoecd/41/50/1859713.pdf.

SAP AG (2005). Powerful Solutions for Enterprise-wide Airline Management. Retrieved 08/27/2009 from http://www.sap.com/sk/industries/aero-defense/BWP_Powerful_Sol_Ent_Airline_Mgt.pdf.

Schaltegger, S.; Burritt, R.; Petersen, H. (2003). *An Introduction to Corporate Environmental Management: Striving for Sustainability*. Sheffield: Greenleaf Publishing, p.21.

Schneider, A. (2009). A Framework of Corporate Sustainability and its Organizational Pre-conditions, 8th International Conference of the European Society for Ecological Economics, ESEE 2009, Biotechnical Faculty, Ljubljana, Slovenia, June 29–July 2, 2009, p.6. Retrieved March 30, 2010 from http://www.esee2009.si/papers/Schneider-Outline_of_a_Framework.pdf.

SearchCIO.com (2009). Definition—Enterprise Risk Management (ERM). Retrieved 08/27/2009 from http://searchcio.techtarget.com/sDefinition/0,,sid182_gci508983,00.html.

SH&E an ICF International Company (2009). Airlines. SH&E Areas of Aviation Consulting Expertise. Retrieved 08/27/2009 from http://www. sh-e.com/expertise_ind_airlines.htm.

Sheehan, N.T. (2009). Making risk pay: the board's role, *Journal of Business Strategy*, 30(1), 33–39.

SMS Project Team of the Air Line Pilots Association, International (2006). Background and Fundamentals of the Safety Management System (SMS) for Aviation Operations, Second Edition, February 2006. p.24. Retrieved 08/27/2009 from http://ihst.rotor.com/Portals/54/Aviation%20SMS%20 Background-Fundamentals.pdf.

Society of British Aerospace Companies (SBAC) (2008). Aviation and Environment. Retrieved 08/27/2009 from http://www-sbac-co-uk.cname. strategiesuk.net/pages/92567080.asp.

Southern California Safety Institute (SCSI) (2009). Operational Risk Management. Retrieved 08/28/2009 from http://www.scsi-inc.com/ORM. php.

Space for Ideas (2010). Edward de Bono, Water is not Soup, Ideas Essays. Retrieved 04/01/2010 from http://www.eastofengland.uk.com/wp-content/uploads/De-Bono1.pdf.

Srivastava, R.P.; Kogan, A.; Vasarhelyi, M.A. (2001). Balanced scorecard approach to sustainability and value creation: a challenge for survival in the new economy (pre-publication version, Kshitij, *The Journal of Eastern IILM Calcutta*, January–March 2001, pp.1–9. Retrieved 27/08/2009 from raw.rutgers.edu/.../2020.2BalancedScorecard-SustainabilityandValueCreation.doc.

Stakeholder Research Associates Canada, United Nations Environment Programme and AccountAbility (2005). From Words to Action, the Stakeholder Engagement Manual, Volume 1: The Guide to Practitioners' Perspectives on Stakeholder Engagement, First Edition, July 2005, p.10.

Stanford University (2009). The Airline Industry. Stanford University's Department of Aeronautics and Astronautics. Retrieved 08/27/2009 from http://adg.stanford.edu/aa241/intro/airlineindustry.html.

Stern, N. (2006). Stern Review: The Economics of Climate Change: Summary of conclusions (PDF). Archived from the original on 2006-12-09. Retrieved 08/27/2009 from http://web.archive.org/web/20061209034512/http://www. hm-treasury.gov.uk/media/8A8/C1/Summary_of_Conclusions.pdf. http://airquality.ucdavis.edu/pages/events/2007/aviation_presentations/ Stewart.pdf.

Stratos (2007). Integrating Sustainability into Business Processes, Case Studies of Leading Companies, Stratos inc., Ontario. Retrieved 08/27/2009 from http://www.stratos-sts.com/documents/Sustainability_Integration_ Study_Brochure_EN_.pdf.

Symreng, J. (2002). Risk-management by Banks, Insurance Companies and Securities Firms, Contractual Savings Conference, Washington DC, May 2, 2002, p.4(17).

TAV Airports Holding (2009).TAV Airports Holding 2008 Annual Report, Annual Reports, ir.tav.aero, 2009.

TAV Invester Relations (2010). Corporate Social Responsibility, TAV Airports Holding. Retrieved 07/28/2020 from http://www.tavyatirimciiliskileri.com/docs/pdf/corporote_social_sesponsibility.pdf.

Taylor, C. (2006). Why Global Warming is Good for Business. CNNmoney.com. Retrieved 08/27/2009 from http://money.cnn.com/2006/04/13/technology/business2_futureboy0413/index.htm.

Thakur, S. (2010). Explaining the Burke-Litwin Change Model, Edited and published by Ginny Edwards, on September 14, 2010, Bright Hub. Retrieved 01/21/2011 from http://www.brighthub.com/office/project-management/articles/86867.aspx.

The Calgary Centre for Non-Profit Management (2001). The Sustainability Model. Retrieved 08/28/2009 from www.thecentrepoint.ca/pdf/sustainabilitymodelOct2001.pdf.

The National Communications Branch of the Department of Immigration and Citizenship (2008). Stakeholder Engagement Practitioner Handbook, Australian Government, p.13. Retrieved 02/03/2010 from http://www.immi.gov.au/about/stakeholder-engagement/_pdf/stakeholder-engagement-practitioner-handbook.pdf.

The Organisation for Economic Co-operation and Development (OECD) (1997). The Future of International Air Transport Policy, Responding to Global Change, Head of Publications Service, OECD, Paris, p.12. Retrieved 05/23/2011 from http://www.oecd.org/dataoecd/21/43/38303767.pdf.

The University of Queensland (2009a). Sustainable Enterprise Management Major/s, Part of the Bachelor of Business Program. Retrieved 08/27/2009 from http://www.uq.edu.au/study/program.html?acad_prog=2268.

The University of Queensland (2009b). Sustainable Enterprise Management. Retrieved 08/27/2009 from http://www.uq.edu.au/nravs/index.html?page=57556.

The University of Queensland. (2009c). Corporate Sustainability. UQ Business School. Retrieved 08/27/2009 from http://www.business.uq.edu.au/display/execed/Corporate+Sustainability.

Thomas, C. (2006). Sustainable Airport Development, p.4., Towards Sustainable Airport Development—Airport Conference Exhibition, Fingal Development Board, Dublin Airport. Retrieved 08/27/2009 from http://www.fdb.ie/Callum_Thomas.pdf.

Torum, O. and Kucuk Yilmaz, A. (2009). Havacılıkta Sürdürülebilirlik Yönetimi: Türkiye'deki Havalimanları için Sürdürülebilirlik Uygulamaları Araştırması, Havacılık ve Uzay Teknolojileri (HUTEN) Dergisi, Cilt: 4, Sayı: 2, Temmuz 2009.

Treadstone 71 (2010). Risk Governance Model. Retrieved from 03/01/2010 from http://www.treadstone71.com/whitepapers/Risk%20Governance%20Model.pdf.

UHY Advisors (2008). Enterprise Risk Management. Retrieved 08/27/2009 from http://www.uhyadvisors-us.com/uhy/Default.aspx?tabid=496.

United Nations Environment Programme Finance Initiative (UNEPFI) (2002). "Climate Risk to Global Economy", A document of the UNEP FI Climate Change Working Group, CEO Briefing. Retrieved 08/27/2009 from http://www.unepfi.org/fileadmin/documents/CEO_briefing_climate_change_2002_en.pdf.

United Nations Environment Programme Finance Initiative (UNEPFI) (2006). Sustainability Management and Reporting: Benefits for Financial Institutions in Developing and Emerging Economies, December 2006, p.2. Retrieved 08/27/2009 from http://www.unepfi.org/fileadmin/documents/smr_benefits_dec2006_01.pdf.

Union of Concerned Scientists (2009). Common Sense on Climate Change: Practical Solutions to Global Warming. Retrieved 09/03/2009 from http://www.ucsusa.org/assets/documents/global_warming/climatesolns.pdf.

Unione delle Università del Mediterraneo (UNIMED) (2009). Assessment of Air Transport Projects in the Light of Global Warming. Terms of Reference. Retrieved 08/27/2009 from http://w3.uniroma1.it/unimed/documenti/TermsofReference.pdf.

United Nations Environment Programme, Division of Technology, Industry, and Economics, Energy Branch (UNEP) (2009). Sustainable Air Transport and Sustainable Airports Issues at Stake. Retrieved 08/27/2009 from www.uneptie.org/energy/act/tp/aviation/docs/Airtp-leaflet.pdf.

University of Toronto, School of Continuing Studies (2008). Certificate in Enterprise Risk Management (ERM). Retrieved 08/26/2009 from http://learn.utoronto.ca/Page1386.aspx.

Van Marrewijk, M. (2003). Concepts and definitions of CSR and corporate sustainability: between agency and communion, *Journal of Business Ethics*, 44(2/3), 95–105.

Van Marrewijk, M.; Merre, M. (2003). Multiple levels of corporate sustainability, *Journal of Business Ethics*, 44,(2–3), 107–119.

Waitz, I.A. (2006). A global balance: aviation and the environment, *Aero-Astro Magazine*, MIT Aeronautics and Astronautics Department. Retrieved 08/26/2009 from http://web.mit.edu/aeroastro/news/magazine/aeroastro-no3/2006aviationandenvironment.html.

Weber, M. (1968). *Economy and Society*. Translated and edited by Guenther Roth and Claus Wittich. New York, NY: Bedminster Press.

Wei, L. (2006). Strategic human resource management: determinants of fit, *Research and Practice in Human Resource Management*, 14(2), 49–60.

Werther, W.B.; Chandler, D. (2005). Strategic corporate social responsibility as global brand insurance, *Business Horizons*, 48 (July–August), 317–324.

Wikipedia (2009a). Economics of Global Warming. Retrieved 08/26/2009 from http://en.wikipedia.org/wiki/Economics_of_global_warming.

Wikipedia (2009b). Corporate Sustainability. Retrieved 08/26/2009 from http://en.wikipedia.org/wiki/Corporate_sustainability.

Wikipedia (2009c). Aviation and Environment. Retrieved 08/26/2009 from http://en.wikipedia.org/wiki/Aviation_and_the_environment.

William Gallagher Associates (2009). The Impact of Global Warming: Property Risk Management Strategies. WGA Publications, White Papers, Risk Management Topics. Retrieved 08/26/2009 from http://www.wgains.com/Publications/WhitePapers.aspx.

Wilson, M. (2003). Corporate sustainability: what is it and where does it come from? *Ivey Business Journal*, March/April, s.1–5.

Wilson, S. (2005). Human Resource Management in the Airline Industry — The Example of Star Alliance. Master thesis, Arts in International Business, Universitat Erlangen, Nürnberg, Friedrich Alexander Universität Erlangen Nürnberg (WISO) pp.2–3., 2005. Retrieved 08/26/2009 from GRIN Publishing, http://www.grin.com/e-book/41155/human-resource-management-in-the-airline-industry-the-example-of-star#.

Wirtenberg, J.; Harmon, J.; Fairfield, K.; Russell, W. (2006). HR's Role in Building a Sustainable Enterprise: Insights from Some of the World's Best Companies, ISE/CHRMS Breakfast Seminar, November 17, 2006. Retrieved 08/28/2009 from http://view.fdu.edu/default.aspx?id=977.

World Economic Forum (2007). Core Global Risks. Global Risk 2007, A Global Risk Network Report, A World Economic Forum Report, January 2007, pp.5–6. Retrieved 08/28/2009 from http://www.weforum.org/pdf/CSI/Global_Risks_2007.pdf.

Yildirim, O. (2009). Sociologist Max Weber and Sociology (Sociology, Anthony Giddens). Retrieved 08/26/2009 from www.felsefe.gen.tr/sosyolog_max_weber_ve_sosyoloji.asp.

Index

For Product Safety Concerns and Information please contact our
EU representative GPSR@taylorandfrancis.com Taylor & Francis
Verlag GmbH, Kaufingerstraße 24, 80331 München, Germany